Bar... W9-CZX-900

Envisioning Collaboration

Group Verbal-*Visual* Composing
in a System of Creativity

Geoffrey A. Cross
University of Louisville

Baywood's Technical Communications Series
Series Editor: CHARLES H. SIDES

Baywood Publishing Company, Inc.
AMITYVILLE, NEW YORK

Baywood Publishing Company, Inc.
26 Austin Avenue
P.O. Box 337
Amityville, NY 11701
(800) 638-7819
E-mail: baywood@baywood.com
Web site: baywood.com

Library of Congress Catalog Number: 2010017678
ISBN 978-0-89503-400-7 (cloth : alk. paper)
SBN 978-0-89503-452-6 (epub)
ISBN 978-0-89503-453-3 (epdf)
http://dx.doi.org/10.2190/ECG

Library of Congress Cataloging-in-Publication Data

Cross, Geoffrey A.
   Envisioning collaboration : group verbal-visual composing in a system of creativity / Geoffrey A. Cross.
      p. cm. -- (Baywood's technical communications series)
   Includes bibliographical references and index.
   ISBN 978-0-89503-400-7 (cloth : alk. paper) 1. Advertising copy. 2. Communication of technical information. 3. Visual communication. 4. Creative thinking. 5. Teams in the workplace. 6. Rhetoric. I. Title.
   HF5825.C76   2010
   659.1--dc22

                                        2010017678

A Dual Dedication:

For Jocelyne

Soli Deo Gloria

Table of Contents

LIST OF FIGURES

LIST OF TABLES

Preface

En*vision*ing Collaboration traces key composing processes of some outstanding writers and artists involved in an advertising agency's successful struggle to prepare technical marketing communication—lawn mower ad campaigns—and present them in a "pitch" to retain the business of a vital national account. Artist-writer teams using aesthetics, humor, and rhetorical moxie to prepare numerous verbal-visual pieces are described and analyzed in the context of this real, successful, integrated technical marketing campaign. The advertising agency site is explained as a system of creativity or community of practice.

Our time demands this research because technology has made verbal-visual composing widespread; collaboration is typically entailed in professional verbal-visual composing, and much money is being invested in verbal-visual communication: print advertisement revenues for magazines alone brought the advertising industry well over $23 billion in 2008 (Publishers' Information Bureau, 2009).

No other book to date presents an ethnographic thick description of verbal-visual composing processes. En*vision*ing Collaboration is qualitative research based upon 460 hours of participant observations and over 7,000 hours of subsequent research. The meticulous depiction of composing processes in their social contexts of production and reception allows much more accurate and informed teaching, training, and practice of verbal-visual collaboration, useful for teachers, researchers, students, and practitioners from a number of disciplines involved with verbal-visual composing. Disciplines particularly involved include technical and business communication, rhetoric and composition, advertising (strategic communication), psychology (collective mind, psychological types, situated cognition), communication (large group and dyadic research, media theory, verbal and visual imagery), graphic design and education (computers [desktop publishing] in education). Technical writers and artists; advertising creatives; and other corporate editors, writers, and artists, trainers, and writing consultants can learn many useful approaches from such a study of verbal-visual composing to fulfill rhetorical strategy.

Although applicable to all subjects of verbal-visual composing, En*vision*ing Collaboration focuses specifically on the marketing of technology. Scientific and technical companies are two of the fastest-growing clients of advertising. For example, between 1997 and 2007, pharmaceutical advertising increased by 330%, spending $5 billion in 2005 alone (Cameron, 2008).

My findings contradict or offer corrections to existing models of verbal-visual collaboration. Furthermore, an extensive literature review found no other study that documents the function of verbal and visual rhetorical elements of arrangement, emphasis, clarity, conciseness, tone, and ethos (Kostelnick & Roberts, 1998) in real composing processes in their actual settings. En*vision*ing Collaboration also investigates the nature of verbal-visual coherence, closure, and completion, and addresses several ethical issues that arose during the composing processes. Based on the findings, a pedagogical unit is proposed that describes and incorporates "gateway activities" (Hillocks, 1995) for verbal-visual composition and collaboration. Students model collaborative moves and verbal-visual invention approaches, and they learn a metalanguage to describe and critique their processes. Student writers and artists are encouraged to collaborate in the "shared territory" (Bakhtin, 1981; Himley, 1991) of the layout grid, where words and images may coalesce.

I hesitated momentarily in selecting the book title because of the World War II negative connotations of the word "collaborate." As someone who had read many books on World War II by age 10, I cringed when I first heard the term *collaborative writing* used to denote group writing, a reaction others (e.g., Stewart, 1988) have expressed in print. Yet we must beat our spears into pruning hooks and swords into plough shares. One of the last weapons to go is words. "Nip, Jerry, kraut," these words lose the kind of edge put on them by life-or-death conflict and become known more for the celebration of life rather than the advancement of death. It is in this spirit that I call this new study of writer-artist collaboration En*vision*ing Collaboration.

I consistently strove to do the most balanced reporting possible during my three months at Heric Advertising and during the six-and-a-half years that followed. However, this research is one version of what happened, reported as carefully as possible from a limited, rather than omniscient, point of view: "We know but in part." This research is not Heric's official history of the process—there is none of which I am aware. Those interested in learning more about the process of envisioning before considering this representation and analysis of collaboration should read first the methods section that concludes this book.

Louisville
2010

Acknowledgments

For their encouragement, inspiration, and support, I wish to thank the many people identified here or not, who helped bring this research to full fruition. At Heric, I am grateful to Jim Montgomery, Steve Douglas, Rick Waller, Des Renfield, and Bob Thompson for their support and contextualizing of the project. I am most grateful to the Heric creatives—particularly Neil Tyner, Jesse Cooper, John Rolland, Angela Chapman, Craig Clayton, and Jason Wells—who, amidst the pressing deadlines of high-stakes improvisation gave me time to document their verbal-visual composing.

I would like to thank the University of Louisville, particularly my chairs Susan Griffin, Dennis Hall, and Debra Journet, who encouraged me in this endeavor, especially in supporting my successful application for three Intramural Research Incentive Grants from the Office of the Senior Vice President for Research. These paid for equipment, a bit of release time, and transcriptions. Thanks also go to Watson Visiting Professor Cheryl Geisler for a prepublication copy of her methods book and to Rodney Dick: while directing his dissertation (2006) the power of moving from a 120-character-line database to Excel became evident to me. Mary Rosner, as with many previous projects, gave me important feedback on my prospectus. Several work study students helped greatly with filing. Nancy Henry literally saved the transcriptions.

I also especially thank Jim Suchan, Professor and Associate Dean of Distance Learning in the Graduate School of Business and Public Policy at the Naval Postgraduate School for his most generous and incisive feedback on a draft of this work. I am also thankful for the thoughtful and meticulous comments of the anonymous Baywood reviewer, an academic and professional graphic artist. I also thank Series Editor Charles Sides and publisher Stuart Cohen for their encouragement and assistance.

I am grateful for the long-standing encouragement of my recently deceased mother, Dorothy Writer Cross and father Arthur D. Cross. I am grateful for the wisdom of my great friend Ted Beardshear. For their inspiration, I thank my wonderful daughters Pascale and Isabelle. Without my wife Jocelyne, her French proverb, "no two without a third," and answered prayers, this endeavor would have never begun . . . or ended.

CHAPTER 1

Introductory *Framework* and *Overview*

When I was a writer, I spoke like a writer, reasoned like a writer and wrote like a writer.

B ut increasingly today I am a composer, and like the music composer, although I don't play all the instruments, I must compose not only for my keyboard, but also for and with the rest of the group. [1]

CONCEPTUAL FRAMING

In 1950, Kenneth Burke defined rhetoric as "the use of *language* as a symbolic means of inducing cooperation in beings that by nature use symbols" (p. 43, my emphasis). In those days, the media were largely populated by *words*—in sound transmitted by telephone and radio, or print in newspapers and books. However, in succeeding decades, developments in technology made television, news-magazines, and picture-intensive newspapers the norm. The personal computer further accelerated the incidence of visual communication; in the last 15 years, the dissemination of desktop publishing and Web authoring software has brought the opportunity for nearly everyone in industrialized countries to combine verbal and visual symbols into texts for a variety of purposes.[2] At the professional level, however, because of the expertise required to produce professional verbal-visual communication, from newspapers to workplace documents to advertisements, we see writer-artist collaboration more widespread than ever, in turn creating the expectation in "readers" for more high-quality verbal-visual documents.

---

[1] Loose imitation of I Corinthians 13:11.

[2] Bernhardt (1996) addressed the impact of desktop publishing on (visual) rhetoric and composition in his "Visual Rhetoric" entry in *Encyclopedia of Rhetoric and Composition*.

1

However, as with the introduction of writing in classical Greece, widespread use of the medium has occurred long before research-informed pedagogy developed in academia. Access to a medium, of course, does not ensure professional competence in either individual composers or in writers and in artists who need to collaborate to produce multimodal texts. The shift in signifying practices and potentials has made it imperative to study expert verbal-visual composing to develop empirically based pedagogy to train effective writers who can collaborate with artists and also make strides through the zone of proximal development to compose professional-level verbal-visual documents individually. Vygotsky defined the zone of proximal development as "the distance between the actual developmental level as determined by independent problem-solving and the level of potential development as determined through problem-solving under adult guidance or in collaboration with more capable peers" (1978, p. 86). In our case, research-informed pedagogy could be developed that incorporates both teacher-led instruction in visual design and performance with the instruction of more advanced peers. The pedagogy could also teach writing students how to learn more from artists when they collaborate with them outside of school and after their formal education in this area ends.

In the last few years, composition studies has begun to respond to this challenge in major ways. A featured article linked to the splash page of the Association for Business Communication Web site noted that the lack of visual rhetoric education leaves business communication students ill-equipped for the workplace (Brumburger, 2005). Kathleen Yancey stated in her 2004 Conference on College Composition and Communication Chair's address, "Composition in a New Key," that our definition of "composing" should now include verbal-visual composition. Grice and Krull, in their introduction to a special issue on the future of technical communication in the journal of the Society of Technical Communication, said that to meet the demands of the information age, technical communicators must become able to use visual design to solve communication problems (2001).

The frequently collaborative nature of such communication was pointed out by the National Council of Teachers of English Guideline on Multimodal Literacies: "Because of the complexity of multimodal projects and the different levels of skill and sensitivity each individual brings to their execution, such projects often demand high levels of collaboration and teamwork." The guideline advocates having students collaborate on verbal-visual projects such as brochures (National Council of Teachers of English, 2005). Yet on this subject, composition studies finds itself in the same place it was with writing 25 years ago: having plenty of helpful analyses of *products*, but no meticulously detailed descriptions of real group composing *processes* in their social contexts.

The many pertinent discussions of features of finished verbal-visual works include Bernhardt, 1986; Donnell, 2005; Handa, 2004; Kostelnick, 1988; Kress & van Leeuwen, 1996; Rosner, 2001; Willerton, 2005). Dragga and Gong's (1989) award-winning *Editing: The Design of Rhetoric* is a theoretical, practical, and pedagogical discussion of verbal and visual aspects of editing, based upon the five canons of rhetoric and an examination of verbal-visual documents. These studies have provided some crucial genre knowledge and general process knowledge that is necessary, although not sufficient for effective performance of a specific process (Hillocks, 1995). We have also had development of several other verbal-visual composing pedagogies to begin to address the critical gap (e.g., Faigley, George, Palchik, & Selfe, 2004; Odell & Katz, 2005; Portewig, 2004; Ramey, 2000; Wysocki & Lynch, 2007), although they are not based on meticulous renderings of expert processes.

Such renderings would be valuable because the differences between visual communication and writing are great, often causing managers of technical communication to hire only people who communicate in their medium: writers hire only writers, visual designers hire visual designers (Carliner, 2001, p. 159). There is little wonder about these differences: each medium encodes reality differently (Carpenter, 1966, p. 162), and mastering one of the media to a professional level typically involves a bachelor's degree or more. Nevertheless, the problems professional writers and other professionals who write are asked to solve frequently involve graphic design, editorial, and tools skills, involving collaboration; even more challenging because *any* kind of workplace collaboration is often problematic. From 1975 to 1995, U.S. industry invested more than $1 trillion in technology, but realized little improvement in the effectiveness of its knowledge workers. Director of the prestigious Xerox PARC, John Seeley Brown, attributed this failure to lack of scrutiny and improvement of collaboration (Brown & Gray, 1995). Why is collaboration frequently so difficult? The flattening of hierarchies has eliminated middle managers who used to mediate cross-functional teams. Research has shown that individuals trained in different disciplines can have more different ways of identifying and solving problems than do people from different countries (Webb & Keene, 1999). In addition, collaborative decision making involves complex skills, including knowing how to interrupt and illustrate with nonverbal means. Performing these skills involves learning to argue, present compelling evidence, and persuade. Unless a group uses these skills, its work cannot progress (Heath, 2000, p. 127). Such group skills, despite their degree of difficulty, are expected by employers in the workplace (Wallis & Steptoe, 2006).

We have learned from the study of the acquisition of writing ability that beyond general procedural knowledge, knowledge similar to the small-group decision-making skills mentioned above, writers, like anyone trying to accomplish any involved process, need specific procedural knowledge (Hillocks, 1995, p. 122). Writers who collaborate with artists need procedural knowledge of a similar granularity. To develop needed courses and curriculums integrating collaboration, graphics and writing, composition studies and other disciplines need meticulously detailed qualitative research on writer-artist collaborative procedures to learn how expert teams work effectively to integrate verbal and visual symbols into messages. We particularly need to learn about the roles of the writers in such groups—what and, more importantly, how they contribute in both the verbal and visual dimensions of the message.

Despite the importance of verbal-visual collaboration, only a few preliminary studies have been conducted, perhaps because, as Charney noted in *Central Works in Technical Communication* (2004) about empirical research in general, "we seem to see so many articles . . . telling us what kind of research to do and so few describing substantive research." Pupipat (1998) studied Thai scientists who cowrote articles that involved graphics. However, he did not observe their actual processes, processes that, regardless, were not notably effective. In the special issue of the *Journal of Business and Technical Communication, Prospects for Research in Technical and Scientific Communication,* Part 2, Haas and Witte (2001) described how engineers and construction workers revised a channel easement diagram and text. However, this study focused upon workers who compose as only a part of their jobs, not expert writers and art directors. Haas and Witte called for more empirical research on collaborative writing (p. 446).

Mirel, Allmenndinger, and Feinberg (1995) investigated their own processes of collaboration in the design of a manual. Based on their experience, they advanced Morgan's three-model view of collaboration (1991), in which (a) writers create material that they give to artists who complete the project; (b) writer and artist each compose drafts, then get together and integrate material; or (c) writer and artist compose together. Mirel and colleagues noted that "because little research exists on collaborations between writers and graphic designers in industry, we cannot make claims about how well each model represents actual production contexts or how demonstrably better one model is than another" (p. 260).

To illustrate properties of visual design, Schriver (1997) discussed her participation in the team revision of a manual. Like Mirel and colleagues, Schriver did not include quotations from collaborative interaction. Allen (2002) also described verbal-visual collaboration, tracing the creation of a book of photo essays by an artist, writer, and layout designer. From the description of methods and quotations, participants appear to have been interviewed only after the process ended. Nevertheless, the chapter provides an important early description of writer-artist-designer interaction.

Advertising creatives (industry vernacular for the artists, writers, and other media specialists who create advertisements) also routinely interact. Vivian reported that in the United States, organizations expend roughly 2% of the gross domestic product on advertising (as cited in Marsh, 2007, p. 170). Between 1997 and 2007, scientific and technical companies were two of the fastest-growing clients of advertising. During this decade, pharmaceutical advertising increased by 330%, in 2005 spending $5 billion annually on such campaigns (Cameron, 2008). John Philip Jones (2004), professor of advertising at Syracuse University, noted that various studies show that the average American citizen daily encounters from 300 to 1,500 ads (p. 12). However, there are surprisingly few research articles documenting creative processes. As Jones said, "We know less about the actual workings of advertising than about the workings of any other business activity that swallows so much money" (p. xii). Surprisingly, composition and rhetoric studies has contributed little to knowledge of advertising generation. Marsh (2007) recently advanced a *"rapprochement"* between the disciplines of advertising and rhetoric by showing how Aristotelian causal analysis could be used by brainstorming creatives to analyze products to later advertise them, a seemingly fruitful idea, although as yet not reported tested by creatives.

Since the 1920s, practical literature has prescribed 4-to-8-step approaches (Marsh, 2007). However, the first fairly detailed description of collaborative artist-writer processes was Johar, Holbrook, and Stern, 2001. This important protocol analysis study describes several phases of the development of ad concepts by five professional artist-writer teams and found that the creative team that invented ideas in the largest number of plot patterns was evaluated the most effective by professionals. Although a groundbreaking work in this area, the study had limitations the authors pointed out: the problem was made up; the creatives were given two hours to do the problem, all teams had to follow a predetermined 5-phase structure of individual and dyadic composing, with a set time allotment for each phase; participants could not ask account managers for more information; participants completed their research after the end of a work day and were tired; and some participants were anxious because they had to compose aloud. The authors called for "more realistic, less time-limited ad creation tasks with more representative and fully developed creative briefs, [and] better simulation of the real-world agency-situated conditions in which creative teams actually work" (p. 23).

Conditions in which creative teams work was the focus of Vanden Bergh and Stuhlfaut's research (2006). The researchers noted that only one other study in advertising research, focusing just on brainstorming, had addressed this broader focus (p. 376). Reviewing 68% (p. 30) of the interviews conducted for the column, "The Moment of Creation," from *AGENCY* magazine from 1991–2001, a column that interviewed creatives about the process they had been involved with of generating award-winning national ads, the researchers to an extent documented part of the model of creativity as social process posited by Csikszentmihalyi.[3]

The authors do not note that Csikszentmihalyi himself (1996) suggested that advertising is not a creative field. Nevertheless, advertising at best adds art, wit, and some bumper sticker wisdom to everyday life. Like art and some of the social sciences, it has its finger on the pulse of the zeitgeist. As McLuhan said, ads are a vigorous dramatization of communal experience; if they weren't, they would quickly lose our attention (1964, p. 203). Csikszentmihalyi implied that

---

[3] In 2004, I independently identified the Csikszentmihalyi model as a valid description of verbal-visual collaboration in advertising I had researched in 2002 (Cross, 2004, February).

advertising is a "shoot-from-the-hip" business and that creatives don't strive for perfection, but on the contrary, creatives often move from agency to agency in search of the environment and collaborators to create the perfect ad. One creative field Csikszentmihalyi included in his study of creativity was business management. If creative processes were identified in this applied area, they also occur in advertising. Moreover, nearly the exact phases in the creative process that Csikszentmihalyi described are found in a description of the advertising creative process from the 1940s, antedating his published work by over two decades (Young, 1944). Clearly, this model of creativity is germane for our purposes.

One component of the social process interrelating with advertising creatives' contributions is the field; that is, the political/economic system of organization(s) that finance these kind of creative works—in advertising, the field includes the agency, the client, the distributor, and the customer. Another is the domain, which Csikszentmihalyi defines as a set of symbolic rules and procedures in a particular discipline (1996, p. 27). One of the important contributions of Vanden Bergh and Stuhlfaut's research (2006) is to show in a general way the field generating advertising ideas and evaluating them. However, this research has a flawed conception of the domain. Where Csikszentmihalyi (1996) defines the domain as the rules and procedures of a discipline that is itself "nested in what we call culture, or the symbolic knowledge shared by a particular society or humanity as a whole" (p. 28), Vanden Bergh and Stuhlfaut define the domain as "culture" (p. 381) and later describe this culture as American popular culture and society (p. 391). Certainly a domain can influence a society and vice versa; however, there is a huge difference between a discipline or industry (e.g., biology, advertising, IT, or insurance) and American society. Also, relying on retrospective interviews in a national trade publication is helpful when no other knowledge exists but is in some ways limited. The method relies upon memories of participants well after the process concluded. Also, the lack of anonymity could cause interviewees to omit anything they considered potentially offensive or that otherwise did not present them in the best light. Ethnographers know that what participants say, do, and think can be three different things; a reason for long-term on-site observations. Another limitation of the study for our purposes is that although the research provides some helpful information on concept generation, it does not specifically focus the roles of artists and writers in this procedure. In recommending further research, the authors of this exploratory secondary research ask,

> What could a deeper examination of the field, the domain, and their interaction with the creative teams reveal about their contribution in specific and the system in general? From the field perspective, much more needs to be known about the effects of social structure and organizations on the development of creativity. What qualities in organizations promote creative inspiration? What qualities restrict it? As for the domain, how do creative persons access the information? (Vanden Bergh & Stuhlfaut, 2006, p. 377)

Answers to such questions are crucial because, as the researchers note, the social systems perspective

> unburdens the copywriter and art director from sole responsibility for the creative process (only in a theoretical sense) and places the responsibility for new ideas on the entire system.
>
> *In essence, it is the entire creative system that is responsible for the generation of ideas and the evaluation or judging of them to determine which ones will survive.* (my emphasis, p. 394)

Although all of the above research provides substantial groundbreaking perspectives, our knowledge needs to be advanced by detached and thorough empirical descriptions and analysis coming from someone not engaged in the collaboration or structuring it from the outside, but on-site, full-time for months to document and analyze social processes involved in creating real campaigns. It is particularly important that the researcher be on-site because composing is social action (Lindemann, 2001, pp. 32–33) and is shaped by its culture: the code of acceptable behavior shared by members of a society (Havilland, 1980, p. 29).[4] Because composing is a sequence of choices, researchers need to understand how both industry and organizational cultures (and the "structure of authority" [Faigley, 1985, p. 7] that support them) can influence verbal-visual group-writing processes, products, and the reception of those products. Research on creativity, though not specifically advertising, has shown that high levels of both personal and organizational factors encourage the most creative performances (Oldham & Cummings, 1996). Studying the functioning of the system of creativity reveals the criteria of the domain or discipline (in this case the practice of advertising) as well as of the field. Fields serve as filters to help us choose what to pay attention to amid the flood of information (Csikszentmihalyi, 1996, p. 42).

Conducting an ethnographic study of advertising creatives working on communications for clients, Pope-Ruark found that three communities influenced their use of advertising genres: their organizational community, occupational community, and the client-ad agency intercommunity (2008). This study uses genre theory to consider important elements found in the domain and field but does not focus on artist-writer relationships or a verbal-visual community of practice. The decisions of members can also influence the "technological lens" of the community of practice. Entire cultures have been differentiated by anthropologists based upon the "distinctive patterns to the interplay of the senses they

---

[4] "Culture" can describe humanity or many of its subsets (Kroeber & Kluckhohn, 1963, p. 367). I stipulate media-based cultures (e.g., visual, print, and oral culture), American popular culture, the discipline (industry, i.e., advertising), and the organizational culture of Heric Advertising, Inc. Miller and Selzer (1985) have described the latter two as "discourse communities."

present" (Howes, 1991, p. 9). That is, members of cultures that rely more upon one medium or a configuration thereof than another culture does may have a different "sensorium," a somewhat different mode of perception and cognition of consciousness (McLuhan, 1964; Ong, 2002). Observations of a community of intensive verbal-visual communicators will allow us to compare different subcultures of composing; for example, compare a community of writers and artists with a community of writers. As Lindemann noted, "We need to know much more about the complex relations between language, [visual] perception, and thought" (2001, p. 93).

What is called for is ethnographic research focused upon verbal-visual collaboration—specifically, "thick description"—which strives to convey the meaning of the recorded act within the social context in which it occurred. Envisioning Collaboration, employing pseudonyms to protect participants and encourage candor, is just such an ethnographic study, which will help us reenvision what Broadkey (1987) calls the "scene" of collaborative writing to include writer-artist dyadic collaboration interrelated with large-group verbal-visual collaboration.

CONTEXTUAL FRAMING

During my 2002 sabbatical, after 240 hours of phone calls and networking to attain the research site, I conducted 460 hours of observations of verbal-visual collaboration at a multiple award-winning regional/national advertising agency while it prepared campaigns and presented them in a pitch to retain the business of a key national account. Advertising is a nearly ubiquitous verbal-visual form of inducing symbolic cooperation, in part because it is a primary way to announce and promote the exchange of goods and wealth upon which consumer societies rely. And for the advertising agency, the most important link in "the endless chain of selling that links the whole advertising business" is "selling the agency to its clients" (Rothenberg, 1995, p. 61).

The Rhetorical Situation of Composing:
Heric Advertising's Struggle to Retain the Agavez Account

In 2002, Heric Advertising (pseudonym) was a full-service advertising agency, over a century old, that conducted planning, design, production, and placement, along with other marketing services, including public relations, sales promotion, Internet advertising, and direct marketing. Heric prized its long relationship with clients, some partnerships having lasted more than 30 years. In the previous two years, its advertisements had won more professional awards than those of any other agency in its city. Heric had $150 million[5] of capitalized billings in

---

[5] Figures disguised to protect anonymity of company. The economic situation represented is accurate, however.

2001, a year CEO Jim Montgomery characterized as "tough." Indeed, 2001 was a tough year for the advertising industry in general, a year that *Advertising Age* reported had included a "disastrous first quarter" (Cardona & Dipasquale, 2002). Adding to the impact of the tech bubble's bursting in 2000, the 9/11 terrorist attacks had precipitated another very large drop in the stock market. Although the economy was technically in recovery, businesses were still spending anemically on advertising. Having national/international corporations as clients is critical to an agency's reputation; Heric lost a very large national account in early 2001 and, as a result, laid off 15% of its 200-person staff. However, expansion and contraction in ad agencies due to accounts coming or going is typical in the industry. As Rothenberg noted, advertising has few cushions others have—only people (1995, p. 22). To attain new business, Heric typically did six to eight pitches for new business a year. Throughout the year, Heric continued to "take a pounding" but landed a large and growing account, and by February 2002, thanks to what the CEO characterized as the agency's "strong work and improved client relationships," was on the upswing. The agency needed to hold onto its existing clients to avoid further decimation.

At this time, Heric got the word that one of its national accounts, lawn mower manufacturer Agavez Corporation (pseudonym), an American-founded company, which had been recently bought out by an East Indian conglomerate, had been downsized and ordered to centralize its advertising by having one agency instead of the current two handle both its point-of-sale (POS) and other advertising. Point-of-sale advertising involves everything in the store and its milieu that communicates to the customers about product assortment, quality, and price. This mode of communication is responsible for one half of purchase decisions made in the store (Soto, 2006, p. 7). For 3 years, Heric had been handling Agavez' other advertising: TV, print, radio, Internet, direct marketing, public relations, and outdoor. However, now Heric had been invited to compete with four other agencies for all of the Agavez advertising business, including the current Agavez POS creators. Heric stood to gain another $1.1 million in billing or lose $2.8 million and likely institute more layoffs in a downward trend. The account was also very important because, as its account manager said, "It's easier to keep business than go out and get new business. So you . . . put an effort behind it" (Audiotape Transcription [TR], p. 686).

A major reason Agavez wanted to consolidate its advertising was to create a "one voice approach," with which an organization tries to "unite brand/image advertising, direct response advertising, public relations and consumer sales promotion into a single positioning strategy at the outset of an [sic] promotional campaign" (Carlson, Grove, & Doerch, 2003, p. 70). Before, Heric had provided the strategic campaigns while a small graphics-oriented agency provided most of the POS materials unrelated to the strategic campaigns. Because Agavez planned to devote most of its budget to POS for reasons noted above, they needed an agency that did excellent POS; Heric was perceived by Agavez to be very strong strategically with non-POS forms of advertising, but weak at the point of sale. Because of Heric's capacity for strategy, however, they were given the chance to translate it not only into other media but also into effective POS merchandizing.

Heric had gotten past the current competition in its first assignment from Agavez—redoing the Agavez logo. Rather than just providing something flashy that had nothing to do with the business, Heric asked Agavez pertinent questions such as, "What does this product stand for?" and "What are you trying to do as a business?" But Agavez had no answers, so Heric conducted focus-group research with potential or current customers and also tested several logos. From this research and conferring with Agavez, Heric came up with the strategic objective to "position [Agavez] as the common sense approach to lawn mowing and own the 'Value' position in lawn mowing category: all the features and quality that you need for a fair price—not necessarily cheap!" The consumer audience addressed was what market research had indicated was the typical Agavez customer: 25- to 59-year-old male homeowners. Most of the intended audience were customers of MegaWorld (pseudonym), a megastore chain discount retailer that sold the largest share of Agavez' products. Heric Advertising wanted to convince Agavez to build its brand equity because in Heric's opinion, MegaWorld was trending toward "owning the [Agavez] brand," in effect. In such a situation, MegaWorld could force Agavez to lower price points and quality (e.g., use cheaper steel to sell at a lower price) to levels destructive to the manufacturer. Agavez, on the other hand, wanted to eliminate consumer perceptions of it as manufacturer of solely inexpensive lawnmowers and to increase perceptions of the mowers' strong features for the price. It wanted to move into the middle price range of the market while retaining its "shelf (selling) space" in MegaWorld.

The friction between Agavez and MegaWorld was endemic of conflicting forces in the global economy, a struggle between brands and huge chain discount retailers. Such retailers buy their goods cheap and sell them cheaper than competitors, flourishing in part by selling a high volume of goods. Manufacturers were drawn to sell their goods with such vendors to sell high volume, and they became dependent upon high volume. As *Frontline* reported, such retailers have shifted the relationship between manufacturer and retailer. Previously, the manufacturer created the product and asked the retailer to sell it. With superstores, however, the retailer determines what sells and tells manufacturers what to make at what quality level and at what prices. When the manufacturer of retail goods had been dominant, retailers were mostly thousands of individual "mom and pop" stores and small chains. However, the low prices of superstore chains drove most of these smaller stores into mergers or out of business. Today a manufacturer may do business with just four or five superstore chains. Once a manufacturer becomes dependent upon the high volume, then the retailer starts "squeezing" them on profit margins (Waller, 2002). Retailers exert huge influence on manufacturers, often having several different manufacturers bid on shelf space at the same time (Smith & Young, 2004).

Such tactics were a major factor in many manufacturers moving to China, where, resulting in part from the forced labor of dissidents including Christians, Falun Gong, and other religious minorities, superstore markups on products had changed from 18%–20% for American-made goods to 60%–80% for Chinese-made goods (Reuter, 2007; Smith & Young, 2004). Another source, *Business Week*, reported the difference in markup as 30%–50% (The China price: Special report, 2004). Such stores often pride themselves on having "loss leader" products: low-end products that the retailer makes no money on but whose prices draw shoppers who often decide on slightly more expensive products after arriving and comparing features. To meet these low price points, big-box retailers require and economically force manufacturers to lower quality (e.g., lower the thread count in clothing). The retailer then may dictate that the house brand become a higher quality product than the outside brand (frequently the manufacturer makes both the house brand and the brand-name product), sometimes causing the store to become a "brand killer" (Waller, 2002). Such tactics have caused some companies that wished to retain high quality to go bankrupt. For example, Rubbermaid was named the most-admired company by *Fortune* magazine in 1994, but 10 years later, after losing shelf space at superstores because it refused to lower quality and price, it was bankrupt, and Wal-Mart was voted the most-admired company (Smith & Young, 2004) as well as the largest company in the *Fortune* 500. In 2002, retail brand-name companies were in a sometimes life-or-death struggle to maintain their reputation while working with megastore chains such as K-Mart, Best Buy, Circuit City, Target, and others that sold most of their products.

Reflecting its need to maintain its volume at self-service MegaWorld, whose stores' floor space averaged over 100,000 sq. ft., Agavez changed its marketing strategy. In 2000–2001, it put 45% of its $5 million Heric marketing budget into brand-strengthening media advertising; 40% into POS; 10% into buyers guides, brochures, spec sheets, and other collateral materials; and 5% into public relations. However, the next year, it cut its Heric budget in half and put none of it into media advertising, 85% into POS advertising that went in retail stores, 15% into related collateral materials, and nothing into PR. Agavez also decided to produce its engine in China, where it could be made 40% cheaper. Agavez' total advertising budget was $20 million, of which $17.5 million went to superstore chain retailers directly to support their presentation of Agavez products.

This shift in advertising emphasis was part of a general trend, reducing "media"—TV, radio, and print advertising—and increasing POS merchandising, for important reasons. In 1998, research on purchasing found that in Europe, 67.2% of brand purchase decisions were made in the store, as were 72% in the United States (De Pelsmaker, Guens, & Vanden Bergh, 2001, p. 350). With advertising costs increasing sevenfold since 1980 and marketing costs amounting to 15% of revenues, marketers have become more accountable for their expenditures (Davis, 2005). For all of these reasons, not long before the start of this study, the majority of consumer-product marketers in the United States planned to increase their POS budgets for 1999, nearly half of them (46.7%) by more than 5% (Schober, 1998, p. 44).

Heric's challenge was to focus largely on POS, but convey on this merchandising vital brand information and selling concepts initially composed for print. Entailed in all was a vision for the brand. Signified by a logo or trademark, brands are (a) goods identified by name as the product of a single company and (b) consumer perceptions of the product. Companies typically try to build brand equity (the aggregate of all differentiating elements of a brand to consumers, retailers, and distributors), which results in demand and individual commitment to a brand. Brand equity develops a loyal customer base and attracts new customers. To the degree a brand does this well, it grows, compared with the competition, and is more profitable (White, 2005). An alternative means of gaining customers is simply to either match or offer the lowest price. However, this approach only builds loyalty to the price, and many consumers are "burned" by purchases of poor quality in this pursuit. An alternative that at least permits the company to retain quality and charge more than the cheapest price is to offer some additional value beyond what the cheaper competitors provide—to occupy "the value position" in the market. In Agavez' case, this value was "all the features and quality you need at a fair price. Not necessarily cheap." It thus differentiated itself from the poor-quality commodity products and also from the high-end "designer" mowers with extra features of interest only to the status-seeking or very serious gardeners. Brand building was a major trend in 2002, as Russell and Lane (2002)·note: "during the 1980s, too many marketers milked their brands for short-term profits instead of protecting and nurturing the brands. In the 1990s, brand building became fashionable again. Today marketers realize the brand is their most important asset." This asset was threatened by the economic impetus to decrease product quality.

Another challenge to creating an effective brand for Agavez was its need to broaden its lawn and garden identity. The company that bought Agavez was going to market many of its outdoor power tools and recreational vehicles (e.g., go-karts) under the Agavez brand name. To simultaneously broaden and reinforce the Agavez brand, Heric planned to construct an integrated marketing campaign. Integrated marketing campaigns interrelate all communication on behalf of the brand: media advertising, promotional, PR, direct mail, point of sale (display), and the like. If this technique succeeds, it builds brand equity by communicating a consistent brand message (Russell & Lane, 2002, p. 68). Different media can emphasize different aspects of brand equity; for example, direct-mail advertising communicates the brand message to existing customers. Print and TV advertising, on the other hand, by focusing on specialized shows and periodicals (e.g., *Field and Stream*) viewed by target markets, communicate to many potential customers unfamiliar with the brand who must decide by what they encounter about the brand (White, 2005).

To prepare for the pitch to keep and expand the Agavez account, seven dyadic writer-artist teams at Heric created numerous ads, including some POS advertising, which they displayed at what the company called "tip-ball" selection meetings overseen by the creative director. Over 17 business days, the competitors were winnowed to three teams. The concepts for the integrated marketing campaigns were first created in verbal-visual print ads before being transposed into messages in other media.

Organizational/Physical Structure

Along with economic conditions, interrelated organizational and physical structures can shape composing practices (Cross, 1988, 2001). A survey of both furthers our understanding of the "scene" of print verbal-visual collaboration in this integrated marketing campaign.

The Heric Building was a seven-story Romanesque row office downtown in a medium-sized southern city. The outside edifice was not especially salient. But inside its narrow foyer, which stretched the entire first level, walking across the polished marble floor that reflected from the walls art, lights, and a striking floral arrangement, and approaching the mahogany elevator housing made a different impression, heightened because of its contrast with the outside. A six-floor elevator ride opened onto the decoratively carpeted floor that housed Heric's senior management. Past the receptionist, to the left, encased on three sides by frosted-glass walls, the office of Heric's President and CEO overlooked the street and lake beyond through floor-to-ceiling windows. A 22-year veteran of the company, an ex-Air Force officer who began at Heric as an account manager and who got to work each morning at 4 a.m., James (Jim) Montgomery had been Heric's sixth president since 1992. He described his job as making sure resources are put where needed and "ensuring that we've got communication flowing every day in all jobs." Communication was critical at Heric, Montgomery said,

> because "we sell ideas," andwe want ideas from everybody, . . . whether they're working on the [project] team or not. . . . Our real world is not here—[it's] our client. And they don't particularly care whether you have white hair or red hair; . . . they don't care where you went to school. . . . [They want to know] 'How are you going to solve my business problem?

Regarding the organization of the agency, Montgomery said, "Our structure is the structure that it takes to get work done for the clients." The company had a formal structure (see Figure 1), with Montgomery presiding immediately over the Chief Creative Officer, Director of Research and Account Planning, Director of Account Services, VP Direct Marketing and Sales Promotion, and VP

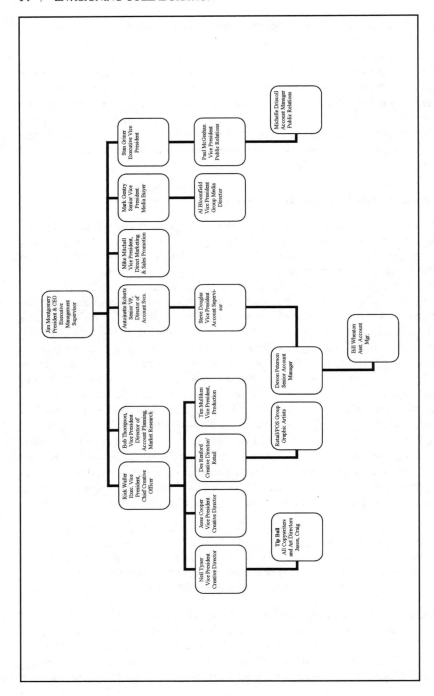

Figure 1. Organizational chart of Agavez mower pitch team, Heric Advertising, Inc.

Media Buyer (of print space and broadcast time for ads). These senior managers, Montgomery said, conferred with each other about the quality of work processes such as pitch preparation processes at Heric, striving for continuous improvement, the goal of total quality management (TQM). Accounts were serviced by account managers, who were the contact to the client; the Chief Creative Officer and creatives; and by people from public relations, direct mail, media buying, and production. But beyond this formal structure were tip-ball meetings, where numerous artist-writer dyads (pairs) presented campaign ideas.

Attending tip-ball meetings could not only be the teams assigned the work, but also managers and production staff. Here the CEO said the purpose was to

> go broad [with] . . . as many different kinds of ideas from as many different people as you can, as long as they fit the boundaries . . . in the [strategy], . . . then . . . refine, select, reject, improve, continue to . . . listen to input. . . . The final decision is with the [Chief Creative Officer], but he rarely does anything in a vacuum . . . . It's a never-ending process for the writers and art directors and designers to communicate with each other so that we can communicate with our clients. (TR 721)

Such a structure is similar to that of successful firms in another fast-developing and changing industry—computer product development—who "blended limited structure around responsibilities and priorities with extensive communication and design freedom to create improvisation within current projects" (Brown & Eisenhardt, 1997, p. 1). This similarity is not surprising, because advertising encounters "a general class of design problems also found in product development" (Johar et al., 2001, p. 2). A midpoint between rigid structure and unstructured chaos was found most successful: "Too much structure leads to mundane products, predictable strategy, and missed market opportunities. . . . Too little structure leads to high costs, missed schedules, and confusion" (Brown & Eisenhardt, 1998, p. 28). Cross-project communication was strongly encouraged.

Although the intention was to have continuous input so that there would not be last-minute changes caused by people withholding ideas or not attending until late, the process was open to change through the last minute. As the CEO said of the creative process described in this book,

> There were still some nights and some weekend work involved. Not four nights in a row, as we've experienced from time to time. And sometimes that happens because of last-minute changes. Somebody will bring in an idea that's late, and everybody likes it better than what we've been working on, so we jump on that.

This flexibility and recursive rather than linear process was one also found in successful computer development teams, who "fiddle right up to the very end" (Brown & Eisenhardt, 1997, p. 9).

Another part of the extensive communication at Heric was one-on-one. As the CEO said,

> In terms of how to manage our people—because that's our most important asset—we do that with a lot of personal attention. This is an open-door place—every office from this one on down. . . . Everybody is in and out of every office. Everybody is talking. Everybody tries to . . . leav[e] the ego at the door. (TR 725)

When egos clash, as artist Jason Wells told me, "neither side wins because they are not willing to listen to the other." This situation would particularly damage Heric. As Steve Douglas, Account Manager for Agavez, told me, "There's a lot of one-on-one stuff that goes on. That's where . . . some . . . decisions get made. It's just kind of talking instead of the big group—[for example] 'Neil, you're not saying anything. What do you think about doing this?' or 'Bob, here's how I think we should do the strategy'" (TR 686). Part of why managers were circulating and talking was that creatives, involved in time-intensive projects under tight deadlines, did not read e-mail much. Steve told me he often wrote out policies but communicated them orally.

Beyond interaction in the workday, the organization provided other opportunities for informal communication by sponsoring a company softball team, golf scramble, and fairly frequent company parties. This company-sponsored recreation also evinced its partly human-relations style of management, which also included e-mails announcing birthdays of employees and humorous e-mails describing new hires or employees leaving to take jobs at other firms. But Heric also encouraged informal project communication, a tactic used as well by product-development firms by having coffee bars situated within the development areas to encourage informal connections and problem-solving on breaks (Brown & Eisenhardt, 1997, p. 9).

Within the organization's macrostructure occurred a range of creative outcomes, as the CEO noted: "Some days you don't feel like it's got a chance of working at all. And some days you're 'Wow, that's perfect.' Most days it's pushing to make it work" (TR 727).

Verbal-visual collaborative endeavors were shaped not only by the organizational structure but also by the definition of the rhetorical situation and campaign strategy. This area was the province of the Vice President-Account Planning and Research, whose office was a brief walk down the frosted-glass hallway. Bob Thompson, who had been with the company for 4 years, had a doctorate in market research from a nationally prestigious university. Thompson had asked Agavez the questions about what their brand stood for and what they wanted to accomplish with their logo. Thompson had commissioned the focus-group research to determine the preferences of their potential customers. He and the Senior Account Manager, Steve Douglas, had come up with the strategy to sell the product mentioned above. The Chief Creative Officer told me that this strategy needed to "marry" two key elements: what the client wanted to say about the product and what the consumer wanted to hear. The CCO indicated in a meeting that the customer wanted to hear not only about the benefit but also the reasons to believe that the product would deliver. Account Planning's research of potential customers typically made the account planner represent the customer in discussions with account managers, who represented what the client wanted to say. Planning "should be able to tell the creative and the client . . . 'Here's how you have to do this so that it's what the consumer wants to hear" (TR 421).

In creating strategy, the Vice President-Account Planning and Research strove for an idea that creatives could visualize and translate into something persuasive. The statement of strategy needed to be sufficiently general to allow a range of responses, but sufficiently specific to avoid "strategic drift." Sometimes to help the creatives visualize their audience and its values, he created "brand personalities." These are TV or movie actors who conveyed in their roles the demographic and psychographic characteristics of the consumers of the product. For example, for Agavez, he encouraged creatives to write to the character played by John Goodman in the TV sitcom *Roseanne*, with attributes of "solid/well-grounded, simple/casual, carefree, reliable, knows what matters in life, laid back, no-nonsense, gets the most out of life." The brand promise for Agavez (the mower "gets the job done without a fuss") plus the brand personality produced the brand position—both the audience to be invoked (Ede & Lunsford, 1984) and *product* to be invoked in the ads to position the product in the minds of the people in the market for the product. Identification, as Burke noted (1962), is necessary for persuasion, and the goal was to convince the consumer that, as the creative with the winning tag line put it, role-playing a consumer, "that mower is all about what I'm all about" (TR 774). For that result to be brought about honestly, the strategy had to be the product of careful research of both product features and audience characteristics.

Another walk down a frosted-glass hall on floor six, passing buttoned-down managers in business casual attire, brought one to the French doors of the office of the co-writer of the strategy, the Agavez account manager. At 32 years old, Steve Douglas was not only an account supervisor but also vice president of Heric. Despite his youthful appearance, his ability to grasp the essential and to lead made him widely perceived at Heric to be Jim Montgomery's heir-apparent.[6] As the chief contact at Heric, Steve spent much of his day talking to clients about their brand and project issues. This communication was vital to Steve's vocation because, as the senior vice president of account services said, "Ninety percent of an account services person's career is plotted by the client relationships he or she develops." Nevertheless, Steve also spent much time coordinating personnel working on the Agavez account because he was responsible for "having everybody else bring their part to the table . . . [and for] bringing it all together." As he said, "You've got to have a relationship, an open dialogue with these people for them to be comfortable with what we're all

---

[6] Douglas became Heric's seventh President and CEO several years later.

doing." Possessed of the salesperson's ability to adapt to the other person's mood and communicate appropriately, Steve was clear, humorous, and when necessary, forceful.

His other duties entailed in working on account campaigns included constructing and reviewing budgets, writing memos, and doing paperwork for the "traffic system" that managed the internal workflow. He led a team of account managers that also included an associate and assistant manager. Because he had several important accounts, his assistant manager did much of the nuts-and-bolts communication with the creatives. However, Steve also coordinated the strategic, budget, and deadline elements of the integrated marketing campaign for the Agavez pitch, conducting several meetings with public relations, direct-mail (sales letter) marketing, media buying, and other managers involved. The 3 weeks before the pitch, Steve averaged well over 60 hours a week on the job. The night before it occurred, he worked until 9:30 p.m. reviewing the work: making sure the boards (pasted-up print ads) were right, that there were no mistakes in the written material, that a caterer was scheduled—"just all the logistics." Although he had a central role in the oral presentation of the pitch, including "doing the ask" (asking for the company's business), he spent no time working on what he was going to say ahead of time because, he told me, he had been working on the account for over 3 years and knew the brand well (TR 684).

From the locus of the management structure and strategy that shaped the verbal-visual collaboration, we next move to the level of composing. The sixth floor, with its skylit Scandinavian wood staircase that circled to the plush seventh-floor client conference room, was Heric's showcase, where deals were signed. Descending, however, below floors that held the direct marketing, public relations, accounting, and production staffs, to the third-floor domain of the creatives, you stepped from day into night—darkness. Instead of fine wood, the elevator entrance was corrugated steel, and one strode/stumbled from one pond of a spotlight's strong light to the next, each situated occasionally down the hall, trained on white walls or concrete floor, creating a wide range of value—grey and black shadows. Because of the single light sources, people walking by tended to have black circles under their eyes. Welcome to the creatives' cave! *Inside* their offices along this twilit corridor, one found much of the same milieu: track lights and Macs illuminating the cherry desks, but darkness surrounding this pool of light, cloaking the exposed rafters and brick back wall. Creatives insisted upon this Soho loft atmosphere, but the IT staff hated it because they couldn't see the backs of the computers they were supposed to install or repair (see Figure 2).

At the end of my interview to do research at Heric, the CEO told me I could return "if I promised not to wear a tie." But jettisoning the tie did not prepare me for the dress code of the creative floor, which, as Rothenberg said of another agency, was "dress . . . less for success than for softball" (p. 221), with many men, for example, in t-shirts and faded jeans, who appeared to lift weights. A

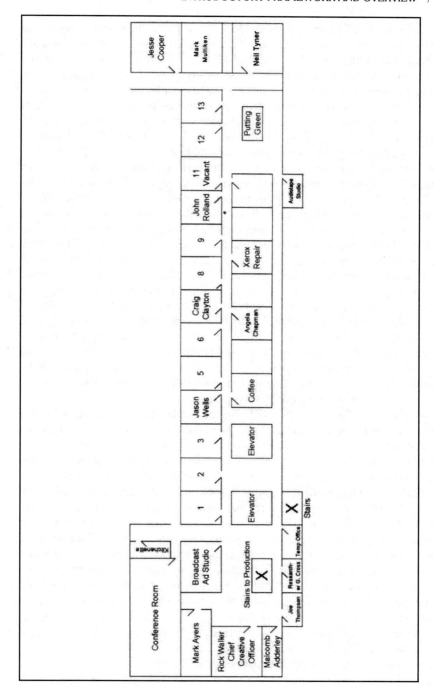

Figure 2. The creative cave, Heric Advertising Agency.

few had shaved heads and goatees, which could make them seem gnome-like in those catacombs or cavemen warming themselves around Mac G4s. Women were more stylishly dressed. The end of the long office corridor opened into a window-lit area with a 15-foot ceiling, where creatives occasionally repaired to inspire themselves for sporting goods or other ads by playing Ping-Pong, putting, or practicing foul shots at a basketball net. Although you blinked at some first appearances (perhaps because you thought you were back on a college campus), what was returned to your gaze was the focused, detached look of a professional. In the cave they were talking business and collaborating on ads at a fast pace.

Writers on the creative floor generated ad concepts with art directors. Once "comps" (unfinished drafts of the ads) had been approved for production by the Creative Director, the art directors collaborated with graphic artists on the fourth floor to do "mechanicals" (final drafts of the ads). A staircase wound upward to this production floor from the other end of the cavernous corridor. Up there, behind the stairs, overlooking the street, was the office of Desmond "Des" Renfield, Creative Director of Design. On the other side of the staircase, in offices along a corridor, resided graphic artists, including computer animation, POS merchandising, and production specialists. Extremely long hours were frequently spent by employees on this floor, in part because production conducted the last phase before the deadline. Halfway back the corridor, the floor opened into a graphics studio with high-resolution printing machines capable of huge posters, large layout tables where ads could be mounted on pasteboards, stacked reams of paper, translucent decals, and multicolored jugs of toner. There were the machines and tools used to shape and assemble Plexiglas and metal end-aisle, H-rack, gondola, and other store displays.

This floor was the destination not only of display but also of other printed creative concepts to be produced. From mock-ups, the Production Director checked all mechanical specs and did high-resolution production, including blowups of materials; he also sent finished materials or files out to the media (e.g., magazines, newspapers, printers of billboard ads). The fourth floor also held the office of the traffic team, who, in maintaining the workflow, continually descended to the creative floor to remind them of deadlines and pick up all the (sometimes myriad) pieces of assigned work from each member of an account team and bring it to the production team. They also brought finished work down to the art directors for their review and signature. Keeping track of hours devoted to each project was also necessary to properly bill the client. In 2002, for the Agavez account, Heric Billing Services charged these rates per hour for the following roles: Management Supervisor (the CEO), $144; Account Supervisor (Steve), $135; Chief Creative Officer, $155; Art Director, $115; Copywriter, $115; Creative Director of Design, $135; Graphic Designer, $115; Production Art, $90; Print Production, $105.

Descending the stairs from Production back to a skylit area before the cave, we see to the right the conference room where creative teams presented their work in group meetings. Outside it, on tables near lounge chairs, were stacks of periodicals, such as *2002 Chicago Creative Directory, AV Video Multimedia Producer; Wine Spectator; Veer Visual Elements Catalogue.* To the left was the office of the Chief Creative Officer, who presided over tip-ball meetings and selected the work for production. Other responsibilities of the CCO were to motivate artists and writers to produce client-buying creative work on strategy, and to recruit and keep good talent. Rick Waller, 44, had directed Heric's creatives for 3 years. Very early in his 23-year career he had also worked for Heric as an art director. Later, as creative director at agencies in large eastern and midwestern cities, Waller had contributed to or was responsible for bringing in $135 million of new business in one year and tripling the capitalized billings over 3 years at another agency, where they had gone 12 for 12 in bringing in new business (where 1 in 5 was considered typical). He had worked on many national and international accounts. The reason he attributed to those agencies' marked growth during his tenure was his approach of tip-ball meetings.

Waller saw the tip-ball meeting, involving all people working on the account and others, as having several advantages. In a traditional mode, teams were pitted against teams for the same account, but they never saw each other's work. For print, each writer-artist team just showed its work on the account to the Chief Creative Officer. The teams were never with account managers, executives, PR people, direct marketing, media buyers, or others:

> You're never really exposed to a wide array of thinking on the brand or on the assignment. Whereas this way you're exposed to everybody in the room's thinking. So it's impossible for you to walk out of that meeting thinking the same way as when you came in. Your idea might still be right-on, but you won't think about it exactly the same way. (TR 414)

Jesse Cooper, an international-award-winning art director, concurred with Rick's estimation of this approach: "Everyone's been sitting . . . in their own little corner working on it, and then you come in and see what someone else did, and it's 'Huh, I didn't even think of that.' And . . . you don't take their ideas, but . . . it will inspire you for something else" (TR 66).

This approach also, Waller noted, helped account managers and creatives work as a team:

> In most of the agencies you go to, it's account against creative. . . . The creatives bad-mouth the account people and the account people bad-mouth the creative people. And there are two separate cycles. . . . The only place they meet is . . . with a client or the creative director and the head of account service. [But with the tip-ball,] everybody is thrown into it together. And they feel an ownership of it because they've been in the meetings. [Account services] understand how it was conceived. They saw how it evolved. So hopefully they know how to help sell it because they've been involved . . . versus just, "here it is, now go sell it." . . . That's demeaning. And it doesn't give [the creatives] the tools they need to help sell it. (TR 414)

Waller also stressed that the exposure helped noncreatives contribute: "this way, everybody is set up to . . . think about how they can help to solve it."

A managerial method that facilitates such input is needed. In quickly changing industries such as advertising, in which the emphasis has shifted from media to POS to the Internet, an often-successful managerial approach is "improvisation." Although applied to product innovation, it is analogous with jazz improvisation, in which one creates music while adjusting to the changing musical interpretations of other group members. It relies upon (a) performers intensively communicating with each other in real time (Brown & Eisenhardt, 1997, p. 12) and (b) within a preestablished song structure. The structure provides boundaries needed for cohesion. The intensive communication, Brown and Eisenhardt note, allows group members to adjust and coordinate. The group can thus accomplish tasks even as the context changes (1997, p. 12). In the case of the tip-ball meetings, the strategy provided the terrain and boundaries. The result of such an improvisational approach in many "high velocity industries" is "rapid, continuous innovation" (p. 13).

At Heric, Chief Creative Officer Rick Waller, a tall ex-athlete who labeled himself a coach rather than a manager, said that the approach also provided a rapid education:

> Why I've been able to hire so many young creatives is because they get so far in that learning curve that they would never get in a normal agency. And they're treated like a regular creative versus a junior creative. But they're exposed to everybody's thinking that you would never get [in the traditional mode].

Along with Waller, CEO Jim Montgomery stressed that the invention atmosphere was nonhierarchical and cross-functional:

> [We] provide an atmosphere . . . that needs to be nonstructured so that the creative direction doesn't become subservient to the strategic direction or vice versa. So that junior people have courage enough to stand up in front of a seasoned guy like Rick Waller and say, "I don't think that idea is good. Here's a better idea and let me tell you why." And . . . blending all the different disciplines that we have in-house together: that's the focus.

The primacy of the idea is typical of advertising agencies in general, according to Rothenberg (1995): "There are few places where money and power are less important than an idea" (p. 109). There was great motivation for creatives to generate "the big idea" because getting their work produced was necessary for retention, raises, and promotion. To get strong ideas, Waller said, it took two different kinds of creatives. One type worked there for a while, then moved on to another agency to further their careers, like surfers in search of the perfect wave, to create the perfect ad. As Waller noted,

> The hard thing about creative [material] is it's you . . . that's put out there, and so if somebody doesn't like it, it's like they're saying they don't like you. And so you're always wanting people to like your creative. . . . Then you do something that has the whole world talking about it. But now— that was two years ago. And now it's three years ago, and I need to do something that's got everybody talking about it. So even when you achieve it, it's so fleeting.

"You're only as good as your last ad," as Waller and other creatives told me, and creatives had to produce many ads per year. Moving "when you're hot," however, could bring about not only new perspectives, but also increased responsibilities and compensation. Waller had moved to Heric in part because employees could own a share of the company and thus reap more from the business they brought in than just a salary.

Along with the "gypsy," Rick said, was another kind of creative at Heric:

> We've got some great creatives . . . who will never leave here just because they're from [this city] and they've got families. . . . And they've reached that point in their life to where they're comfortable with themselves, and they've accomplished what they want to accomplish. . . . They still want to . . . do great work, but it's not about going out there and proving to the world that I can do it. . . . You need to have the people . . . who give you that base and give you . . . the soul of it. But then you've always got to make sure you've got the people coming through that are always going to keep it fresh and keep pushing everybody who's there. . . . Unless they are growing, you're not getting new thinking.
>
> "Ignorance is bliss" . . . for creatives because . . .[when] you're young, . . . you don't know rules. . . . The worst thing about creative is when you start limiting yourself "because we presented some like this, and they didn't like that, and then we tried something like this and they didn't like that." So you start limiting the area that you'll think [in]. . . . And then you start just narrowing and narrowing that box. . . . Hopefully, what jump-ball does is you've always got people who don't know the rules, and so they're always trying stuff that's different. You have an idea like this (pointing to a new ad)—you wouldn't get that if you were working on the brand all the time because you know they like to see a big *product*. [But] you know it's got to be all about the *benefits*.
>
> What you hope is that when someone leaves . . . we bring in somebody who is just as good or better, and they just keep growing it and building it. . . . A lot of agencies will hire people [when] they look at their book and go "I would have done something like this." *I* want to hire people who do stuff—it's like, "How did you come up with that? How did you get there?" . . . And hopefully if everybody you hire is something different, you're going to keep expanding and expanding everybody's view.

Another value of the tip-ball approach, Waller said, was the volume of material created by dyadic and large-group collaboration:

We pitched [a client] and we won it. In the middle of the meeting, the client goes "How much longer did these guys have to work on this than the other agencies that presented?" And the consultant goes "They were given the brief at the same time," and the client goes "They did all this in the same amount of time as these other guys did? . . . The last thing on their mind should be, "Man, do they really want this business?" It should be . . . "They'll move heaven and earth to get this business." Because every client wants to feel like they're your most important client, whether they're your smallest client or your biggest client.

None of them want to be the only one with you, and if [you]'ve got other brands that they respect . . . , that's a plus because they judge themselves by the quality of the other clients you've got. But at the same time they want to think that they're your most important client. So . . . you want to wow them; you want to deliver on the strategy. You want to have some stuff in there that's a little bit edgy and is pushing the strategy. But then you need to have stuff that's right in their safe zone that they just go "that's a no-brainer, I can run that tomorrow." [Also] there's just something that will make them laugh and lighten it up.

Advertising is one industry where fun is an element. As Jim Montgomery, CEO, described the pitch process: "Get all the ideas out, have some fun with each other. Have some fun with the client. Make the work as good as we can make it." However, to select the campaigns to present to the client from the many generated in tip-ball meetings, the Chief Creative Officer said he kept the focus on the aim of the discourse (Kinneavy, 1971). Art and entertainment in the service of persuasion were constantly in contention with art and entertainment for their own sake. As Waller said, "If a client says, 'Why would you recommend that?' you have to be able to say why. And it can't be because it's cool or . . . hilarious. It's always got to be based on a strategy and how it's going to deliver that strategy." This point of view is consistent with research on effective advertising (e.g., Johar et al., 2001, p. 2), and the conflict between the creatives' tendency toward aesthetics vs. the account managers' insistence upon strategy that sells the product is well documented (Koslow, Sasser, & Riordan, 2003).

The discourse aim was not expressive either, for the Chief Creative Officer: his ad agency was not to be emphasized over the content:

You see a Wieden & Kennedy [ad from Nike's agency] and you go "Oh, that's a Wieden & Kennedy." I've always tried to not have a style. . . . I think the style should come from the brand. . . .To me that's how you do—maybe not . . . award-winning work, but work that works better. . . . You don't really try to make them wear clothes that they shouldn't wear. I don't try to dress it up so that everybody knows I did it. (TR 413)

For Agavez, unlike for some higher-end mowers, it was important to stress quality:

You've got to build in the quality because at the price point they are not going to grant you that quality. So you've got to get in the warranty . . . and all those things which will then justify spending that little for a mower. (TR 420)

His concentration upon persuasive strategy resulted in Rick not searching first for personnel whose greatest strength was dazzling technique. Trained as a commercial artist, Rick felt his solo work as a junior creative doing art and copy together helped his career because

it was more about the concept than the execution . . . .You can hire people [temporarily] to *execute ideas.* But to *come up with ideas*—right now, we've got a lot more writers than we do art directors, and that's just because I hire people based on ideas, not whether they're a writer or an art director. (TR 424)

It is within this system of creativity, economic context, and rhetorical situation that En*vision*ing Collaboration provides the first extensive documentation and analysis of expert artist-writer collaboration, documentation necessary to derive and analyze procedural knowledge in order to improve and teach both collaborative and individual verbal-visual composing.

OVERVIEW OF THE STUDY AND COMPLETION OF THE FRAMEWORK

My overarching research question is "how do art directors and writers collaborate within an organizational culture to create effective persuasive and informative verbal-visual messages for client/manufacturer, retailer, and consumer?" My research does not repeat the previously stipulated models of other advertising and verbal-visual researchers discussed above, but instead generally documents an actual process of verbal-visual creativity involving dyadic, large-group, and interorganizational collaboration. Moreover, it meticulously documents the verbal-visual composing processes of two artist-writer teams, focusing especially upon the visual and verbal skills writers need to successfully compose verbal-visual texts.

It also evaluates the degree of mindfulness and in turn effectiveness of selected dyadic and associated large-group collaborations. The most successful teams are those that stay mindful, heedfully interrelating regarding a common, accurate task representation (Asch, 1952; Cross, 2001; Weick & Roberts, 1993). People are heedful when they are critical, careful, consistent, purposeful, vigilant, and conscientious (Weick & Roberts, 1993, p. 361). Weick and Sutcliffe expanded the definition of mindfulness in 2001, including among other qualities "a more nuanced appreciation of context and ways to deal with it, and identification of new dimensions of context that improve foresight and current functioning"(Weick & Sutcliffe, 2001, p. 42).

Mindfulness is devoting the time and concentration to read situations accurately and adjust one's response appropriately, avoiding premature responses. As Thera notes,

> A specimen of research that is to be examined with the help of a microscope has first to be carefully prepared, cleaned, freed from extraneous matter, and firmly kept under the lens. In a similar way, the "bare object" to be examined by wisdom, is prepared by Bare Attention (mindfulness). It cleans the object of investigation from the impurities of prejudice and passion; it frees it from alien admixtures and from points of view not pertaining to it; it holds it firmly before the Eye of Wisdom, by slowing down the transition from the receptive to the active phase of the perceptual or cognitive process, thus giving a vastly improved chance for close and dispassionate investigation. (1996, pp. 34–35)

The premature response, on the other hand, normally involves a miscategorization or "normalizing" of the phenomenon observed and enacts routine activity and thoughts that have been used in the past when encountering the category of phenomena ascribed. Using such associative thinking simplifies life and allows us to take on other tasks. However, prematurely triggering associative thinking can perpetuate and enlarge mistaken or incomplete first observations and errors of judgment (Thera, 1997, pp. 51–52). Many accidents in organizations are not sudden, random occurrences, but rather are "incubated" because anomalous data that indicate danger are lumped together with typical data and responded to in routine ways (Weick & Sutcliffe, 2006, p. 517).

In collaboration, it becomes easier to make these errors in judgment because to communicate, people shift from perceptually based knowing to categorically based knowing. As the need to coordinate increases, people, by communicating via categories, distance themselves further from their initial perceptions of phenomena, reducing their awareness of those phenomena (Weick & Sutcliffe, 2006, p. 520).

Thus, it is imperative to identify, evaluate, and if possible help increase mindfulness in a collaborative activity prone to oversight through miscategorization. A key research question of this study, then, is how mindful are the interactions of dyad members and between the dyads and the large group?

To provide a detailed view of verbal-visual collaborative composing, the following additional research questions are addressed as well:

- To what degree is the composing visual? Verbal?
  - In ad concepts?
  - In discussion topics?
  - In intradyadic communication?
- How do the verbal, visual, and verbal-visual rhetorical elements of arrangement, clarity, concision, emphasis, ethos, and tone factor into the composing processes and products?

- What is verbal-visual dyadic invention?
  - What are commonalities in the sequences of invention?
  - What is the function of pauses?
  - What is kept? What is discarded?
  - What kind of audience analysis was used?
  - Were any transferable principles of verbal-visual invention used? For example, in his Aristotelian analysis of advertising product analysis, Marsh wondered, "might other heuristics of invention, such as the topoi, also be effective in product analysis and idea generation?" (2007, p. 184)
- How is power handled among collaborators?
  - To what degree are collaborators supportive? Assertive?
  - How is conflict managed?
- How mindful and productive are the dyads? Or the large group in decisions that involved the dyads?
- How do the findings of this first extensive study compare with existing models of verbal-visual collaboration and creativity (e.g., Csikszentmihalyi, 1996; Mirel et al., 1995)?
- How do artists and writers who come from very different communicative traditions and mental models create a common text representation that assimilates and accommodates rhetorical elements effectively?

To answer these questions, En*vision*ing Collaboration includes five additional chapters that compare the approaches of two accomplished dyads within the creative system. Chapters 2 and 3 document in detail the verbal-visual composing process for the Agavez Campaign of 20-year veteran supervisors in the advertising business who had worked together as a creative team for many of those years. Their approach relied significantly upon large-scale collaboration. Chapters 4 and 5 will describe the composing process of a young, new, but highly successful artist-writer team who focused on creating an idea that addressed all audiences in the correct relationship and proportions. This team could be described as convergent thinkers—people comfortable making quick decisions and coming to closure so they can move on to something else. Chapter 5 will also describe the conclusion of the Agavez campaign, including the evaluation of the finalists meeting, the pitch (presentation) to the client, and the outcome.

Chapter 6 will conduct a cross-case analysis (Miles & Huberman, 1994) of comparable aspects of the creative teams, addressing the above research questions. After examining the collaborative behaviors of writers and artists, I will reconsider the traditional concept of "writer" in the context of these cases. I will relate findings to pertinent research in technical and business writing; and rhetoric and composition; and also to some key findings in visual design, anthropology, media theory, neurolinguistics, advertising, and psychology. In addition, from a managerial standpoint, by examining the relevance of the account manager's creative brief to the rhetorical problem and the extent to which ads generated addressed the brief and any aspects of the rhetorical problem not represented by the brief, the book focuses upon the degree of mindfulness and in turn *effectiveness* of the individuals, dyads, and large-group collaborations (Cross, 2001, Weick & Roberts, 1993; Weick & Sutcliffe, 2006). The book will expand the notion of mindfulness to address ethical dimensions. It will also evaluate the results of the tip-ball approach with regard to its degree of success with clients and cost to personnel.

Chapter 6 will also include recommendations for pedagogy, including a unit on verbal-visual individual and collaborative composing with gateway activities (Hillocks, 1995), recommendations for improved verbal-visual composing in the workplace, recommendations for further research, and a final thought regarding the extent to which a discipline centered upon written composition should venture into visual design.

The Appendix will describe my methods of gathering and analyzing data, then provide a rationale for my mode of presentation, and reflexively consider the observer's influence on the observations. It will additionally honor the contributions of the support team to this 7-year study.

CHAPTER 2

Ping-Pong, Part I:
Collaborative Brainstorming of
an "Insight-Intensive" Team

Although Rick Waller, Chief Creative Officer at Heric Advertising, mildly discouraged creatives from continually working in the same teams, he allowed it. Friends since middle school, the first artist-writer team we will consider, creatives in their early forties, had worked with each other most of their professional careers. Such lengthy experience, the literature on mindfulness suggests, could be a liability because their work routines could obscure the nature of the problem at hand. A more "loosely coupled" team might "increase the number of ascertaining moments and the proportion of those moments that are directed at weak signals of developing problems" (Weick & Sutcliffe, 2006, p. 521). On the other hand, the reason this artist-writer team had been *able* to work together for so long was that they had been very successful in doing so. Their work routines were very efficient and effective once the problem at hand had been accurately diagnosed.

On Thursday, February 14, 2002, a day after the Brief Meeting, where the Account Manager had discussed the campaign strategy and rhetorical situation, copywriter Neil Tyner met with art director (visual artist) Jesse Cooper to brainstorm ad concepts for the Agavez pitch. That they worked together was also predictable because of their previous successful collaboration for Agavez products—Agavez had been "their" account. In an interview, they described Heric's *current* dealings with Agavez:

> Neil: Basically, we're trying to keep the business.

> Jesse: It's almost like we're chasing [the] business over again, track[ing it] down and competing with a couple of other agencies for it and—

> Neil: That's always weird, just because it's kind of like your wife saying, "Well, I've got three other guys. . . . I really love you, but I'm thinking . . ." [laughter] Just the fact that she's got three other guys, waiting there, is not good.

To retain the business, Heric was asked to create an integrated marketing campaign for Agavez' line of lawn mowers. The assignment was challenging because in composing the ads, the creatives had to serve all primary audiences: (a) the client, who decided whether the advertisements were ever shown to the public or not; (b) the client's customer—MegaWorld—the big-box retailer of the technology, who had its own ethos if not ego; and (c) the customer, who bought the mower.

To initially provide the competing ad teams with the rhetorical situation, the Account Manager wrote a creative brief based on qualitative research on past purchasers and other potential purchasers of the lawn mowers. This document had been presented the day before in the Brief Meeting (see Figure 3).

The Account Manager not only gave teams the brief, but he also circulated the qualitative research that was much of the brief's foundation. In the main, the brief was helpful to creatives. Its brand promise, "Agavez gets the job over so you can do more desirable things," interrelated product and benefit—not an easy task. However, gaps existed between the brief as presented and the research, seemingly because the research reported somewhat conflicting attitudes. While the research reported prospective consumers seeing grass cutting as a "comfortable escape," the research also suggested that they just wanted to get the job over with and forget it. In the struggle to pull together a coherent strategy from this contradictory data, in his oral presentation of the written brief to the teams, the Account Manager stressed the latter, saying the consumers "hate to mow their lawns." Simplifying the complex data in this manner, as the mindfulness literature suggests, made it easier to coordinate the eight competing teams and numerous other managers and staff involved. But such categorizing, even though the qualitative data it was drawn from was circulated to creatives early in the process, caused oversimplification that contributed to some later problems, probably, because as Weick and Sutcliffe (2006) assert, "we don't see through concepts, we see with them" (p. 518).

The creatives were asked to come up with preliminary versions of campaign concepts for tip-ball evaluation by 2/22/02, nine days after the Brief Meeting. Tip-ball is a metaphor referring to the head-to-head competition in the event that begins or resumes a basketball game when possession has been disrupted, when an official throws a ball up between two players, one from each of the opposing teams, who try to tip the ball to teammates. Neil and Jesse's ensuing preparation for the tip-ball meeting can be seen in Table 1 and Figure 4.

Neil and Jesse had prepared for many previous tip-ball meetings in their lengthy careers. Tall and balding, favoring untucked Arrow shirts, jeans, and boat shoes, Neil was by turns serious and deadpan, this demeanor frequently broken by rapid, nearly concussive belly laughs. Possessed of a strong work ethic, he generated many ideas across many media in intensive brainstorming sessions, and in campaign meetings made many practical recommendations that evinced his supervisor rank for a decade to that point. Neil's verbal-visual writing skills

1) Communication Objective: To own the "Value" position in lawn mowing category: all the features and quality that you need for a fair price—not necessarily cheap!

Target audience:
(a) Male, 15-59
(b) High school grads or some college
(c) Blue collar or mid-managerial
(d) Work hard for money and live within means
(e) Strong family values
(f) Believe simple things matter most
(g) Traditionalists
(h) Laid-back, casual
(I) Don't take life too seriously
(j) Dependable, loyal
(k) Commonsense-like
(l) Take pride in how they live but don't worry what people think about them
(m) Maintain their lawns
(n) But want to get on to things they like more
　(I) Being with family and friends
　(ii) Hunting and fishing
　(iii) NASCAR
　(iv) Car repair/restoration
　(v) Relaxing
　(vi) Other hobbies

2) Brand Promise: Agavez gets it done so you can move on to more impt things

3) Reasons to Believe: All features you need at a reas. price
(a) Briggs & Stratton and Tecumseh
(b) 2-yr. warranty
(c) 30 years exper. building mowers

4) Brand Personality: smart, simple, no-nonsense

5) Campaign Elements:
(a) Print (mag and news)
(b) Serious focus on instore POS

Figure 3. Pertinent elements of the Agavez creative brief.

Table 1. Overview of Jesse and Neil's Collaborative Process During
the First Part of the Agavez Campaign, 2/13-3/6

2/13/02	Creative Brief Meeting: Situation, Purpose, Audience, Ad Strategy Defined: For selling low-end to mid-priced lawnmowers: "Get it over with and do something you want to do"
2/14	Jesse and Neil's Concept-Generating Meeting
2/14	Neil generates lines for evolving concept
2/15	Neil meets with Jesse, goes over lines
2/15-20	Jesse creates ads from lines and concepts
2/20-22	Jesse reviews progress with Neil, finishes ads
2/22	Neil and Jesse pitch ads with other teams in Tip Ball Meeting
2/27	Neil and Jesse pitch ads with other teams in Second Tip Ball Meeting, three campaigns of theirs selected to continue
3/6	Neil and Jesse pitch ads with other teams in Third Tip Ball Meeting, three campaigns selected to continue

had been honed by writing scripts for ABC-affiliate TV news while on summer internships during his years spent earning his bachelor's degree from a flagship southern state university. Neil's major competitive recognition, including national Clio and ADDY awards, along with 10 Clio Finalist awards, was first-rate.

For Jesse's work in graphic design at Heric and previously at one of the top agencies in the United States, the artist had won both national and international awards. Sporting an artist's gotee, Jesse had a laid back comportment, yet was industrious and unsparing of himself. He had earned an art degree from a regional southern university before working as a professional art director for 20 years.

FIRST AD CONCEPTING SESSION, 2/14: FORMING A MENTAL PICTURE

Since both Jesse and Neil were Vice Presidents, holding roughly equal rank, each had a large corner office on the end of the creative floor near the Ping-Pong and basketball area. When Neil came in to begin brainstorming preliminary concepts, Jesse was working with his Macintosh G-4 at a broad, C-shaped redwood desk. Atop the Mac glinted a bronze bowling trophy; several decorative

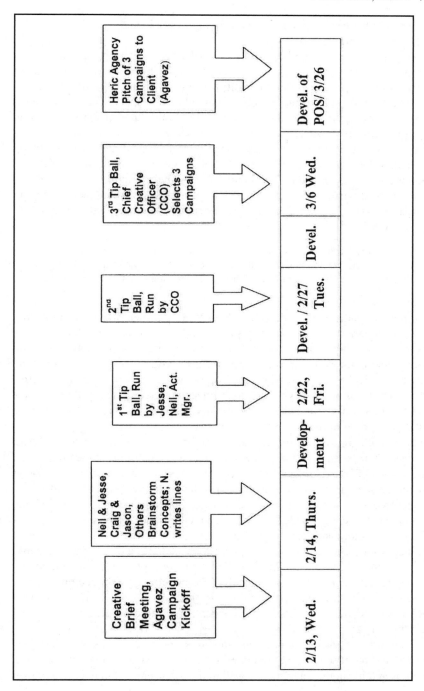

Figure 4. General Timeline of Composing Process, Agavez Campaign.

bowling balls Jesse had designed lined the windowsill, including a clear Plexiglas ball encasing a flaming locomotive.

Taking a chair across the desk from Jesse, the copywriter opened an 11 × 14 sketchpad. Neil's sketchpad would come in handy because the processes of advertising concept generation frequently begins by creating a visual concept of the ad, "form[ing] a mental picture of how the basic appeal can be translated into an effective selling message . . . [then] while thinking of the visual form, find[ing] words that will best reinforce and work together with the visual." Alternatively, one derives headlines from the basic appeal and then comes up with images that "fit these headlines" (Russell & Verrill, 1986, p. 411). Neil and Jesse generated concepts in both directions during their session.

The received wisdom in advertising is to generate numerous ideas during an advertising session, as award-winning advertising practitioner and educator Otto Kleppner noted:

> The creative leap is a period of free-association and brainstorming. No idea is too silly or farfetched . . . to be suggested. The crazy idea may be just the spark that leads to that illusive [sic] "great campaign." (Russell & Verrill, 1986, p. 411)

A rapid-fire game of Ping-Pong was how Neil described revising with his old friend and collaborator, and the metaphor could be used to accurately describe every phase of their collaborative interaction in the following account. But although one might expect the artist and writer to produce volleys of images and words respectively, in the session, the copywriter proposed more than words. And the artist did not always reply with images, although nearly three-fourths of the comments in the meeting were about visual matters, the copywriter contributing over 51% of the total visual comments.

In these exchanges, consumer attitudes that the creative brief reflected clashed: there was the imperative of focusing on the image and capacity of the product, all the quality and features the consumer needed to get the job done, yet on the other hand foregrounding the recreation activities the consumer preferred and would move on to do afterwards. In the session, 12 complete print ad and point-of-sale (POS) concepts were generated or otherwise focused upon. The veteran collaborators moved rapidly and recursively from concept to concept.

To begin the session, both creatives began sketching and talking. The copywriter started in a visual mode about his first concept, describing the visual relationship between product and benefit. The benefit (e.g., barbequing) would be shown in the foreground, the mower in the background, "out of the way, where it should be." For this visual concept, Neil quickly generated his first line, a throwaway.

Continuing the visual composing, the artist pointed to his sketches (see Figure 5) and proposed "a real bold graphic . . . right in front": in one ad, a set of golf clubs and in another, a barbeque grill in the foreground, and in both a mower

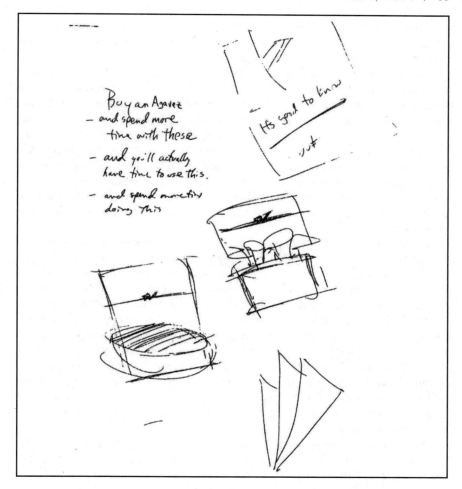

Figure 5. Jesse's preliminary sketches.
Reprinted with permission from Heric Advertising, Agavez Corporation.

in the background, seen through a window. Persisting in prioritizing product and benefit through their spatial positions and visibility, Neil then recommended putting the mower in "a shelter." Jesse added, "with the handle sticking out." Neil added another visual design element, however, that "there's some long grid thing going on in the foreground" (TR 32). The grid idea would later turn up as a different ad.

So from the copywriter's initial idea of small visual representation of mower and large representation of recreation, came two separate ad concepts, the "icons" ads, in which the recreation implement partially obscured the mower, and the "graph, chart ads," where the mower was inset into a small segment while the recreation was displayed in a large segment.

Because the product was partially hidden while the benefit was emphasized and the copy line would call more attention to the product, but negatively, these ideas visually communicated the Brief Meeting characterization of the consumer hating mowing. Be that as it may, in the Brief Meeting, Neil had said that past work with Agavez management had taught Heric creatives to show the mower: Agavez wanted the mower to be "the hero." Evident here were unresolved tensions caused by trying to address what the creatives perceived were mowing-hating consumers and the mower-loving manufacturer/client, both crucial audiences of the same ad.[1] Also contributing to the tension was the need to show the consumer that the product had sufficient features and quality to get the job done.

Responding to the opposite pole from consumer recreation, the next concept, brought up by Neil, was a "big hero thing about the mower." The "product-as-hero" ad was clearly a genre the dyad had produced many times previously. In the present instance, the approach of showing a large product but no benefit seemed an intentional reversal or obversion of the large benefit/small product approach that came before it. In both cases, Neil was relying upon routinized invention concepts/routines—both the hero approach and what he later called flip-flopping a concept. Neil thus was "encoding stimuli [what he knew about Agavez and its customers] in ways that match context with a repertoire of routines" (Weick & Sutcliffe, 2006), but not first resolving conceptually the underlying tensions between the client's need to show the mower and the perceived customer's desire to do the minimum of thinking about and physical labor with the mower.

Tweaking the standard approach to accommodate what he perceived to be the consumer preference of recreation over mowing, Jesse quickly added, "but we're going to talk about golf . . . something a little less literal . . . . It's got whatever horsepower, this and that, if you really care. . . . Not something more product focused. It's good to know Agavez is whatever it is, it's always good to know Agavez." There then ensued a 34-second pause.

Putting a slightly different spin on Jesse's golf topic, Neil served by integrating "reasons to believe" from the brief into the following headline: "The Agavez is reasonably priced, comes with a two-year warranty and 30 years of experience. [Jesse began to interrupt but Neil finished the thought] . . . [but] is that what you really want to talk about when playing golf?"

---

[1] Neil said in a later interview that consumers should be emphasized more than the client, though the client needed to be addressed as much as was necessary (TR 189).

But after a 16-second pause, Jesse said that Neil's headline was "just too literal," presumably wanting to keep in the concept the attention-getting contrast of a large, detailed, flashy picture of the mower (to placate the manufacturer) but vague words indicating a lackadaisical attitude toward mowing (to placate the consumer). This approach was more in keeping with the genre of magazine ads, while the large product picture and reasons to believe was used more in POS ads. Neil said he would continue to work on this concept later.

Pointing to his sketch, Neil then reverted to visually emphasizing the benefit, in this case a scene of people having a cookout at home, with the mower's handle just showing from the garage. Focusing down, Jesse suggested showing this scene through the window from inside a house, creating through the frame of the window a tighter, more cropped image delivering greater visual impact.

After a 35-second pause, Jesse briefly mentioned hanging signs in different departments. Neil changed the subject to the third concept, beginning with the visual: a tree or branch that looks like a golf club, and the line, "Agavez gets the job done fast." Providing visual variations on this concept that yoked similarity with contrast, Jessie and Neil suggested other natural phenomena that would assume the shape of recreational equipment: clouds and mountains. "But it has to be fairly ingenious," Neil said after a 14-second pause. Developing this scene, Neil suggested a man mowing his lawn and looking over his shoulder at ethereal golf clubs.

They then discussed the sports they would choose for the ads—golf, hunting, and fishing "because [ad agency management] want to tailor [the ad] to the magazines." To reach middle-income males who hunted and fished, Heric planned to advertise in *Field and Stream* magazine. But beyond these sports with smaller followings, they decided to add softball and watching TV to reach more of the target "demo," or demographic/psychographic group.

Neil then again switched to composing words for a visual scene, generating, then refining a headline: "'Agavez gets the job done fast.' You put a product statement there and whatever warranty . . . 'gets the job done fast so you can move on to other things.'" Here Neil again mentioned the "reasons to believe" and planned to put them in the ad, but he did not get around to it before the evaluation meeting. He suggested applying this line to the visual where the lawn mower is "sort of hidden."

Next surfaced a line that may have predated the present campaign. Bringing in previously discussed visuals, Neil suggested a vivid grilling scene with the mower mostly hidden, barely visible in the garage, the contrast driven home by the line, "Another satisfied Agavez owner." Neil wanted to add another line, "He's working hard," but Jesse felt they only needed the line and a photo of someone having fun; "It just ends in the shot." It appeared that Jesse here was objecting to "gagging the gag," that is, unnecessarily pointing out the humor in a line and ruining its effect. Jesse and Neil then visualized other situations that would work with the line, such as people playing softball, people fishing. For the first time in the session, a verbal line generated several different visuals and ads.

That "He's working hard" didn't work for the "satisfied owner" ads, Neil agreed, but he added that they should show a tractor at the bottom of the ad [presumably below the framed shot of recreation] and a line to "drive home the strategic point that 'you've got more important things to worry about.'" Jesse agreed. After a 53-second pause, however, Neil added that the latter line would be better explained by a pie chart. Here we see the writer visually emphasizing his verbal idea, in this case the low priority of mowing. Upon mentioning this visual approach, Neil started sketching pie charts, then Jessie did as well. Neil proposed that "the skinny part of" the pie chart was a picture of cutting grass. A bigger slice was family. Bigger yet was golf (see Figure 6). Jesse responded with a visual addition: "Put in a little small [slice] that says in-laws or something like that?"

> Neil: Yeah, that would be fun. So it's like Agavez . . . .
> [a 25-second pause ensues], writes, "Agavez makes life easier . . . . so you
> can move on to all the things you want to do."].

This headline was straight off the brand promise in the creative brief. It also tied into Neil's comment earlier that they had the opportunity to do the more important things they had to do: "It's like we could take [pointing to the line he just wrote] this for a positioning line so that it works over all the other products, like they're asking us to do."

In writing this initial version of a positioning (tag) line (the tag or slogan that often accompanies a company logo in an advertisement; e.g., GE's "Imagination at Work"), Neil had moved beyond the visual/verbal mode of composing the pie chart concept to verbally contextualizing the concept within the larger market strategy for the entire Agavez power tool line. Words were the chosen medium to locate the ad concept in the "big picture"—Agavez' marketing strategy. Words are typically used in this fashion as tag lines, perhaps because they can be used in radio as well as print and video.

After the discussion of the pie chart above, Neil paused, sketching a bar graph with several small bars and one very large one.

> Neil: And then if you do a bar graph that same way . . .
>
> Jesse: That should be like two pie charts [points to his sketch of these], one where it's mostly cut grass. And then the other one, as a comparison.
>
> Neil: I would think it gets . . .
>
> Jesse: [finishing the other's sentence, something each member of the veteran pair did often] It's busier, but if you have one it just . . .

Here Neil gave visual advice to the artist. But rather than to continue to argue about two pie charts, Neil changed the subject slightly, focusing upon both visual

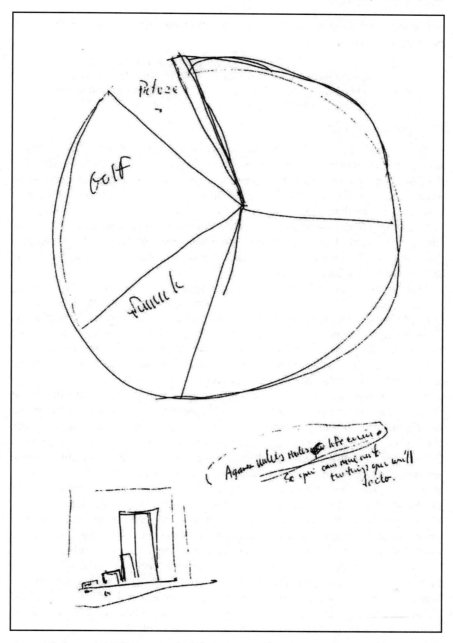

Figure 6. Neil's preliminary sketches.
Reprinted with permission from Heric Advertising, Agavez Corporation.

and conceptual conciseness by trying to eliminate the conflicts in the initial pie chart concept:

> And maybe it's just the golf. We can get rid of all that, just strip it down and it's just the picture of the—the smallest sliver is the cut grass part and then the whole entire other thing is golf. So we don't get involved in—well who's more important, family, golf, product, whatever.

> Jesse: Yeah, yeah.

This revision was validated by qualitative research circulated to the creatives, noting that the target audience highly valued spending time with family. Neil then brought up a bar graph that presented the same idea as the pie chart. Jesse asserted that in this chart they could use three elements to compare, including a tiny "in-laws for dinner" bar.

Continuing in the visual mode, moving from one visual genre to another as an idea generator, Neil drew a different arrangement of the bars on his sketchpad. Jesse said he liked the arrangement and then drew a variation of the line graph, an "area block" or band chart, on his sketchpad.

Neil wracked his brain for other graphs to try. Seeking the available means of persuasion, he asked me for graph ideas, but I declined to give ideas because it would have influenced the study. To avoid the evidence with the audiotape, Jesse jokingly encouraged me to write something and drop it on the floor. Having gotten a good laugh at my expense, the pair resumed dyadic brainstorming.

Continuing the visual mode of composing, Neil suggested a horizontal bar graph, and Jesse further developed it by recommending 3-D.

Neil then returned volley with another visual concept, "the split thing," one that, although he did not mention it, was "in the air," in a series of commercials during the 2002 Winter Olympics that were going on and one that he had been the first to suggest to other Heric creatives. The copywriter gave the example of a half-tractor, half-golf cart image. Here we see the copywriter suggesting a visual intertext that drew its authority from its use in a venue that, along with the Superbowl, was the Olympics of advertising. Jesse liked the idea and added that this concept would translate well into store displays, one of the key campaign objectives. Neil affirmed that they would have to involve the concept with point-of-purchase advertising. Consideration of the rhetorical situation seemed to lead Neil back to considering audience, and he looked at the creative brief.

Dropping the topic and reverting to a previous idea, Neil said, "This graph thing could be really cool. I'm not sure it's as right at the target, though . . . household income [HHI] between thirty-five thousand and fifty. . . . It's blue collar; midmanagerial. But I don't know that they can relate to it and understand it. Play devil's advocate is the only thing that I can think of."

Neil's decision to go ahead with a possibly inappropriate approach may have been caused by the different educational and work experiences of the two audiences within the demographic group addressed. More midmanagerial than blue-collar workers would work with charts and graphs. Whether or not to address the more graph-literate audience was another problem stemming from the disparate constituencies in the target audience.

Moreover, Neil and Jesse's approach, one shared with most creatives at Heric and the received wisdom in advertising, was to present a number of ads at the Chief Creative Officer's tip-ball ad selection meeting. Quantity seemed more important to Neil and Jesse in this case than did suiting the message to all target audiences. Their previous successful repertoires engaged on the "consumers hate mowing" notion. Perhaps not prematurely engaging or engaging repertoires at all would have helped: "When people move away from conceptuality and encoding, outcomes are affected more by the quality than by the quantity of attention," Weick and Sutcliffe assert (2006, p. 514). However, they also note that routines are necessary to live.

Still in a visual mode (most likely pursuing "the split thing"), the copywriter next recommended that the art director draw a mower with shapes on it that looked like recreational paraphernalia. To help them visualize, Neil took from the metal bulletin board an old riding mower ad, from which Jesse sketched a tractor mower that had a grill-top roof. Neil worried, however, that this visual was "too corn[y]."

Jesse countered by reverting to an idea they had successfully used earlier with the client, simply headlines and "hero" shots of the mower, as Jesse described it, pointing to the old ad where he would insert the headline next to the mower.

Neil then returned to developing his idea from earlier in the session about parts of the mower being made to look like golf paraphernalia, pointing at a part of the mower that resembled a golf ball. Jesse added that they could make a switch look like a golf tee. Neil agreed, "something that takes that natural form."

Continuing to mix the contexts of mowing and golfing, Neil suggested showing someone wearing golf shoes and driving a riding mower or pulling a push mower. Jesse developed this idea, suggesting a tight shot of the golf shoe. Neil responded, "That's kind of 'so what?'" Then Jesse suggested a variation, a person driving a tractor in his pajamas. Perhaps in part because of the abruptness of Neil's response, the idea did not generate a lot of enthusiasm. There was the longest pause of the session, a minute and 46 seconds long.

Neil looked at the brief again, while Jesse stared at the blackboard with the ads on it. They were diverted by an employee who brought in MegaWorld's floor layouts and display specifications, "planagrams" for the campaign. With the arrival of planagrams, the topic shifted to in-store displays—the POS merchandising.

Putting "shelf toppers" advertising Agavez mowers in different departments in MegaWorld, or "cross-selling," was discussed first. Jesse suggested the line/concept, "Buy an Agavez and spend more time doing this." The message could be put on a "dangler," a sign hung from the ceiling over grills or other recreational products in any leisure department in the store. Jesse suggested hanging a steak picture, but Neil countered by suggesting a replica of a steak with the Agavez logo on a grill. Neil also suggested hanging a fish with the same logo from a fishing pole in sporting goods, and a similar scenario and line for hunting. In the concept, each media element completed the meaning of the other: "These" referred to the picture in the danglers or the product the dangler overhung. The headline, on the other hand, associated the image with the product. Moreover, in all these cases, the line was heuristic, generating visuals for several ads, as had "Another satisfied Agavez owner."

Jesse proposed putting a "dummy box" in a stack of boxes in the sporting goods area, but Neil challenged this idea because they would need permission from whoever's product they would stack the box on top of, and because it interfered with people accessing the product, something MegaWorld wouldn't want. Here Neil's knowledge of and experience with retailers guided the dyad mindfully, demonstrating "a more nuanced appreciation of context and ways to deal with it" (Weick & Sutcliffe, 2006). Jesse then suggested putting something on the floor. In golf sections of sporting goods departments of stores, there was often a practice putting green. The artist suggested having a straight line run the length of the green to the hole, and he began coming up with headlines, though nothing that worked well. A 32-second pause ensued.

Neil then countered by reversing Jesse's idea of "golf shoes to cut the grass," proposing "maybe (if you flop this) so it's saying like this is the other side of the coin, like a, you know, you can't go play golf because he's got to cut his [grass]—oh I don't know. Some of this is like a TV spot." The wind leaving the sails of that idea, Neil was becalmed for 55-seconds.

Changing the media topic to print ads, Neil reverted to his idea of making shadows or other visual entities near the lawn mower resemble golfing or hunting scenes. However, showing that he was thinking visually from a process as well as product standpoint, he said that though he could write headlines for the shadow ads, the visual concept would take Jesse a lot of time to create; Jesse replied that was OK, all of them took a lot of time. Neil then repeated and wrote this idea in his sketchbook. He then went back through his previous pages, numbering each sketched and scrawled concept.

Having refreshed his memory of all proposed concepts, an act of mindfulness to avoid reinventing the wheel, Neil changed the subject briefly back to the barely visible mower in the garage: "Needs a really fun headline, and I just don't know what the words are coming from." During the ensuing pause of a full minute, Jesse walked over to the metal bulletin board and surveyed past ads. Jesse next proposed a reverse psychology concept where lawn mowing was facetiously seen as superior: "'Spending an afternoon along the rolling hills or chasing some dumb ball. What would you rather do?' You see a guy playing softball . . ."

After an 11-second pause, Neil changed the topic, reviewing the consumer's mindset, or at least the one he hoped to project: "[You] spend some money for this thing. You've got it and don't really want to use it, but you're glad to have it. It starts every time."

After another pause, 20 seconds long, Jesse and Neil each brought up ads they had done for previous Agavez campaigns. There was another pause, 15 seconds long, as Jesse checked his computer to verify that they had covered that ground 2 years before. Neil suggested another idea that Jesse dismissed as "old . . . stuff" they had done for Agavez for a mower it sold under the name of a different company. A 54-second delay followed.

Jesse, after another pause, suggested putting a picture of a mower on a golf ball. It was not clear that this idea was further developed. An 18-second pause ensued.

Neil wrote on his pad, "Dependable because you aren't."

After yet another pause, 32 seconds long, the winds of inspiration having subsided, Jesse exclaimed, "Break!" and they ended the session. As Wells, Burnett, and Moriarity (1995) note, the brainstorming process of analysis, juxtaposition, and association is mentally tiring, and people may get to a point close to quitting where they draw a blank. This is a necessary part of the process (421). When a number of pauses had occurred halfway through, Neil consulted the brief, helping to revive the brainstorming to approximately double the comments[2] made before the ideas ran dry. However, the brief was not consulted at all for the first fifth of the session. Moreover, the brand promise's interrelation of the product and benefit was not focused upon by the artist-writer team during the session.

Table 2 explains the composing moves employed by subjects in the study. These moves are numbered "up the ladder of abstraction," the most abstract being identifying the rhetorical context of the problem but no solution yet, and least abstract, most tangible move is completing the advertisement for submission for departmental evaluation. Completing body copy and subheads to support headlines is considered at the same level of abstraction as completing a visual.

Figure 7 shows the progression of composing moves in Neil and Jesse's 2/14 brainstorming session. Neil reviewed the creative brief again at increment 118 and revived the session.

SUMMARY OF ARTIST-WRITER BRAINSTORMING

In beginning to investigate the nature of this artist-writer brainstorming, we must note that both creatives were fully involved: Neil and Jesse each made about half of the comments uttered in the exchange (53.3%, 46.7% respectively). Although Neil spoke more, more of his comments (86 vs. 72) also were not

---

[2] The transcription of the session was initially segmented into verbal and visual comments and entered into an Excel database. These comments were then each classified a number of other ways, including as composing and collaborative moves, discussed on the following pages.

Table 2. Jesse and Neil's Composing Moves

9—Writing down the rhetorical problem and target audience and/or consulting creative brief

8—Identifying music appealing to various demographic strata

7—Searching Internet, etc. for ideas about the problem and audience

6—Writing positioning lines (concepts about product for campaign or across campaigns)

5—Creating preliminary ideas for the campaign that employ other media (e.g., radio) or sections of the genre of the same medium as the print ads

4.5—Doing thumbnails (concepts for individual ads)

4—Writing headlines

3—Discussing and/or finding images of product in image banks for manipulation to flesh out the thumbnails

2—Writing subheads and body copy

2—Creating visuals

1—Creating penultimate layout with elements either in place or described

0—Laying out visuals and words tight (finished) in the final products

---

applied in final versions of the ads that resulted from their collaboration. But he originated more concepts (8/66%) than artist Jesse (4/33%), although each contributed to the development of all concepts. Each contributed approximately half of the comments that were applied in finished ads (Neil 32/50.8%, Jesse 31/49.2%).

To further trace the overall shape of this brainstorming session, we can examine the incidence of different collaborative actions. Four collaborative "moves," identified by Burnett (1994) in studying written collaboration, were employed by the artist and writer.[3] At different times, the creatives *offered prompts* to each other, encouraging the other to contribute more; *contributed information*; *directed* the collaboration; and *challenged* the other's idea. Directing each other was the most frequent move (46.92%) as collaborators suggested adapting the document or plans by changing, adding, or removing. Contributing information to each other was second (25%), as ideas were fleshed out by facts, suggestions, observations, summaries, syntheses, or metacognitive comments

---

[3] Collaborative moves are another way of describing the comments of collaborators by not focusing upon the production of generic elements and analysis of the rhetorical situation per se, but rather upon cooperative techniques. Normally each comment during the brainstorming entailed both a collaborative move and a composition move.

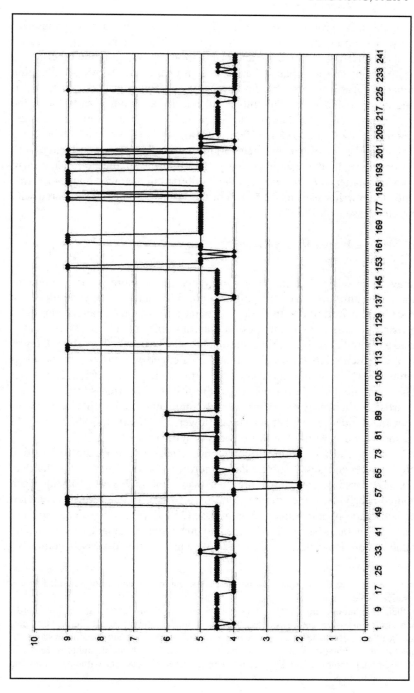

Figure 7. Neil and Jesse's composing moves 2/14: brief increasingly consulted to generate ideas.

regarding the task, group, or document. The third most frequent collaborative activity was offering prompts to each other (16.2%)—reinforcing or neutral comments, requesting clarification and elaboration, encouraging the other to say more about both text and plans. Lastly, a significant activity was challenging each other (11.8%)—recommending alternatives, offering critical questions, or asserting an opposing view. This move did not occur so much as to block the meeting.[4] Constructive conflict over ideas can enhance group-writing processes, as Burnett (1991), Cross (1988, 1990a, 1994a), Karis (1989), and others have noted, increasing involvement, generating more ideas, and surfacing submerged conflicts. In the meeting, nearly three-fourths of the comments were about visual matters (74.7% vs. 21.8%),[5] addressing layouts, images, charts, and fonts. Copywriter Neil made 51.8% of the visual comments, compared with Art Director Jesse's 48.2%.

Collaborative Roles in Visual vs. Verbal Composing

It may seem surprising that the copywriter made more visual comments than the artist, but those numbers alone do not fully indicate the strength of the writer's visual contribution. In their collaboration on visual matters, the artist unsurprisingly made more comments contributing information (9.6% vs. 8.3%), but he also offered more prompting comments to the writer (8.7% to 4.8%), fewer directing comments (16.2% vs. 19%), and challenged the writer's visual ideas fewer times than the writer challenged the artist's (1.5% vs. 6.6%). The writer could have not challenged the expertise of the artist on the artist's turf at all.

The artist challenged the writer's verbal comments more than vice versa as well, but the incidence of both was much lower: (7.9% artist, 3.9% writer). In other respects, the artist did less with words than the writer.

When we look at the combined collaborative moves (see Figure 8), we find that Neil challenged Jesse substantially more (7.9% vs. 3.9 % of individual moves), and Jesse offered more prompts than Neil (5.7% vs. 10.4%). Each contributed nearly the same amount of info, 10.9% vs. 12.2% respectively. Neil offered substantially more direction than Jesse (25.8% vs. 19.3%). Gauging from their actions in the session, Neil appeared the more dominant of the two in the collaboration. However, an almost exactly equal portion of Jesse's comments

---

[4] These percentages do not total 100 because some comments could not be coded as any collaborative move.

[5] In their interaction, the collaborators communicated about layouts mostly in words, but such comments were not considered "verbal" comments about word elements of ads, e.g., the headlines. If the team described a scene first, they were envisioning a scene, so the object of their thoughts was visual at that point, even though the thoughts were put in words. Additional comments (3.5%) regarded procedures or concepts without mentioning verbal or visual matters.

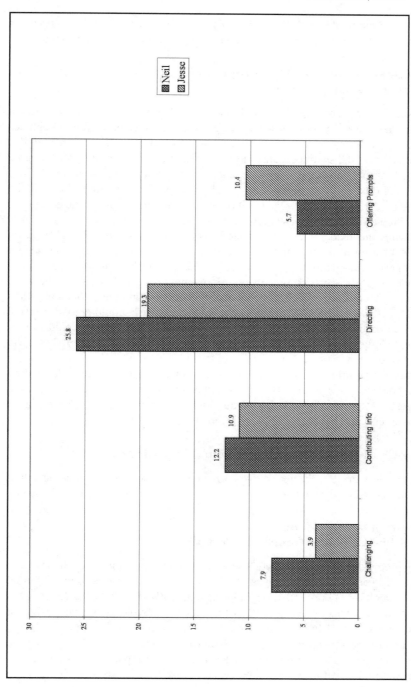

Figure 8. Verbal and visual combined percentages of collaborative moves, 2/14, Neil and Jesse.

was used in the final ads. Still, this 50-50 artist-writer contribution is a surprising outcome because nearly three of four comments addressed visual elements.

Rhetorical/Grammatical Description of Verbal and Visual Comments

Another way of examining verbal-visual collaboration is to note how much discussion occurred regarding rhetorical/grammatical elements. *Visual* cognates of the above terms have been developed by Kostelnick and Roberts (1998). Arrangement is the spatial organization of visual elements. Clarity "is the degree to which visual language enables readers to understand the message." Conciseness is the necessary amount of visual language for a situation. Ethos is the amount of credibility of the visual in its rhetorical situation. Tone is the designer's attitude toward the subject as revealed by the design elements chosen. Emphasis is drawing the reader's eye to selected visual elements (pp. 437–440). Jesse spent over a third of his comments (40.1%) on arrangement, suggesting layout was central during this invention process. Next was emphasis: 23.52%. Neil expended slightly fewer comments on arrangement (35.4%), but about the same as Jesse on emphasis (22.7%). Neil devoted more comments to clarity than Jesse did (7.9% vs. 5.9%). This outcome leads one to ask, could clarity in visual design be particularly important to writers because of the attention paid to it in writing? Could this concern transfer into the visual realm? Figure 9 shows the incidence of the various comments.

When we combine rhetorical/grammatical comments and comments of their visual cognates (see Figure 10), we see that arrangement and emphasis were strongest, categories that involve layout—where words and images are placed (arrangement) and how large they are (emphasis).

Some Characteristics of Verbal-Visual Invention?

From this overview, we now move into evidenced conjectures about the nature of verbal-visual invention that we will investigate further in succeeding chapters.

Wellspring of Invention: Visual Precedes and Generates Verbal?

The preponderance of visual comments suggests the importance of the visual in composing verbal-visual messages. Furthermore, the visual preceded the verbal in the generation of concepts three times as frequently (9-3; 75% vs. 25%).

Moreover, when we look at the occurrence of layout (a visual design or scenario) and verbal lines, when we look at the sequence, we find that layout came before the invention of lines in 80% of the cases (14 vs. 3.5). When we look at the cognate area with the highest incidence of a particular collaborative move, we find directing-arrangement visual is by far the largest—23 for Jesse

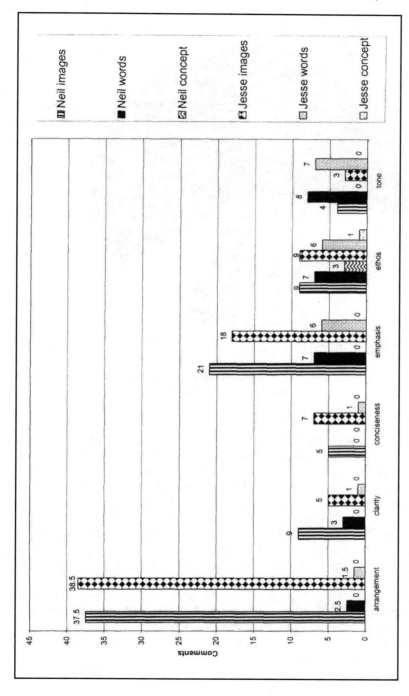

Figure 9. Visual cognate and written rhetorical-grammatical elements, 2/14 Neil and Jesse—arrangement has highest incidence in verbal-visual invention.

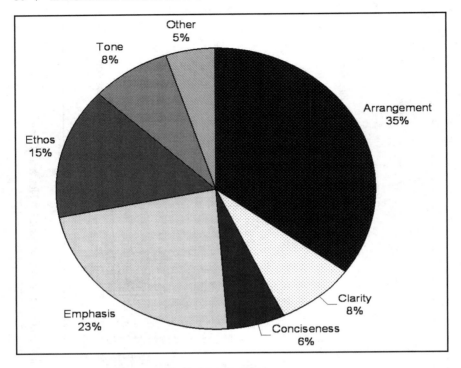

Figure 10. Combined written and visual rhetorical comments,
Neil and Jesse combined 2/14.

(21.7% of his comments, 10% of Jesse and Neil's total comments), 21.5 for Neil (17.6% of Neil's comments, 9.4% of Neil and Jesse's total comments). The point is that invention was predominantly visual and occurred in the realm of layout/scenario most often, merging the classical canons of invention and arrangement. Of the 10 most frequent moves, four were visual arrangement across a number of moves, three were visual emphasis, and all but two were visual. And those eight most frequent moves composed nearly nine-tenths (88.2%) of the aggregate number of move-coded comments in the top 10 categories. All of these findings support the conclusion that the visual was by far the more important in generating ad concepts.

However, not all that was generated was used. Although there were more visually initiated comments used in the final ads than verbally initiated comments used (39.5 [63.7%] vs. 25 [36.3%]), the visually initiated comments that were discarded were also more numerous than the verbally initiated comments discarded, by almost a 2:1 margin (102.5 [66.1%] vs. 52.5 [33.9%]). The incidence of both used and unused visually initiated comments likely occurred because there was also about the same percentage of more visually initiated comments (144 [62.4%] vs. 79 [34.1%]).

Verbal Origins of Some Verbal-Visual Ideas

Layout discussions were primarily about visual matters, but a series of images were each matched with the words "Another satisfied Agavez owner." However, initially, Neil brought up this line to add to the image of a mower handle sticking out of a garage.

Extensional Properties of Point-of-Sale Compositions

Also evident in the session were the different rhetorical properties of point of sale advertising. For instance, Jesse proposed putting a "dummy box" in a stack of boxes in the sporting goods area, but Neil, drawing on his knowledge of retailing, challenged this idea because they would need permission from whoever's product they would stack the box on top of, and because it interfered with people accessing the product. As the creatives considered the feasible surfaces to display their messages, the physical dimension of the rhetorical situation, which included not only location in layout but also location in the physical world where the sign would be read, came into sharper focus. Point-of-sale advertising, a very different rhetorical situation from standard print, included what Hayakawa calls the "extensional meaning, . . . that which it points to in the physical world," much more (1978, p. 52). In that way, it approaches the properties of speech where the speaker may point to an object or use props.

Another way extensional meaning was involved is when the pronoun in the slogan of a sign hanging from the ceiling referred to a recreational implement in close proximity below it. The fishing pole, in one case, was used to provide tangibility and to identify the product with the benefit spatially, both by its proximity to the fishing pole and sporting goods department. If persuasion involves identification, and the mower customer identifies with the fishing department, perhaps the mower would be identified with the benefit.

Retention of Inscribed vs. Stated-Only Comments

Did writing the idea down or drawing it during the collaborative session make a difference over saying it in terms of whether it was kept in the final ad? Yes, but not how we might expect in a session where the visual dominated discussion. Comments that were said but not written down or drawn were more likely to be kept than ones that were drawn or written down (12.4% vs. 16.1%, respectively). But the largest percentage of dropped comments were said only as well (43.1%), while a substantial percentage of discarded comments were written or drawn (28.4%). Of the written or drawn ideas retained, they were about evenly split between written (14/51.9%) and drawn (12/44.4%), with one comment both written and drawn.

Generative Principles of Verbal-Visual Brainstorming

Some concepts generated multiple executions or concepts. For example, from the principle of small visual representation of mower and large representation of recreation came two separate ad concepts: the "icons" ads, in which the recreation implement partially obscured the mower, and the "graph, chart ads," where the mower fit into a small segment while the recreation fit in a large segment. Immediately after these concepts were begun, Neil, from a visual standpoint obverted the small product-large benefit visual concept, generating the mower-hero ads with visual depiction of large product and no benefit, although the benefit was to be discussed in words. This reversal seemed to be intentional, a systematic movement from one approach to in some ways its opposite; Neil here engaged an invention routine that had worked in the past. One visual idea in this case began three ads in quick succession.

What is the invention process and power of concepts that have several executions? Were there any commonalities in the generation of potentially fruitful headlines and visual concepts? Although, as I note below, no ad addressed the entire complex rhetorical situation, Neil and Jesse responded to their partial understanding of the rhetorical situation with strategies that did produce attention-getting lines, images, and concepts. In the cases of the "big benefit, little product" visual concept and the "Another satisfied Agavez owner" headline with recreation benefit showing, *contrast* was their generative principle of both the primarily verbal and the primarily visual approaches. We visually juxtapose small product and big benefit in the first concept, showing the proportions of each as promised in the brand promise. We juxtapose in Schriver's sense (1997) words and pictures in the Satisfied Owner series, the contrast being what we expect the words to introduce to us and what is really introduced.

This generative principle of contrast was responsible for the origination of the most ad concepts (7/13, 53.8%). It also was used the most in the development of many concepts: in 87 of the 201 comments involving generative principles (43.3%). The generative principle of contrast or difference, of course, is ancient. Although not previously identified as such for verbal-visual arguments, it is one of the classical common topics, or topoi (Corbett, 1990, pp. 106–107). Contrast is also used in the classical canon of arrangement or *dispositio,* according to Kenney, who noted that cartoonists engage this principle in their designs; Kenney also notes that cartoonists use topoi, but he explains topics as political commonplaces, cultural allusions, character traits (2004, p. 323). Regarding the disposition of the two concepts, we can say that difference is used from an argument standpoint to stress benefit over product. We can also say that the principle was used to allot and distribute space to be devoted to product and benefit—a lot of space for the benefit, little for the product; benefit foregrounded, product backgrounded.

Similarity/Contrast, a fusion of the two seemingly contrary principles, was the second-most frequent generative principle and topic, originating four concepts and used in 64 of 201 comments involving generative principles (31.8%). Neil used this invention principle in the surreal tree branch/golf club and motor switch/golf tee or "something that takes on its natural form." He ironically juxtaposed, using contrast (golf tee built on mower, golf club sprouting from tree branch), but got away with the incongruity because of the similarity of the natural form of the recreational implement and the object (mower, tree). This principle was also apparent, although not as developed, in the split concept, and the "wrong uniform" concept where someone wore golf shoes or pajamas to mow the lawn.

Another generative principle for Neil was *obversion*: after coming up with an idea, considering what he called "the other side of the coin," or "flop[ping]" (as in flip/flop) the idea. The *American Heritage Dictionary* defines "obvert" as turning something to show a different side or view (2000). The obverse is considered the counterpart of a previous statement. On 2/14, after coming up with the idea of someone cutting their grass wearing golf shoes, illustrating the idea of someone getting the job done fast to get on to what he preferred, Neil considered the obverse, showing someone unable to play golf because he had to mow his lawn. The large-product mower-hero ads were generated immediately after large-benefit, small-product ads. This approach was used in seven comments involving generative principles (3.5%) and was half-responsible for the hero concept.

A related technique is to facetiously argue the inverse, the opposite of what one intends. In brainstorming, Jesse engaged this reverse psychology of *facetious inversion* to generate the following headline idea: "Spending an afternoon along the rolling hills . . . or chasing some dumb ball—what would you rather do?" Although the approach was used in only three comments involving generative principles (1.5%), it did generate one of the 13 ad concepts (7.7%).

Another means of invention for Neil and Jesse was using one member of a class of things, then another member of the same class of things. In brainstorming alternatives, Neil moved, for example, from one visual chart genre to another— from pies to bars—to asking the researcher for other examples. In another instance, he moved from one recreation to another: adding cross-selling shelf talkers to grills, then fishing poles, and such. As would be expected, this approach did not generate new concepts, but it was used in 31 (15.4%) comments involving generative principles that created many variations on established themes.

In addition to the 201 comments involving generative principles, there were 28 other comments, devoted to procedural or other support matters. Thus a little over a tenth (12.2%) of comments was devoted to procedural matters, while comments involving generative principles dominated the meeting.

Effectiveness of Verbal-Visual Brainstorming

Having established the general nature of this collaborative verbal-visual brainstorming, we now turn to the question of quality: how effectively did the ads address the sometimes clashing attitudes of the audiences?

Let us first look (see Table 3) at the distribution of comments that addressed the audiences:

In this first invention session, the primary audience is the customer, with the client a distant second and MegaWorld a slightly more distant third. Neil favored the customer a little more, and Jesse the client. Jesse addressed nearly 16% of his comments to audiences other than the customer.

The sometimes conflicting or ambivalent attitudes of their different audiences made it difficult to create an ad that appealed to everyone intended. Jesse and Neil resolved their dissonance by creating a range of concepts that appealed to different constituencies of that audience. To appeal to the manufacturer's desire to show the mower, there was the mower-hero concept (its lines, though, spoke to the "mower-hating" consumer, even as the spiffy image spoke to the manu-facturer). For the mowing-hating consumer, there were the "Another satisfied Agavez owner" and the foregrounded recreation concepts. For the midmana-gerial audience, there were bar graph and pie chart concepts. For what the creatives believed to be the less graph-literate blue-collar audience, there were the other concepts.

The concepts generated addressed various constituencies in the demo, but most of them alienated someone. The mowing-averse might be turned off by the flashy mower shots. Some people in the blue-collar audience might not completely understand the chart ads. The manufacturer would be alienated by the fore-grounded recreation, pie chart, couch potato, and reverse psychology ads. Even the mower-hero ads would have lines not about mowing or disparaging it. For example, below, Neil and Jesse got off track by stressing the mower haters more than reasons to believe that the mower would function efficiently, reasons that would attract both the client and the consumer wanting to get the job over with.

> Neil: [Proposes specific reasons to believe] "The Agavez is reasonably priced, comes with a two-year warranty and 30 years of experience."
>
> Jesse: Something like that that . . .
>
> Neil: "Is that what you really want to talk about when you're playing golf?"
>
> Jesse: Like, don't worry where you're going with it. . . . [But] that's just too literal.

Table 3. Audience Most Benefitted by the Creative's 2/14 Comment, in Numbers of Comments

	Customer	Customer & Agavez	Agavez	MegaWorld & Agavez	MegaWorld	Customer, MegaWorld, Agavez	MegaWorld & Customer	Total
Jesse	69 (67.6%)	16 (15.7%)	9 (8.9%)	1 (1%)	6 (5.8%)		1 (1%)	102
Neil	86 (71.7%)	20 (16.66%)	6 (5%)	1 (.8%)	6 (5%)	1 (.8%)		120
Total	155 (69.8%)	36 (16.2%)	15 (6.8%)	2 (.9%)	12 (5.4%)	1 (.45%)	1 (.45%)	222

Putting in the above reasons to believe, the warranty, and experience facts, might have attracted the mower manufacturer as well as both the consumer who just wanted to get the job over with and the consumer who saw mowing as a problem-free "comfortable escape." However, Jesse believed instead, reflecting the Brief Meeting, that the audience "dread[ed] cutting lawns"(TR 100). Here, the Account Manager's binary categorization of conflicting data encouraged a response that did not address the audience fully.

With another ad concept, Neil planned to put these facts in and Jesse did not object; however, Neil did not get to it before the evaluation. Neil did not write down his intention to add reasons to believe, and it could have been difficult to remember if the ideas were not written down and the artist did most of the final work on the piece. In the intended ad, words provided the "hidden parts of the product"—the selling points, such as a 2-year warranty and 30 years of experience that the image of the mower could not show. Including these words, Neil's intended ad was much better than his executed ad.

The incomplete arguments and execution may have been the result of the dyad's prioritizing quantity over quality, or the outcome of a very rapid game of Ping-Pong that in 45 minutes generated 12 concepts and the beginning of two others, one every three and three-quarters minutes, on average. This count does not include the various spin-offs of some of the concepts. For example, the POS "Spend more time doing this" concept generated eight versions. The creatives' approach of generating as much as possible while brainstorming reflected the received if not always well-taken wisdom of some advertising textbooks.

CHAPTER 3

Ping-Pong, Part II: Development, Elaboration, and Evaluation of Concepts by an "Insight-Intensive" Team

Neil's Composing Lines, 2/14:

Kind of what we do is . . . we'll come up with the ideas, and then I'll go back and try and flesh them out. And then I'll show them to [Jesse].

Neil's description of the dyad's typical process fits their actions on 2/14–15. The afternoon after the morning's brainstorming session, Neil, alone at his PowerBook G3 laptop in his office, typed 20 lines, tag (1), or different passages of body copy of multiple sentences. Of those, 18 were presented at the tip-ball ad selection meeting verbatim. He did not linger over his sketchpad that held scrawled drawings and notes from the morning meeting: "just looked through it real quick just to see, 'oh yeah, those are those four that I thought would work.'" Neil's notations served as a memory cue rather than a self-contextualized message. As he told me, if a week elapsed between when he wrote and when he consulted them, he could not decipher them. Here are the layout ideas and copy Neil produced the afternoon of February 14 (see Table 4):

Only one positioning tag came from the morning's meeting, and a headline mentioned that morning came from an earlier campaign; however, 13 of the 15 headlines Neil generated that afternoon addressed concepts from the morning's session. So the "aha" moment for *concepts* came to Neil and Jesse when they were working together, but for the *lines,* it came when Neil worked alone; as Neil said, "I took from [the morning's] things we did and just . . . tried to flesh some of them out." An example of something developed from a kernel idea in the morning session was what developed from the line, "Agavez makes life easier." Neil had envisioned using the same headline with several visuals, but since he was doing

Table 4. Copy and Layout Ideas Neil Generated 2/14/02
(Boldface is Neil's Emphasis)

---

headlines are done in some kind of form look.
Pie chart . . .
Research indicates Agavez owners would rather spend
less time in the yard and more on the fairway.

Bar graph
Studies show that Agavez owners have nice looking lawns and even better looking
fish.

Other graph
A recent survey says guys like a nice lawn and a six point buck.
But not necessarily in that order.
Tag line: Agavez makes life easier.

Icon visuals with tractor in background.
Head:
Lawns are our life. Not yours.
tag:

Incredible shot of guy fishih (sic.), hunting, golfing, running . . . Inset of
manicured, freshly cut lawn.
Head:
Another Satisfied Agavez owner
Tag:

(Beauty shots of mower)
Don't worry, big guy. You'll be back holding the remote in no time.
Our philosophy towards building mowers can be summed up in one simple
statement: Cutting grass [profanity deleted].
The kind of lawn mower you own says a lot about you.
Such as "I'd rather be doing something else besides mowing the lawn."

Do instructional like. . . . .

Head:
Agavez presents
"A helpful guide to golf: getting more
        distance off the tee."
Copy: If you're hitting the ball properly yet your shots landing short, then you may
        be underclubbing. This means using the wrong club for the wrong distance.
        Practice with different clubs. You'll learn how far you can drive the ball with
        any given club. This, friends, can help you get more distance on the ball.
        If you are, however, unsuccessful . . . just smack the heck out of it.
Line of copy at the end: You've got better things to do than cut grass. Trouble free
        starting and cutting Agavez mowers. Get mowing with an Agavez.

Table 4. (Cont'd.)

Tag:

Agavez presents:
"Grilling out: Choosing a great steak"

Friends, choosing a perfect steak for grilling is not
complicated. Try a New York Strip—a boneless cut from
the top loin. A Porterhouse . . . that's a strip and filet
separated by the bone in the middle. Or a T-bone . . . like
a Porterhouse except with less meat on the sides.
Regardless, we hope this helps you with your next
Barbecue. Join us next time when we discuss "Choosing
A Gastro-intestinologist."

Line of copy at end:

Agavez presents:
"Hang gliding for beginners"

Quote with the mower and subhead.
"Honey, weren"t (sic) we going shopping for shoes today?"
"Aren't we supposed to have tea with your mother today at 4:00?"
"I don't know, I think I have a Dentist appointment at 4:00."
"Hey, I thought we were gonna hang those pink curtains today . . ."

**We know you'd rather be doing anything than cutting
grass.** So buck up, pardoner. Our mowers give you trouble free starting and
cutting. And if you're looking for value and performance, there's
nothing like an Agavez. Better features at a better
price. Get it over with an Agavez.

Well, the floor does need refinishing. And I've really gotta get the bathtub
grouted. The roof needs new shingles . . . and I'm supposed to have tea with
your mother at 4:30. . . .

---

that with "Lawns are our life, not yours," he decided to do headlines for each
graph ad, the "Research suggests . . ." lines. As Neil told me in a subsequent
interview, "too many campaigns are all sort of the same, so I mix it up, [use]
different styles."

Neil composed his copy on the computer. He said he used to compose only
on a sketchpad and said when computers arrived that "I'll never do this," but
now "it's all I do." Smoking also used to be necessary for Neil to compose, but

the arrival of a nonsmoking policy changed that. So Neil was not superstitious about what was needed to compose, he told me.

Of Neil's headlines generated for the February 15 meeting with Jesse, 14 went to the tip-ball meeting for evaluation. One line, "Lawns are our life, not yours," came from a previous Agavez campaign—it was the tag line there. Only one additional line to the 14 was in the tight collection that was presented. Additional material from a previous Agavez campaign was the "Agavez presents" ads, originally written for radio but not chosen in an earlier tip-ball.

To this point, Neil and Jesse's creative process was not atypical. Studies of creativity suggest that after preparation and incubation comes insight. Working on the Agavez campaign before and attending the Brief Meeting provided preparation, and the intervening night provided incubation; insight occurred in the brainstorming meeting and Neil's fleshing out the lines. Some evaluation had also occurred in that Neil had not written lines for and thus dropped certain concepts. The function of Neil and Jesse's next meeting was more of this phase— evaluation of what had been produced—and the final phase, elaboration of the selected materials, would follow (Csikszentmihalyi, 1996).[1]

FEBRUARY 15 EVALUATION OF LINES MEETING: CUSTOMER SUPPLANTS CLIENT

On Friday, February 15, the dyad met again to go over Neil's lines in Jesse's corner office, replete with glistening bowling paraphernalia and a record turntable that had (r)evolved into a jaunty clock. Neil rapidly communicated his copy and layout ideas. Jesse helped Neil refine one sentence of copy, encouraged him to rework a headline, and suggested an alternative example for a headline. Because most of this session constituted Neil reading his lines, only the key points of the collaboration will be examined.

Unlike Neil and Jesse's meeting the previous day, the pair did not sketch (or put feet up on Jesse's desk, in Neil's case) but instead responded to the lines Neil had generated. In Flower and Hayes' terms, they were more in a translating and reviewing than generating mode. Neil consulted the creative brief at least once to remind himself of the rhetorical target. However, he appeared to be "reading through" the concept that the consumer hated mowing.

The session produced fewer than a third of the comments of the previous day (69 vs. 221[2]), suggesting an approach that narrowed progressively as text representations (Flower, 1994) became clearer. In contrast to the brainstorming session, where 71.4% of the comments were not incorporated into the final

---

[1] Although Csikszentmihalyi did not include advertising in his creativity study, with the exception of evaluation, similar phases of the creative process were identified by ad copywriter James W. Young in 1944, well before Csikszentmihalyi's studies.

[2] Only used and dropped comments counted.

version, on February 15, a total of 75.4% of the comments delivered or supported ideas were incorporated into the ads presented at the tip-ball evaluation meetings. Neil had the higher number of incorporated comments at 41 (59.4% of all comments used or discarded from the meeting). Jesse had 11 (15.9%), which was unsurprising because his role was to review the lines that Neil read at the meeting. The large number of ideas that were incorporated shows the linearity of the process at this point: following a traditional brainstorming approach of "going broad" before one "goes deep," Neil and Jesse, after going broad with many ideas, went deep with fewer though still numerous ideas.

Although the subject of a majority of comments (53.6%) was copy—verbal messages for the ads—visual matters were addressed by nearly 4 out of 10 of the comments (39.1%), suggesting the importance of the visual, even when one is focusing on words in a verbal-visual document. Concepts with no predominant verbal or visual characteristic composed the rest of the accepted or rejected comments (7.2%). Surprisingly, the copywriter contributed 71.5% of the visual comments used in final ads (15), again suggesting the importance of the visual to a writer in dyadic verbal-visual ad collaboration. Unlike the previous day, however, the copywriter did not contribute many visual comments that were dropped (2 vs. 63.5). All of the visual comments of the writer regarded layout. The writer's total comments were split between visual layout concerns (19, 42.2%), and headlines, subheads, tag lines and body copy—word concerns— (26, 57.8%). The artist's comments were devoted more to word concerns as defined above rather than layout concerns (11/8). However, of the verbal comments used, the copywriter contributed 82.1%.

Further analysis of the comments reveals more of the distinctly different collaborative roles the artist and writer played, Neil primarily directing and Jesse in a supporting or occasionally challenging role. In fact, Neil devoted nearly all of his comments to directing (50 of 51).[3] The copywriter even directed the visual discussion, contributing directive comments on arrangement (6), tone (6), and emphasis (4). However, he was extending ideas that had been agreed upon in the brainstorming session, so he was not the sole originator of the ideas expressed in many of his comments.

For example, on 2/15 Neil recommended both the layout and tone of an ad:

> Then I just thought we could do something with beauty shots of the lawn mower, however you want to art direct it. And it's just headlines, some kind of gnarly headlines like the first one: "Don't worry, big guy, you'll be back holding the remote in no time."

This was a layout concept they came up with together the day before. From a tonal standpoint, Neil recommended lines that were "gnarly," surfer slang that

---

[3] All 71 comments entailed some collaborative move and were thus counted.

in this case meant both excellent and risky (MSN Encarta, 2006), the risk in this case being completely alienating the customer from the topic.

In the following instance, however, Neal alone came up with the layout and accommodated the old radio concept to it after the brainstorming session:

> An instructional ad, . . . sort of like "how to do this." And then down here you've got a little thing about the lawn mower. So it's . . . "Agavez presents a helpful guide to golf. Getting more distance off the tee." And then there's this copy about how to get more distance off the tee. And then when you come down it says "you've got better things to do than to cut the grass. Trouble-free starting," blah, blah, blah. And now there's this whole thing on how to do all these things that you want to do.

> Jesse: Yeah. That'd be cool.

Neil's additional visual directives regarding the ad included:

> As long as [the golf visual] is, like, sort of, like, separated by "Agavez presents." Whatever and then down here we've got our bold subhead that says, "You have more important things to do than mow."

Neil envisioned the picture in the ad depicting the golfer in several stages of teeing off. This arrangement set him up for his explanation, joke, and sales hook at the bottom of the ad.

As in the gnarly example, tone was also important in Neil's concept:

> Neil: Maybe one of them's an older looking ad.

> Jesse: Right.

> Neil: Just takes on the look or whatever.

But in this instance, Neil used both words and picture to create the desired tone. Neil strove for a retro looking ad that mimicked the straightforward, informative tone of a set of 1960s *Golf Digest* instructions, yet added a humorous twist. Neil had passed on to Jesse some golf pictures that would help create this tone. The finished image in the ad inset numbers with no corresponding or inferable explanations next to the shoulder, elbow, and knees of a golfer in midswing. Most of the body copy in this ad and the "choosing the steak" ad provided useful information about the topic. But the retro and incongruous tone of the illogical "how-to" visual was also mirrored by the ad's informative then homespun language:

> Practice with different clubs. You'll learn how far you can drive the ball with any given club. This, friends, can help you get more distance on the ball. If you are, however, unsuccessful . . . just smack the heck out of it.

Neil used visual tone to reinforce verbal tone here to create more impact—"technical" advice about improving one's recreation, coupled with humor, stressed the benefit associated with the product.

More often than not in their interaction, the artist offered prompts—supporting comments—(10/19). Jesse's role here was dramatically different from the brainstorming session the day before, when the largest number of comments he made were directing, primarily on visual matters. In three instances, however, he challenged Neil's verbal ideas, and five times he gave directions regarding the tone of the images (2) or words (3). Below we find Jesse creating the appropriate verbal/conceptual emphasis for one of the "how to" ad ideas:

> Neil: And then another one, which I didn't flesh out: "Agavez presents hang gliding for beginners."
>
> Jesse: Uh-huh.
>
> Neil: That one's kind of over the top, but cool . . .
>
> Jesse: Maybe . . . like "*next week's* hang gliding for beginners."
>
> Neil: Yeah, or maybe, maybe, how to do . . .
>
> Jesse: And maybe that's over the top.

Because an ad devoted to "hang gliding for beginners" would depart from the humorous yet informative "how to" concept into the absurd—go over the top—setting an inappropriate tone for selling a relatively expensive power tool, Jesse recommended the appropriate emphasis by keeping the joke but putting it in a harmless place. Of course in this instance the visual and verbal are related—by reducing the concept to a subhead, Jesse also eliminated the visual/ rhetorical negative impact created by an entire layout.

When he wasn't sure the line worked, Jesse also challenged Neil:

> Neil: And then we have just, like an incredible shot of a guy fishing, hunting, golfing, running. I was thinking this one even says, "Another satisfied Agavez owner." I think it needs some kind of contrast. Like I was thinking if it was inset to show that he's already cut his lawn and he's out there doing that. Do you know what I mean? Just something.
>
> Jesse: I don't know.
>
> Neil: Maybe it's just simple—I'm not even sure that's—I mean, let's just do it up.
>
> Jesse: Yeah, I don't know. I *guess* it can sell a lawn mower.
>
> Neil: Yeah. I just wanted to make sure that people know that. I'd say the line's not right because it needs to be—it's like he's done with it and he's out there and it needs to communicate that.
>
> Jesse: Yeah. Yeah.
>
> Neil: So maybe that line needs something more. Okay.

The connection between the product and benefit was tenuous in the ad, as Jesse noted and Neil recognized. In the final rendition of the ad, the lawn mower was inset at the bottom. The tag at the bottom read, "Agavez makes life easier." The words still did not link the product to the benefit with much clarity or force. Neil himself, in a 2/18 interview, said that the tag was "a little vague." Coming up with a tag line that represented the position that there were more important things to do than cut grass, yet was general enough to sell other Agavez power tool products, was very difficult, particularly because for POS material, ideally, the tag had to be "crystal clear . . . exact" (TR 86). Before, it was easier because they were just writing positioning lines for a lawn mower.

Although Neil here was trying to satisfy the needs of the client to appeal to a broader audience of Agavez customers at the risk of not "grabbing" the lawn mowing customer, in most of Neil's copy generated the afternoon of 2/14, the audience that predominated was the customer. Comments that addressed customer concerns prevailed (47/69,68.1%), as they did in the brainstorming session. Jesse and Neil integrated 39 such comments from 2/15 into the final ads that they presented in the tip-ball selection session. The client (Agavez, the mower manufacturer) was addressed in 7.2% of the comments, and both client and customer were addressed in 17 of the comments (24.6%). Of course, comments that simultaneously addressed both audiences would seem to be important in resolving the competing audiences problem. However, most of these comments either addressed golf or showing the mower. Golf was said to be "huge" with Agavez management, and it was the fastest growing sport in America, thus likely to be one of the "other hobbies" that the brief asserted would interest mower buyers. Although of interest to both audiences, the relationship between product and benefit was not clearly defined in the ads.

The creatives had accomplished part of their objective for the meeting by its end. Neil communicated the *many* creative, humorous lines and new concepts he had generated the day before. This copywriter was clearly gifted in his ability to quickly come up with numerous persuasive and entertaining lines that addressed at least one key element of the conflicted desires of the manufacturer and customer audiences. By the time Neil presented his lines on February 15, he had developed concepts generated in the brainstorming meeting: the icon ads, mower-hero ads, the graph ads (pie, bar, line), and the "Another satisfied Agavez owner" ads. Layout ideas were coming along.

On the other hand, he had cut several concepts: the tree branch/golf club ad; the mower mostly hidden by the garage; the "split thing" (half a tractor joined to half a golf cart); Jesse's "reverse psychology" ad extolling lawn mowing in the rolling hills; the "wrong uniform" ad in which the consumer mows in golf shoes; the "dependable Agavez," mower-on-a-golf ball; and the couch potato concepts. The couch potato and dependable Agavez ads were old concepts that had already been executed. But because he had cut the other concepts, and because of his directing role in this session, Neil had exhibited a large influence on the process to this point. Undaunted by the numerous concepts and executions entailed in Neil's copy, Jesse exhibited a strong attitude and work ethic, helping the campaign gain momentum.

However, ongoing problems continued. In their drive to produce many concepts and executions, including three graphs, Neil and Jesse did not concern themselves with trying to reconcile the competing audience interests. Neil delivered his lines, and Jesse listened, only challenging Neil on one topic. In this session, the client's interest in showing the mower and giving reasons to believe was supplanted by the need to stress the recreational benefit to the consumer, a need also stressed in the Brief Meeting.

After this Friday session, I asked the dyad about where they were going from there. Neil said that they would continue with their typical approach. Their standard process was to brainstorm ideas together, Neil fleshing them out alone (particularly the copy), then showing the result to Jesse, who would put visuals with the words in constructing layouts. Depending on how much time they had, Neil would refine the headlines in the layouts and they would determine what they liked the best.

Neil planned to write more headlines and send them electronically. He said they might get together Monday morning and brainstorm more. Jesse said brainstorming would be easier Monday because "we've got some in the bag, . . . the pressure's off." The deadline for submission was in 7 days, a "huge amount of time," according to Neil, although he said they had other accounts due in the midst of that. As Neil had just gone over 20 headlines, tags, or sections of body copy, I asked how many they would present in the tip-ball meeting in order to gauge the extent of the winnowing process.

> Jesse: Just whatever looks good.
>
> Neil: Yeah, whatever. Then sometimes we'll kind of sniff around and see what everybody else has. Then we're, uh, "Oh we'd better do some more."
>
> Jesse: We'll walk in there sometimes with . . . 20, 30 ads . . .
>
> Neil: Now with this one, we'll probably just not even—we might not even just govern ourselves on this—just come in with everything. Just maybe it will help somebody else start an idea or this could go with that. Just because this is a pitch. Because we want to . . . get as many ideas out there and see what's working.

Neil later questioned whether some of these ideas would work, mentioning the "You'd rather be doing anything else than cutting grass" series of the mower-hero concept specifically. "It seems a little flat," he told me, but after mentioning it might lead someone else to a good idea, he laughingly added that, alternatively, the art direction could be so great that it masked that the line wasn't a "really good idea." Neil's gut instinct about the concept was accurate: the ads were flawed in several ways, discussed in the conclusion. However, perhaps because of all of the other concepts the pair was developing, Neil did not follow up on his intuition by examining the concept's relationship, or lack thereof, with all data about the audiences.

Beyond stressing quantity, it is clear here that the dyad saw their products as not something they owned, but something that others could couple to their work or use as a springboard into their own ideas. Neil and Jesse's approach was more large-group collaborative than dyadic in that the responsibility for content was not just the dyad's. The team was more open to large-scale improvisation in real time; it was less concerned about "staking a claim" on dyadic ideas.

Although Neil had hoped to contribute even more copy before the evaluation, most likely because he had three other accounts due in the intervening days, he did not. But just as Neil had previously worked up the copy, to deliver the copy and concepts Jesse now created the layouts.

MERGING PICTURES AND WORDS:
2/16–2/22

The layout has several functions in advertising, according to Wells and colleagues (1995, p. 467). It translates a visual concept for others so that the idea can be discussed before money is spent on the production. After approved, it provides a guide for production people handling typesetting, finished art, photography, and paste-up. In some cases, it also provides a guide for a copywriter to create copy to fit into its spaces. It is also used for cost estimating.

In advertising, the process of creating layouts normally includes the following steps:

1. **Thumbnail sketches**. Both art directors and copywriters, if involved this early in the process, create "miniature versions of the ad, preliminary sketches (more like doodles) that are used for developing the concept and judging the positioning of the elements" (Wells et al., 1995, p. 468).
2. **Rough layouts**. Done by hand to size, but without a lot of attention to how they look. The art director works out size and placement some more.
3. **Full-blown comprehensives**. Type is set for display copy, though greeking[4] used for the rest. Greeking should be the right size and resemble the typeface intended for the ad. Comprehensives are used for people who can't envision the ad from the semi-comp and for new business presentations and agency reviews.
4. **Mechanicals**: "Camera-ready copy" quality (Wells et al., 1995, pp. 470–471).

---

[4] Greeking is blocks of nonsense text placed in a preliminary layout. This placement lets a composer concentrate on the overall visual appearance before laying out the actual text.

When we see the linearity of this typical process, we should not be surprised that Jesse and Neal's process had been fairly linear so far.

Between the Friday, February 15 and Wednesday, February 20, Jesse worked largely alone with the lines and concepts to create the layouts. To do so, he used Quark Express and Photoshop on his Mac G-4. At 9:30 a.m., Wednesday, 2/20, Neil dropped by to review the 17 layouts Jesse had created, including the following:[5]

One layout was a circular image of a fishing float bobbing on top of concentrically rippling water. Inset into the round image was a wedge-shaped partial view of a lawn mower. Below the image, a scientific-looking black-bordered box included the words "Study 126" and a headline placeholder for "Studies show that Agavez owners have nice looking lawns and even better looking fish." The company logo and the tag, "Agavez makes life easier," completed the layout. Because it was hard to identify that the round image was intended to be a pie chart, Neil vetoed this ad, although Jesse thought it might be further developed. At one point they reconsidered rendering the concept as a simple sketch, but this never happened. A related layout that went no further was three vertical bars, a small one with a lawn mower in it, a small black bar, and a large bar of the now-cropped fishing float image. Below this image was the same kind of "scientific" headline box described above. With no vertical axis or marked horizontal axis for the bars, it was hard to identify the image as a bar graph.

Other developed layouts included a line graph created by a combination of two images: below the line, the angular border (the bottom one-third of the page) was grass. Above the angular border was an image of a 10-point buck, head framed by a dip in the line. However, the line was only suggested by the angular border, it was not drawn. Below was another scientific-style box with the headline, "A recent survey says guys like a nice lawn and a six point buck. But not necessarily in that order."

Like the bar graph and pie chart, there were no clear x- or y-axes, ticks, or values that would identify the images as bar or line graphs or pie charts. For this reason, it was difficult to understand the concept of the ads. Other ads, however, were clearer. Jesse put one of Neil's gnarly lines—"Honey, weren't we going shopping for shoes today?"—over a jaunty image of a lawn mower, with the subhead, "We know you'd rather be doing anything than cutting grass."[6]

---

[5] Because of the cost of image royalties, not all ads can be shown here.

[6] To create the jaunty, heroic image (see Figure 11) for a previous Agavez campaign, Jesse had hired a Detroit automobile photographer specializing in "light painting." In a dark studio, the photographer set the camera lens open, then used a hose with an intense light shining through it, filtered through various prisms, to expose only parts of the mower, creating highlights on tires and chrome that more resembled the play of light in a painting than the broad, flat light of a photograph.

Figure 11. Version of mower-hero ad.
Reprinted with permission from Heric Advertising, Agavez Corporation.

Conversely to the hero emphasis on the mower in the "excuses" ads, Jesse also developed four "Yards are our life, not yours" icon ads, where an overhead shot of a basketball swooshing the net obscured most of a mower below it, and in three other layouts where a mower was obscured, mostly blocked from sight, by a TV remote, a golf ball, and a bottle of beer, respectively. Jesse also had begun some other layouts by putting in Neil's lines and in one case choosing an appropriate script font to convey the retro "helpful guide" ads.

Throughout the rest of that day, Neil occasionally dropped by Jesse's office and made suggestions about the developing visual delivery systems for the copy. Most of the activity from this point on in the collaboration involved Jesse's creating full-blown comprehensives of the concepts. Jesse said that, "anymore," he created ads that were pretty finished because he could do the images assembled from the Internet quicker than sketching, and they looked better. However, he also contradicted himself by saying that he wondered whether all the work involved in creating the concepts nearly tight was worth the trouble. It would appear that to create a "very rough" rough using Photoshop and

Quark was not difficult or time-consuming, but doing so upped the ante, the expectations of the Chief Creative Officer and other decision makers, so one in the end had to spend more time coming closer to finishing the concepts for an initial presentation.

The magazine print ads were by nature not only more finished but also more conceptual than their newspaper counterparts. Jesse saw the rhetorical situation of the print ads for a magazine as less immediate than the newspaper's. Magazines were more about positioning than announcing sales and prices because magazine ads had to go in a month before publication whereas newspaper ads could go in even the same day of publication. So the layouts he was composing stressed positioning (TR 102). This consumer awareness of the brand and product was critical because "if you don't have [it], sales will plummet" (TR 102).

For this reason, Jesse felt that "a good idea" was most important in creating an ad. He said the POS, the store display aspects, could be worked out later, but they first needed an idea "clear, concise, that drives home your strategy right away, like 'Lawns are Our Life, Not Yours.'" (TR 106). Here Jesse referred to the "good idea" as verbal.

EVOLUTION OF A GOOD IDEA: THE "LAWNS ARE OUR LIFE" CAMPAIGN

Both Neil and Jesse felt that the "Lawns are Our Life" icons ads were their strongest campaign. Because of their preference for this ad concept, although it is beyond the scope of a study of collaboration to trace his every individual move or all of the dyad's ads, we will examine aspects of Jesse's production of an advertisement created from this icon concept, in which a recreational implement (e.g., golf ball) hid much of the mower. We can summarize the evolution of the document to this point as follows:

> 2/14: Jesse had the idea of putting a large graphic, such as a golf club, right in the front of the picture. Neil also wanted to foreground a leisure pastime (golf, barbeque) and hide the mower in the garage with only the handle sticking out. Jesse also drew a grill and in a separate picture clubs foregrounded or framed through a window with the mower off in the distance, nearly on the horizon.

> 2/15: Neil independently added the headline, "Lawns are our life, not yours," words that served as a tag line in a previous campaign.

> 2/15 or 2/18: Jesse developed the iconic "pop art" concept of the golf ball with mower hidden behind it; he talked to Neil in the hall about the idea. Jesse shot pictures of the golf ball (also in separate images, a remote control and a beer bottle) on the windowsill of his own residence, rather than spend a lot of time on the Internet looking for images that were not exactly what he wanted. In selecting these images for his layout, Jesse sought

"something simple and graphic that got to the point real quick." He also shot pictures of lawns to use in the layouts.

2/20: Jesse created his first comprehensive of the golf ball icon ad (see Figure 12). He used his photo of the golf ball on his windowsill and took another picture of grass and added it onto his own lawn. He also used Photoshop's layering function to put the lawn mower mostly behind the golf ball.

Figure 12. First version of icon golf ball ad.
Reprinted with permission from Heric Advertising, Agavez Corporation.

In the resulting image, a close-up of a golf ball on an indoor windowsill obscures all but the handle and front left corner and wheel of an Agavez push mower located outside. The golf ball takes up approximately half of the area of the 8 ½ × 11-inch comprehensive (comp). Lawn extends back from the mower into two groves of trees.

Jesse said he used reverse type, hard to read in anything other than small quantities, because the amount of copy was minimal and because a distinct break was needed separating the image and the copy portion of the ad. Jesse felt serifs were "frills" that "dress[ed] up the font" and instead used sans serif type because it was simpler, straighter, no frills, as the brief called for to reach the customer. All caps also had more visual impact, making a "loud statement" (TR 107).

The visual dominance of the golf ball, like the mowing-disparaging subhead in the mower-hero ads (see Figure 11), emphasized the customer at the expense of the mower-loving client.[7] Jesse was aware of this emphasis, as he told me in an interview a few days later:

> Jesse: All the clients . . . like to see their product. So probably one short-coming with this icons campaign is you don't see much product. . . . They'll say . . . "Strategically, you're on, but I can't see my product." So we'll show it to them like this first, and then I know we're going to come back. . . . I'd rather start this way and maybe they'll—they might buy into it. . . . It's all about compromising. (TR 101)

The huge lawns in the background that extended to large groves of trees were also something Jesse anticipated revising in the ad: "These lawns are a little too nice for our target. . . . How many middle class guys have a lawn like that?" (TR 108).

From these responses, it is clear that Jesse saw ad creation as a recursive, social process. With the number of ads and projects he was responsible for, he did not have time to fully render all of the concepts. He continued to develop the layouts and consulted briefly with Neil on February 21. By February 22, the day of the first tip-ball campaign evaluation meeting and one week after Neil had gone over his new lines with Jesse, the artist had produced 16 fairly finished layouts.

Revisions made to the golf ball icon ad were increasing the size of the bottom rectangle to accommodate the insertion of the "Agavez makes life easier" tag line under the logo. This action enlarged the headline by 20% to roughly 18-point type. The amount of image in the ad shrank by 3%, and the golf ball shrank slightly, as did correspondingly the mower it largely obscured. However, the image was still striking, and the more-visible headline drove the message home more forcefully.

---

[7] Figure 11 could also be seen as sexist, but studies by a retail expert suggest that American men in general dislike shopping (Orlando, 2007).

TIP-BALL EVALUATIVE MEETING 2/22/02:
"I'M SURE WE'LL SEE A LAWNMOWER
IN HERE REAL SOON"

The current chapter will discuss how this meeting impacted Neil and Jesse's ads. More details of the tip-ball meeting will be provided in subsequent chapters. At 11 a.m. on Friday, February 22, Steve Douglas, the Account Manager, and 16 other Heric employees assembled in a large conference room to present and evaluate ideas for the Agavez campaign. Since the highest-ranking creative, the Chief Creative Officer, was in Chicago on a TV shoot, Vice Presidents Neil and Jesse ran the meeting and reviewed the ads. The work of seven creative teams was presented by one or more team members. After that, Neil, Jesse, and the account managers met and chose which ads to continue to develop.

The presentation procedure was that each creative team laid its ads before Neil and the creatives who stood or sat near Neil at one end of the conference table, then presented its ad concepts to the group. Neil presented his team's ads last, and he led off with the icons campaign. He briefly explained the concept of "what you want to do"—the recreational implement—foregrounded to the point of hiding the lawn mower, but, as had Jesse, he questioned how long the mower would be nearly completely obscured: "The whole thing about it, you don't see the lawn mower. I'm sure we'll be seeing a lawn mower here real soon" [laughter].

After Neil and Jesse finished presenting their ads, the other creatives left. In all, 87 concepts and tags had been presented. Neil felt "everybody was on the strategy: Everybody nailed it." In a subsequent interview, Neil praised the account managers' ability to "narrow. . . down exactly what the focus is so there was no question" in the creative brief. "Sometimes you'll get some briefs which stress 'quality' and 'excellence,' . . . very nebulous things. . . , so . . .[ideas generated] are all over the place." Neil felt nothing could have been added to the brief (TR 188).

Staying to evaluate the ads along with the Agavez Account Manager were the Assistant Account Manager, Vice President of Public Relations, Group Media Buyer, and Chief Media Buyer.

The evaluation meeting began with a discussion of how the ads would be presented. Some would be suitable for high-gloss magazine inserts, but since Agavez had not given the agency much of a print budget, this approach was dropped. The Account Manager brought up the criterion of being able to "blow out" the campaign idea in POS displays, advertising, as well as other media (e.g., radio, TV, print). Some clever lines were discarded because they could not conceptually carry a larger campaign (TR 138).

Neil asked Steve, the Account Manager, what he felt about the icons ads. The predicted issue surfaced:

Steve: I don't know—do you think you can do it and still get a full shot of the product in there? Because you know you're going to have an issue.

Neil: What we [will] show is, we cut off a third of the product and see how that turns out.

Jesse: Or we show an inset down at the bottom.

Steve: We could do something like that.

Another Neil-Jesse idea, the "things you never want to do," (dental appointments, hanging pink curtains, etc.) was discarded because unlike the fun-focused campaigns, this subset of the "mower-hero" ads was not advertising fun that could also be offered in a contest as a possible benefit of buying an Agavez mower. It is evident that, as the Vice President Media Buyer told me, the campaign was an entity with many entry points through different media—print, radio, promotions such as contests, and the like. Here the PR element of the integrated marketing campaign limited what could be used as a print ad concept.

The Group Media Buyer questioned how the icons campaign would carry over into radio. Neil countered that radio wasn't the problem, rather it was showing Agavez that Heric could do good POS. However, Steve and the media buyer noted that the agency needed to show Agavez that Heric could do an integrated campaign, with the concept integrated into several media. A tension here was that creatives emphasized the visual for good POS to the point that campaigns did not translate into a verbal medium like radio.

Evaluating another of the Neil-Jesse ads that Steve liked best, Neil said their bar graphs needed work to be comprehensible to the reader, whom he doubted would be able to read bar graphs. But Neil chose to let the Chief Creative Officer decide which Neil-Jesse ad was best, and they mailed the ads judged worthy of further consideration to the Chief Creative Officer on location in Chicago.

As the only creatives in the post-tip-ball evaluation meeting, Neil and Jesse had the advantage of the ability to further explain and defend their concepts and negotiate modifications in the case of the icons ads in order to stay in the running. Yet they were not overtly biased; in fact, Neil brought out a weak point of their chart/graph concept that nobody else surfaced. Neil and Jesse also had more experience working with Agavez than any other creatives, having worked with them for nearly 3 years, becoming fully aware of their "pet peeves," according to Neil (TR 188). However, most of that work was for a mower under another brand name with another brand image to uphold. The dyad had only created three billboard ads for Agavez, Jesse told me.

The very possibility of Neil and Jesse's biased influence dissolved in the wake of the events that followed. Chief Creative Officer Rick Waller said he never got the packet of winning ads in Chicago, and when he arrived back at the agency Monday he called for a second tip-ball in which he would have all creatives present their material again, and he would reevaluate everything himself, deciding what would be developed further into the lead campaign. Account Manager Steve felt this extra meeting was "kind of dysfunctional."

During the two and a half business days between the first tip-ball and the second, Jesse revised the icon ads. He knew that the Chief Creative Officer would want to see the product more, so he adjusted the golf ball icon ad to make the grass catcher, the top, and the right front side of the engine visible, while the golf ball obscured the rest. He did this by shrinking the golf ball and windowsill by 20% (90 points), enlarging the mower by 7% (40 points) and partially moving it away from the golf ball. He told me in an interview that the Agavez campaign was visually oriented because of the need to translate the concept into store displays. As Jesse said, "Just a headline in Sears, . . .[8] no one is really going to look at it" (TR 229). It was important, as Jesse told me in an interview, that they create a consistent visual image for Agavez—a"family feel"—so that one could see an Agavez ad in a magazine and go into the store and see similar display advertising that would allow the customer to differentiate the Agavez product from the other mowers for sale. The problem with a different company doing Agavez' POS advertising before was the lack of such a cohesive, integrated campaign.

Although Jesse had emphasized the product a little more visually, he had left out the "reasons to believe" that Neil had recommended early in the process. In their place was greeking that said, "this is not live copy. It is greeking and is for position only."

SECOND TIP-BALL MEETING, 2/27/02: "ROMANCE THE PRODUCT"

When Jesse and Neil's turn came in the tip-ball meeting conducted by Rick Waller on 2/27, they presented their icon ads first. They held the ads up and explained them, then pinned them with magnets to metal boards running along the walls of the room, illuminated by track lighting.

The limelight showed that although they had made the lawn mower bigger, the golf ball still obscured one third of it. And the reasons to believe the brand promise—Agavez gets it done so you can move on to enjoy life—were absent. Waller's response was that these ads needed to "romance the product." The Chief Creative Officer reminded the creatives that "Agavez loves the product," and of the previous campaign where they hired the Detroit light painter to beautify the lawn mower. Jesse responded that he was just trying to sell an idea and that he would put more product in the ad. Putting product in the ad was crucial also, the Chief Creative Officer pointed out, because they weren't trying to sell just any lawn mower, they were selling the Agavez product. Waller

[8] Sears is not "MegaWorld," the chief retailer of Agavez products.

criticized the "Another Satisfied Agavez Owner" series because it did not show the product except in an indistinct inset; instead, it featured the owner engaged in deep-sea fishing, diving, or some other kind of recreation. A customer should be able to go into a store and remember amidst several other brands that Agavez was the lawn mower he wanted.

However, on the plus side, when another creative team later mentioned giving away free golf balls with the purchase of an Agavez, the Chief Creative Officer said that Neil and Jesse's ad would work well with that because it featured recreational implement icons. This ad could be tied into a promotion in that way.

At the end of the meeting, Neil and Jesse's work—the satisfied customer, the "mower-hero" campaign, and the icon ads—were selected by Waller to go forward to the next evaluation, where the final three campaigns would be chosen. Three other dyads' material, involving a number of other potential campaigns, was also selected. Neil and Jesse began to think more about "blowing out into POS" the icons campaign.

Over the next week, in the icons ads, Jesse "moved things around just so the product ha[d] more dominance" (TR 268). For the golf ball ad, to avoid a busy image, he removed the background photo of grass and trees, both because the trees seemingly sprouted from the mower handle and also because in order to maintain visual perspective with the trees, the mower would have to have been small, and visual impact would be lost. Cropping out the trees and adding a brighter grass background image from the Internet brought the golf ball into more prominence, because the golf ball and windowsill, which had since 2/26 replaced the rectangular subhead background, now took up two-thirds of the vertical space in the ad, the largest since the golf ball, windowsill, and headline rectangle took up two-thirds of the space in the first comprehensive 2/22. Unlike 2/22, however, in the backyard behind the windowsill, visually above the golf ball, the mower was nearly 100% visible and reasonably sizable, although still much smaller than the golf ball (see Figure 13).

In arriving at his final version, Jesse had experimented with making the mower equal in size to the golf ball, but his design principles ultimately ended this gambit to please both client and customer: A good picture, he told me, needed "one dominant visual. . . . If you have them both giving the same impact, . . . it's not going to grab me" (TR 269). The visual needed one center of gravity, and the headline, "Lawns are our life, not yours," determined whether mower or recreation was the center. Since the photo was shot from the perspective of the customer, recreation loomed larger than lawn mowing.

In other minor changes, Jesse followed the directives of the Chief Creative Officer and also worked to simplify the ad as much as possible "to increase the odds of someone looking at it." Most magazine copy and ads, Jesse told me, were cluttered and distracting: "If [magazine readers are] seeing a bunch of busy ads, busy copy, all of a sudden something simple might catch their eyes. . . . Just

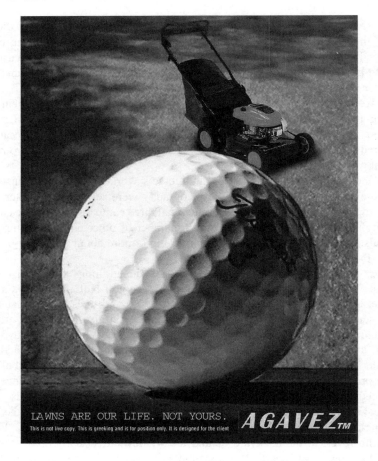

Figure 13. Final version of icon golf ball ad.
Reprinted with permission from Heric Advertising, Agavez Corporation.

give them something to stop. If they're flipping through that magazine, the last thing they're looking for is your ad" (TR 271).

In visual matters, Neil and Jesse considered using the line Waller came up with in the meeting as the tag line: "We spend a lot of time on these mowers so you don't have to." However, it was too long to be a tag, and so they decided to use it as a headline for another mower-hero ad. The tag became "We always work so you can play." (TR 273). Another that Neil considered was "Agavez always works so you don't have to" (Fieldnotes [FN], p. 95).

To show how the icons campaign integrated into PR promotions, Neil and Jesse produced the POS idea from the initial brainstorming meeting: danglers placed in sporting goods departments of MegaWorld, which would cross-sell with the following headline around the bottom half of Jesse's golf ball image: "Get an Agavez and spend more time with this." Along with the subhead, "Better Features, Better Price," were the logo and the new tag.

Other POS concepts Jesse rendered in Photoshop were "Get an Agavez and spend more time doing this" fish and remote-control shelf talkers: placards that would stand on aisle shelves. Also generated was "Another Satisfied Agavez Owner" 2002 Buyers Guide, sporting a shot of a young man deep-sea fishing, joyfully gripping a rod bent from a catch on the line. The tag was "We always work so you can play." Also using the previous headline was an image of an announcement of a "free fishing expedition" on a sign on a pedestal, flanked by a grinning angler with a rod and a tackle box. Another picture showed a grinning boy leaning on an Agavez push mower with the sign, "The Agavez mower WIN A KID for the summer sweepstakes." Another approach to the buyer's guide cover was a light-painted hero shot of the mower.

3/6 TIP-BALL MEETING:
THE END OF THE LINES AND A NEW ASSIGNMENT

At the meeting time, 3 p.m. on March 6, the conference room was empty, smelling faintly of smoke. On the metal boards behind seven chairs on the left side of the long glass-topped cherry table were pinned numerous mower ads. A bright yellow lawn mower hood sat on a table pushed next to the conference table. Creatives in blue jeans and buttoned-down managers arrived, and by 3:11, they were discussing the campaigns.

Rick Waller, critiquing another team's ideas, mentioned that the line was too generic. When Neil urged them to use "trouble-free starting," Waller said to include data to back up the claim—something about the kind of starter on the mower, for example. One couldn't just claim that. All of these grounds were critical in answering the question of "Why an Agavez" rather than another mower. At that point, the Account Manager mentioned a newspaper article reporting the recall of 95,000 Agavez mowers for leaky gas tanks. The team focus dissolved momentarily into sidebar conversations. It should be noted that product recall numbers, however, suggest that Agavez had about the average number of recalls for their lawn mowers. Some high-end mowers had more. For better or worse, product recalls have been a fact of life for gasoline engine products.

The group regained focus and began talking about another campaign and then POS. Waller stated, "We're making our decision based on how the ideas worked for POS. . . . We shouldn't be deciding on ads, we should be deciding on point of sale. That's the assignment" (TR 281). Though they came up with some acceptable POS ideas, Neil and Jesse had devoted little time to them compared with their numerous ad concepts and executions. Strategically this may have been a mistake because the brief did stress in large bold type at the bottom that the campaigns needed to stress POS.

It was brought up that in reality, MegaWorld would not allow elaborate store displays—Heric had tried it with the Agavez sub-brand, and MegaWorld wouldn't give them space. But the ad agencies competing with Heric for Agavez' business would try to do dazzlingly elaborate floor displays, so the leaders asserted that Heric needed to come up with something strong.

In this decision meeting, although transferability into POS was the chief criterion, not duplicating the same thing in three different campaigns to be presented to the client was also important. Furthermore, showing the mower was important. Of the Neil and Jesse campaigns, the "mower-hero" and "another satisfied Agavez owner" campaigns were not clearly linked to POS, and so they were not continued. Rick Waller said that he liked the icons ads, but they repeated the same approach as two other campaigns—one created by a POS specialist—that he liked more. He wanted something different, and he chose to modify an existing second campaign created by the POS specialist to stress that one could afford more fun if one bought an Agavez. This campaign eventually coalesced behind the battle cry, "Neighbors, why pay more?" Thus at the end of the 17-day composing process, Neil and Jesse's original ads, though finalists, were eliminated from the pitch material.

However, because of Neil's uproarious, clever lines and Jesse's clean iconic impact, and in part because its originators were too busy developing the other campaign, the "Neighbors" campaign was assigned to Neil and Jesse to "blow out" into POS display advertising. This campaign was a fully large-scale collaboration involving the Chief Creative Officer and two dyadic teams. Regarding POS, Neil told me after the meeting that it involved a more "down and dirty" kind of copywriting than he normally did, involving bullet points. For Jesse, it was also "more technical" in that he had to create art that went on display racks. As Neil said,

> We don't usually do that. . . . Jesse does a little bit of it, and we have done it, but basically, what we do. . . [is] radio, television, print, posters, brochures, . . . [POS] is a more specialized part of this business. . . . Those guys [whose two campaigns won] just automatically do [it]. (TR 352)

CASE CONCLUSION

Let us return to the overarching question of this inquiry, a question we hope will add pieces into the mosaic-answer of the larger question: what is verbal-visual collaboration? Our more specific question is how do art directors and writers collaborate within an organizational culture to create effective persuasive and informative verbal-visual symbol structures for client/manufacturer, retailer, and consumer? Neil and Jesse's collaborative approach does not fit the three models Mirel and colleagues (1995) posited as a starting-point taxonomy based on their own verbal-visual composing—Morgan's three-model view of collaboration (1991), in which (a) writers create material that they give to artists who then complete the project, (b) writer and artist each compose drafts then get together and integrate material, or (c) writer and artist compose together.

In a typical process for them, Neil and Jesse did something substantially different from the models proposed above, beginning with attending a brief meeting conducted by an account manager for the campaign, there gaining input from other account executives, media buyers, public relations specialists, and other creatives. Neil and Jesse next collaboratively brainstormed concepts and a few lines dyadically, and then Neil wrote copy alone. For concepts, the "aha moment," generating new concepts, came in the collaborative brainstorming, but for writing, in Neil's copywriting alone. Then he and Jesse met and evaluated copy, then Jesse found or drew images and produced layouts for the concepts and copy, which he and Neil tweaked to get ready for the evaluation meeting with the Chief Creative Officer, who, with input from perhaps 20 other creatives, decided whether the campaigns were to be further developed. What this process adds to Mirel et al.'s initial conception is a fluctuation between large-scale, dyadic, and solo composing.

Neil and Jesse's composing process repeats a standard pattern of creativity identified by Young in 1944, more recently summarized as preparation-incubation-insight-evaluation-elaboration (Csikszentmihalyi, 1996). Working on the Agavez campaign before and attending the Brief Meeting provided preparation, and the intervening night provided incubation; insight occurred in the brainstorming meeting and Neil's fleshing out the lines. The function of both the subsequent meetings with Jesse and the tip-ball meetings with the large group was the evaluation of what had been produced, and then the elaboration of the selected materials followed.

Neil and Jesse's approach also helps substantiate the assertion of a respected advertising textbook that after coming up with the kinds of materials found in the creative brief, the next step is to create a "mental picture of how the basic appeal can be translated into an effective selling message. . . . The most important thing in visualizing is to imagine the kind of picture you think would express your idea." This visualizing may be recorded in words or sketches. From there, creatives generate specific words and visuals for the ad. After getting the concepts, words, and visuals, all are developed further into a layout whose conventions include the headline, illustration, copy, and logo; there also may be a subhead, several different illustrations, and other elements (Russell & Verrill, 1986, p. 411). This approach describes the general phases of Neil and Jesse's composing process, although not the specific collaborative or creative moves they used to generate their ideas.

During brainstorming on 2/14, visual topics predominated, even though the artist and writer contributed an equal number of concepts and made close to the same number of comments. Nearly three-fourths of the comments were about visual matters, and the copywriter's share of the visual comments was 51.8%. But just those numbers do not indicate the strength of the writer's visual contribution. In their collaboration on visual matters, the artist made more comments contributing information (9.6% vs. 8.3%), but he also offered more prompting comments to the writer (8.7% to 4.8%), fewer directing comments (16.2% vs. 19%), and challenged the copywriter's visual ideas fewer times than the writer challenged the artist's (1.5% vs. 6.6%). The copywriter also could not have challenged the expertise of the artist on the artist's turf at all.

Moreover, when one compares the number of the copywriter's 2/14 visual comments with the number made in the individual compose-aloud protocol that the copywriter completed as an experiment after the end of the Agavez campaign (Cross, 2008), the difference is substantial. In his protocol, Neil made no purely visual comments per se, although he did generate two rough layouts in Quark Express. Neil's interaction with Jesse brought him even more into the visual realm, to the point that he contributed over half of the numerous visual comments. What was at work here? Perhaps it was the zone of proximal development: When challenged by a more visual person, Neil directed his thinking even more visually, rising to the occasion. Brainstorming with the artist, the copywriter even generated a visual concept for which he lacked words! Jesse also became more verbally oriented.

However, it is important to identify what level of skills was required of Neil. His visual skills were at the concept stage, at the ideation stage. His most frequent visual comments concerned layout. But for writing, his technical skills, while including concepting, also extended through the finished stage— he had to have the technical knowledge to produce grammatical, persuasive, attention-getting lines. To be sure, in small part, Neil's technical prowess was due to spelling checkers: Neil's capacity to misspell at the invention stage was the source of some significant comic relief for the dyad. But it also pointed out Neil's use of writing as a mnemonic cue for later development rather than an instrument for fully rendering some invented material but perhaps not capturing everything generated. Neil captured and developed a large number of ideas.

Beyond generating layouts that led to lines, what other techniques of verbal-visual invention were employed by the artist-writer team?

- Contrast: The big benefit along with small product in the icons and graph, chart ads created attention-getting contrast, difference used to stress product over benefit. Though not previously identified as such for verbal-visual arguments, it is one of the classical topoi and also used in the classical canon of arrangement.
- Similarity: The tree branch that looked like a golf club was one concept employing the topic of similarity, in this case of form, yoked with the contrast of ideas.

- Using different members of the same class of things: for example, trying pie charts then line and bar graphs and considering any other chart or figure to inset product and benefit images into in order to stress the benefit over the product.
- Obversion: Considering the "other side of the coin"—showing someone wearing golf shoes mowing his lawn, then showing someone at the golf course who can't play because he has to mow his lawn.
- Facetious Inversion (Reverse Psychology): Making the following proposition tongue in cheek: "an afternoon along the rolling hills . . . or chasing some dumb ball," which would you prefer?

To what degree are these generative principles visual or verbal in these cases? We can't say the large-benefit, small-product visually originating concept (used in icons, and graph ads) is a purely visual concept, because it needs a line ("Lawns are our life. . . ; "Studies show . . . ") to explain what it illustrates. We can't say "Another Satisfied Agavez Owner" is only a verbal concept, because it needs the beautiful fishing and golfing shots to complete the idea. They are not purely visual or verbal concepts, but they originate in either the verbal or visual.

Why are they generative? In the case of small-big, because it is a pattern that can be used over and over. In the "Satisfied Owner," it is the surprise element that can be done across many different scenarios, making it a widely applicable juxtaposition, similar to Rowland B. Wilson's famous, richly generative line found in 60s and 70s American magazine ads: "My life insurance company? New England Life, of course. Why?" asked the split second before someone was about to be obliterated in a freak accident he or she couldn't see coming but others could. The means of demise were many: a 1250-pound swordfish dropping on its proud angler; a wrecking ball swinging toward the smug executive sitting near his high rise corner-office window, talking about his life insurance on the phone; and so on. Neil's line, like these, required a kind of scene to complete its meaning, but there were a number of instances of that kind that would work. Surprise, contrast, similarity are transferable to many different scenes, ancient principles that have been identified before as generators of speech and writing; but they are in these examples *verbal-visual* generators as well.

One constraint on the verbal-visual messages the dyad generated needs further considering, as I have noted elsewhere: "because of the widespread use of multiple media communications that include written texts, it is vital that we consider an overlooked facet of the writing context: how other media in such communications alter and/or supplement the characteristics of the written text" (Cross, 1994c, p. 225). The fact that the print ads Neil and Jesse generated were part of a larger rhetorical campaign restricted the conditions of signification beyond the limits entailed in the magazine ad. The ads had to transfer well into POS, and the "excuses" campaign was cancelled when it didn't support PR promotions. The icons ads were continued for a while because they did transfer into POS promotions giving away recreational implements such as golf balls.

The creatives worked also in POS to contribute to the integration of print and store displays. As they considered the feasible surfaces to display their messages, the essential nature of the rhetorical situation, which included location in the physical world where the sign would be read, came into sharper focus. Point-of-sale advertising included much more of what Hayakawa calls the "extensional meaning, . . . that which it points to in the physical world" (1978, p. 52). In this case, the rhetorical situation became a part of the available means of signification. Expanding the typical self-contextualized conditions for signification of writing, POS writing becomes a hybrid form approaching the properties of speech where the speaker may point to an object or use props.

Beyond a description of verbal-visual properties of the collaboration, we need to evaluate the effectiveness of this dyad's composing. As research noted previously suggests, the most successful teams are those that stay mindful; that is, heedfully interrelating regarding a common task representation (Asch, 1952; Cross, 2001; Weick & Roberts, 1993). At Heric, the creative brief supplemented by qualitative research of consumers was the intended task representation. But these documents included numerous and sometimes contradictory consumer attitudes and client preferences that had to be translated verbally and visually into a coherent persuasive message.

As it was, no ad concept Neil and Jesse generated adequately bridged all constituencies. Furthermore, no ad provided data—the facts about the mower—to support the claims of various headlines. Thus, the arguments were incomplete, unlike the arguments in ads that were actually used by the client, which included verbally the reasons to believe. The incomplete arguments may have been the result of the dyad's prioritizing quantity over quality, or the outcome of a very rapid game of Ping-Pong that generated 12 concepts and the beginning of two others, one every three-and three-quarters minutes, on average. This count does not include the various spin-offs of some of the concepts. For example, the POS "Spend more time doing this" concept generated eight versions.

The creatives' approach reflected the received wisdom of generating as much as possible while brainstorming. Creativity publications and Web sites often feature Linus Pauling's quote, "The best way to get a good idea is to get a lot of ideas." As Pauling won two Nobel prizes, one cannot discount this scientist's approach. But perhaps in advertising it is better to keep more focused on the problem, come up with fewer ideas, but each hit the nail on the head both conceptually and in the final product. This is not to say that Neil and Jesse's highly inventive use of classical topics was inappropriate—these techniques just needed to be based on a more thorough audience analysis. Before engaging principles of invention that related rhetorical elements in salient ways, the dyad needed to attend more to the rhetorical situation to solve the problem of appealing to clashing audience constituencies.

In Neil and Jesse's case, was the brief an effective preparation? Stressing that mowing was not one of the "more important things in life," the brief to a degree brought on Neil and Jesse's overemphasis on recreation. Although lawn mowing is not sufficient for the good life for lawn owners, it is necessary, so it is still very important. To a degree, the oral presentation of the brief also encouraged Neil and Jesse's response because in the Brief Meeting the Account Manager said that potential customers hate mowing their lawns, an opinion expressed in the qualitative research that conflicted with the "mowing as comfortable escape" attitude summarized elsewhere by the research. The challenge was to represent this consumer ambivalence. It is not surprising that the brief did not do so. The tendency of human beings to change represented reality in order to fit our conceptual categories is a concept that can extend as far as the realm of science: some scientific images have misrepresented the shape of chromosomes in order to make them easier to understand and remember. These images represent a range of phenomena in a generalized, simplified manner (Rosner, 2001, p. 396).

Moreover, the danger of responding too quickly to problems is inherent in "operating adhocracies," smaller organizations that deploy client-based project teams that must nimbly adjust to changing circumstances (Mintzberg & Quinn, 1988). A danger for managers in adhocracies is reaction to problems rather than proactive analysis. This seemed to affect both Neil and Jesse as well as creative brief writer Steve Douglas. As Jarvis, paraphrasing Mintzberg, notes,

> Concentration on action may actually limit the organization's flexibility and ability to respond creatively to the pressures of its environment. Action may focus on known solutions which may be marginal rather than new ones. (Jarvis, 2005)

Maintaining mindfulness was especially challenging in this kind of fast-moving organization. Although Steve Douglas related the product and benefit in the brand promise in ways that would assuage the conflicting audiences, and Neil and Jesse at the end conveyed the brand promise in their tag line, "We always work so you can play," the visual of the large golf ball somewhat hiding the smaller mower did not convey that subordination but rather more of the view that the customer hated mowing. And visuals typically are more powerful than words: for this reason, images are normally used to get people's attention in print ads (Russell & Verrill, 2002, p. 451).

Although the visual gets our attention, frequently from predominant appeals to the emotions or our sense of virtue, words can provide logic and argument to complete the expression and fulfillment of the purpose of the ad. Greeking, in focusing only on the visual form of blocks of text, eliminates a semantic aspect that is crucial in communicating a verbal-visual concept; it institutes a form-content split of a much greater magnitude than the meaning/grammar and meaning/style splits that composition studies has previously considered (e.g., Gage, 1980; Knobloch & Brannon, 1984). Although, of course, verbal-visual composers should be aware of what the greeking characters stand for in the text, even at a macrolevel it can be important to know where the page break falls, where the photo nests, whether the tone of the font matches the tone of the words, and so on. In the Agavez campaign, greeking was particularly problematic because creatives walked a tightrope, trying to balance client vs. customer, product vs. benefit. In a persuasive endeavor of such scope, all verbal and visual resources extant need to be used.

Neil and Jesse needed to provide sufficient evidence supporting the brand promise that their chief creative officer would be convinced. Available space held by the greeking on the icons ads was small, but Neil could have, in his words, "shoehorned in" the reasons to believe. It is quite possible, often a problem in drafts, that Neil and Jesse subconsciously felt those reasons to believe were in the layout because the composers intended them to be there—they were in the pair's internal text representation. Most likely, what interfered with a fully mindful ad was what Bourdieu (1984) calls "habitus," assuming too much knowledge from those less familiar with our ideas.

Neil and Jesse's case suggests that the composing together of an artist and writer involves not only the creative process identified by Young (1944) and Csikszentmihalyi (1996) but also cognitive processes identified by Piaget (1971), in this case regarding verbal-visual text representations. Piaget noted that for cognition to occur, knowledge structures are necessary, for example, the classificatory scheme that naturalists assimilate their perceptions of phenomena into. Having this preexisting structure in relation to the present activity, we can undergo the cognitive processes of assimilation and accommodation (pp. 4–5). "Assimilation" is the reshaping of the mental representation of a currently perceived object to fit the existing cognitive structures in the perceiver. Taking place concurrently with assimilation is accommodation, in which the perceiver's cognitive structures change to accommodate novel aspects of what is being perceived.

It may seem that in principle, Piaget's theory (depending upon knowledge structures, including classificatory schemes) is antithetical to mindfulness. But it is not. When cognition works properly, assimilating novel material changes the system of categories to accommodate the existing material. Although data change when extracted from their context and are assimilated into such a system, in accurate assimilation, these data are not overlooked or "rammed" into existing categories that they don't fit. The new data change the categories, subdividing them and adding new ones. Weick and Sutcliffe would argue that a fully mindful person draws distinctions in the data observed, but relies little upon categories that, as Burke told us previously, may conceal more than they reveal. Weick and Sutcliffe encourage more distinctions in categories and thus more categories, but say that the finer the distinctions in categories, the closer they become to nonconceptual differentiation—distinctive data that are not grouped into categories.

The problem with categories that fine is that, nearly data, they are at so low of a level of abstraction as to be useless. If I just reported processes of composing with no themes or trends, the level of abstraction would be so low that it would be very difficult to discern the shape of the forest from the trees. Barabas (1990) showed that analysis is the value added to reports—we need to have some generalities, some conclusions to draw from myriad data. For this reason, categorization is necessary at a level of abstraction to be useful yet accurate. Such categorization allows us to respond to reality with effective routines or to devise new responses as needed.

Piaget calls these knowledge structures, including category systems, "schema"; they are internal representations. One can infer schema—in the form of text representations of participants—in group composing as well (Cross, 2001). These schema are typically put on paper because, as Baron and Misovich (1999) note, if collaborators intend to share their cognitive structures, these structures must take on a specific form (cited in Weick & Sutcliffe, 2006, p. 520). Layout is an organizing pattern: a sort of knowledge structure, that must assimilate verbal and visual components and accommodate itself to them, the pattern reflective of the schema in the joint conception or collective mind of the artist-writer dyad.[9] One can see how collective verbal-visual creative thought evolves in considering again the actions of Neil and Jesse described so far.

For the dyad, the 3 p.m. Creative Brief Meeting provided novel information (the situation, purpose, and audience of this particular Agavez campaign) that Neil and Jesse separately assimilated over the rest of the afternoon into their preexisting understandings of the rhetorical situation of the Agavez mowers account. The Brief Meeting that stressed the product benefit and that consumers hated mowing changed Neil and Jesse's mower-hero approach, which stressed the reliability of the mower that enabled one to move on quickly. After the meeting's preparation, each "slept on it," going through a period of incubation that night. When they got together to collaborate at 9 the next morning, Neil and Jesse each sketched partial and abbreviated layouts to communicate to each other and capture for themselves their initial ad ideas. These sketches served to help them assimilate the new ideas and accommodate their preexisting ideas about Agavez (including an old tag line that became a new headline) to the new information and new assignment provided by the brief.

At their brainstorming meeting, Neil and Jesse in sharing their developing insights—ideas and sketches—came up with collective preliminary visual concepts, many of which Neil then went off and generated insightful lines for. He also accommodated old radio material to the new rhetorical situation, turning it

---

[9] For more on collective mind, see Weick and Roberts (1993) and Cross (2001).

into the "helpful guide" print ad concepts. Then in their evaluation meeting the next day, he and Jesse selected (assimilated) the best lines and the new "helpful guide" idea into the collective print concepts. The sharp, polished words helped make the originally fuzzy concepts distinct, as Jesse next accommodated the visual concepts to the words in comprehensive layouts that Neil reviewed. When the fishing and hunting graph and chart layouts didn't communicate well, Jesse chose a basketball picture that did (whose verticality worked in a bar graph), and Jesse accommodated the line, "Studies show that Agavez owners have nice looking lawns and even better looking fish," replacing "fish" with "jump shots." During this elaborating process, layout (however partial or abbreviated initially) provided a common text representation so that writer and artist could coordinate their activity together and apart and contribute heedfully both verbally and visually (within the limitations of their audience analysis and memories) to their collective design. Thus, the collective schema kept evolving as the pieces were assembled. Typically, the key elements of the concepts accumulated and integrated gradually from rough sketch to finished lines to finished layout, rather than being worked out in a thumbnail sketch in the brainstorming meeting, as occurred with the next dyad we will examine. Unfortunately, some remained in the internal schema rather than making it into the text.

To conclude this first in-depth description of verbal-visual dyadic composing in context, it is important to note that 10 of 13 concepts (76.9%)[10] began with a visual scenario. As Flower and Hayes (1984) note, the visual representation is fairly far removed from the linguistic features of continuous prose (p. 144). However, the visual representation is very much closer to verbal-visual text. Neil and Jesse started with pictures or visual scenarios and worked their way into words in nearly all cases; rough pictures and locations provided the context and impetus for the generation of words, although not always their full rendering. Moreover, working together, the writer suggesting many visual scenarios and the artist accommodating the writer's line to the new visual concept, their roles as writer and artist became less distinct, more interchangeable and collective.

In taking several initial ideas into the developed concept stage, Neil and Jesse may be described, using Csikszentmihalyi's typology, as insight-intensive (1996). Because they were going forward with five different concepts, including several executions for each, Neil and Jesse as a team could be considered divergent thinkers: thinkers who are broadly creative, generating numerous alternatives from a stimulus, an approach used in the arts and humanities. Advertising has been described as a balance of divergent and convergent thinking

---

[10] These figures include two concepts half-begun 2/14 but completed later; in one case by the Chief Creative Officer and others in later tip-ball meetings. Also, the line for the POS concept, "Buy an Agavez and Spend More Time Doing This," came after locating the shelf talkers in other departments of the store was suggested for cross-selling. Although the actual layout did not come first, the scenario did.

(Vanden Bergh & Stuhlfaut, 2006, p. 377). Convergent thinkers gather a series of facts to solve a problem, an approach used more in math, science, and technology. Effective advertising uses innovation to make a strategic argument to sell a client's product or service. Divergent thinking is expansive, resisting closure; convergent thinking is tightly focused, striving for the "right solution" so that one can move on.

In this instance, part of Neil and Jesse's resistance may have been not taking time to think through the conflicted rhetorical situation entirely. On the other hand, their willingness to include some ads they doubted in the hopes it might push someone else or could be used by someone else shows not only their focus on breadth vs. depth, but also their commitment to large-scale collaborative rather than solely dyadic improvisation within the creative system.

The next chapter will describe an artist-writer team bringing a much more convergent approach to the Agavez account.

CHAPTER 4

"We Had One Idea That We Liked a Lot": The Invention of a Preparation- and Evaluation-Intensive Team

THE COPYWRITER

With the bearing, appearance, and focus of a professional golfer, at age 29, Craig Clayton, Associate Copywriter, was the "young Turk" among the creatives at Heric. One of the "people coming through" the agency that Chief Creative Officer Rick Waller said "keep it fresh," this rapidly rising star soon resigned to take a job in a larger city that was a regional center for advertising near the East Coast. Craig left Heric before the presentation to Agavez but after co-creating three ads that were chosen to be among the 11 presented from 71 entries.

Modern poetry classes had helped Craig most from his BA in English from a well-respected southern private university. This poetry "look[s] at language in a completely different way, and . . . good ads can do that," he said. The basic unit of meaning of a poem was likely a part of this difference; although the basic unit of prose is the sentence, the basic unit of poetry is the phrase (Smock, 2005). Advertisements typically work with highly compressed catchphrases.

Craig completed his formal education with one year's study at an advertising specialty school. A headline-writing class was most helpful there because for one project, the only visual allowed was the product: "It just . . . forced you to think of how to make the words work real hard." One ad for this project was for a motorcycle, but speed could not be communicated visually. So Craig appealed to the sense of touch: "At 130 m.p.h. the goose bumps fall off" (TR 407).

After ad school, Craig had an internship that turned into a job. During this time of intensive study and practice, he was able to create a strong portfolio of ads. Not long after that, he took a job at Heric. At the outset of the Agavez campaign, he had been in the advertising business 2 years. His work during those years was thus characterized by Heric's Chief Creative Officer in his announcement of Craig's departure: "You could always count on Craig to come up with . . . great ideas that could help take this agency to the next level" (E-mail, 3/12/02).

Approach: A Convergent Thinker

Suggesting his tendency toward convergent thinking, Craig said a winning ad concept should be the "creative execution of strategy" (TR 399). He preferred print to television copywriting because "if you're given 30 seconds to explain an idea, it's really easy, but if you ['re] boxed in—you've got one line and one visual—it's more of a challenge. It . . . forces you to come from a better direction."[1] Craig was very careful to base his ideas squarely on strategy, but he preferred to communicate them indirectly: "Leave it so that the reader has to do a little bit of investigating on his own, . . . and he thinks he's smart . . . for figuring it out, . . . leading them down the road to discovery rather than forcing them."

Visual images also played a crucial role: "The perfect headline ad for me is one where the visual plusses [powerfully augment] the line and the line plusses the visual." Although clients liked tag lines, the short slogans accompanying the logo, Craig did not see the utility of them normally. He was taught in advertising school that "if you can't 'Just Do It,' just don't": "unless . . . it's going to be a catch phrase, in the next Webster's, then . . . it just doesn't buy you much. . . . Because you've only got three of four words to work with; . . . it's just . . . really crazy syntax-wise, which I love, [but] the consumers don't get it."

Sources of Material

To come up with effective ads, Craig mined his dreams, writing down ideas that had come to him in his sleep. He also used four other invention techniques. One was beginning with "the visual execution, because . . . I just have more fun doing that, [and] if you can come up with a visual solution or a visual idea, that is so powerful . . . . People just don't want to read headlines anymore, so if you[r] visual . . . will stop them and . . . communicate your strategy . . . , it's usually better." In doing this, he did not sketch beyond stick figures. Mostly, he "ke[pt] it in his head and told the art director." If that didn't work, he wrote headlines, a task he said that came easy to him, but because of the power of the visual today, "they're becoming less and less effective." Another visual technique if he was "completely stuck" was to go to a Web site that had stock photos, flip through those, and if "a neat visual pops up, I'd say, 'what if the line were this?'"

Craig's primary techniques for generating headlines were brainstorming and word association, a form of clustering in which he put the name of the product in

---

[1] This essence-generating constraint was likely one reason that creatives at Heric invented their integrated marketing concepts first in the genre of print ads.

the middle of a page and then drew lines off it to qualities such as "dependable" or "cheap." One then drew lines from those words to newly associated words, and "about five steps away from where you started, you come up with a word that could lead you to the really cool thought." At his previous agency, he had also brainstormed with the other writer there each by writing on Post-it notes 100 lines apiece—100 different versions of a basic idea—then each putting his on the wall outside the door to the other's office. Each writer selected three by his door for the other to rewrite. "It is kind of like poetry in that the word, [e.g.,] whether you use 'like' or 'love,' . . . completely changes the feel of the line. . . . I'll spend a lot of time massaging a line."

Writers didn't brainstorm per se with other writers at Heric now, Craig said, because the tip-ball meetings made everyone more secretive and possessive. To assist his self-evaluation and revision, Craig had read at one point a checklist for the perfect ad, but he couldn't remember it; and said knowing when he was onto something was "more just a gut feeling," which he confirmed by taking a concept or line to peers to see if they gave it "that first look, and they all respond positively" (TR 401).

To get to that positive response, he needed a working relationship with an artist in which it was OK to "throw out stupid ideas, and you know that each is going to laugh them off. . . . You don't fear that 'you're a dum[my]' . . . response" (TR 400). Craig's collaborator told me the way he assessed whether he was on the wrong track is when Craig gave him a quizzical look. The easiest collaboration Craig had ever had was with an art director at an agency he had worked for previously who had "the same age, same ambition, same goals, same everything, and everything we worked on came like that," he said, snapping his fingers.

Normally, however, Craig's dyadic creation process with an artist was to meet and brainstorm, go away and come up with something better, meet and brainstorm again, and reiterate as long as necessary. For Craig, what was needed by the artist, beyond empathy and technique, was also the creative ability to communicate the concept quickly rather than just "make things look pretty." Craig had worked with his Agavez campaign collaborator, Jason Wells, constantly during the preceding year. Craig was both a great writer and a great concept guy, although he "*sometimes* didn't know how to make it work in the visual sense," Jason told me [my emphasis].

THE ARTIST

Winner of OBIE and ADDY awards, Jason Wells was an art director in his late thirties who had worked for Heric for a year and a half. Jason was described by the Account Manager as "exactly the type of guy that buys an Agavez," not only a fact (he owned an Agavez tractor mower) but a tribute because of the values and wisdom of the psychographic profile. Jason's current position had come via more circumstance and experience and less higher education than Craig's. Early, Jason had never considered going into graphic design, but he did a drawing in middle school that was identified as outstanding for Jason's age, and he was put in advanced art classes. After graduating from high school, he pursued a commercial art certification at a community college for a year, then left for automotive school, where, he told me, he learned that it was a lot more fun to work on his own car than on someone else's.

He returned to the community college and completed his art certificate, winning a school competition there. Jason sometimes regretted not earning a 4-year degree because of his long road to becoming an art director. He began work at a type house, setting linotype and keylining. The business was one of the first in his city to use Apple Macs and Quark Express. After work, Jason spent many nights at the office until midnight learning MAC graphics. Leaving the type house, he spent 2 years as a production artist, completing others' ideas, a job he hated. He next became production art manager at another agency, working there 7 years, then moved to a smaller ad agency where he could try out his own concepts and was eventually promoted to Senior Art Director. After 2 years in that role, he joined Heric and had recently been promoted to Associate Art Director.

According to Neil, Jason was known as "The Champion of Photoshop," because he made some submissions to meetings look like finished ads, although he also used his excellent freehand skills to sketch concepts (see Figure 19, p. 102). Jason said for the most part he could present *drawings* within the agency because most of the staff, including the Account Managers, were "pretty visual." However, tip-ball meetings caused him to set the bar "higher and higher" because the best art directors in his region would be putting their concepts on the wall next to his. Moreover, clients often had a hard time understanding ad concepts unless they looked nearly finished. However, it was a waste that "a lot of these things that people have spent hours pounding . . . out on the computer . . . don't go anywhere," he noted, but said tip-ball forced his dyad to be on strategy or out of the running.

He preferred the shorts-and-untucked-shirts dress code of the creative floor, where he could "throw . . . a CD" into his computer and compose ads while listening to music. Often, breakthrough insights came on the 25-minute drive home, a drive he never remembered, which "kind of scared" him. Another time ideas surfaced was when he was with his children. Jason also kept sketchpads by his bed and TV.

"I'm not a writer," Jason told me. He had trouble making an oral presentation of his work in community college; his instructor said artistic people were typically introverts who had to force themselves to verbalize. So to create ads, Jason needed to find a copywriter whom he "clicked with." This kind of collaboration was like a good marriage, both Jason and Craig independently said. Both were approximately the same "rank" in the organization, so there was no power differential. Craig would come up with a concept, and Jason would "plus it," then vice versa, he told me. They could also evaluate the potential of the campaign and how the concept branched out into various key elements. Normally, Craig came up with the ideas: "He's great at [saying] . . . how something can be done differently, which is what you are looking for."

Wearing a fishing hat in an office adorned with images of hot rod engines, drag racers, and Ed Roth Rat Finks, Jason did not look like a person who had pulled himself up by his own bootstraps from the lower provinces of the graphic world through talent and fierce determination. But looks are deceiving. And no one appreciated the creative process more intensely than he did, because of what it had taken to earn it.

OVERVIEW OF COMPOSING PROCESSES

To prepare ads, Jason and Craig took steps noted in Table 5.

PREPARATION AND PRELIMINARY IDEAS

During the Creative Brief Meeting Wednesday, 2/13, Craig came up with his first idea: the line, "Just because lawn mowing [profanity deleted], it doesn't mean your mower has to." That line was a throwaway, but at home that night, he identified the essential relationship between the product and benefit: "It's kind of the *chore* you have to go through before you can get to the *reward*." He thought of it in conjunction with a visual concept:

> A rat in a maze . . . so this [pointing to his drawing; see Figure 14] would be a half-mowed lawn and this [pointing to path line] would be overlaid. And so he's got to start here. And he's got to finish doing all this stuff before he can get to his reward which is his fishing rod.

> Or [Craig continued] he's mowed all of this lawn except for this one little swatch and the swatch there would be a headline . . . "It's . . . four steps to get to go fishing." [see Figure 15]

He also briefly thought of the image of a mower with a fishing pond on it but concluded people would not make the connection between images.

Earlier that day at work, Craig had also met with artist Jason for a few minutes after the Creative Brief Meeting to discuss the new campaign. In the halls of Heric that day, the dyad had heard Neil recommend doing the "split thing," combining images to create a startling synthesis, an idea that was "in the air." "Move," (2002)[2] a spectacular Nike ad being shown then during the 2002 Winter Olympics, transformed one image into another: a running, pivoting boy into a

---

[2] This commercial may be viewed on *YouTube*. Retrieved March 20, 2009, from http://www.youtube.com/watch?v=_jT82oU3kv4

Table 5. Overview of Jason and Craig's Collaborative Process During the First Part of the Agavez Lawnmower Campaign, 2/13-2/27

Large-Group Preparation

2/13   Agavez Account Brief Meeting, 3 p.m.

Dyadic Preparation

2/13   Craig and Jason talk quickly after meeting about initial ideas for Agavez campaign

Incubation

2/13   Drive home for both.

Individual Insight

2/13   At home, both Craig and Jason think of ideas

Dyadic Insight, Evaluation, Elaboration

2/14   Craig and Jason collaborate in two sessions.

Large-Group Evaluation

2/22   Craig and Jason present ads at Tip Ball 1—all sketched

Individual Elaboration

2/22   Fri. Jason on own in office from 1:15–5:27 p.m.[a] develops ads for 2/27.

2/25   Mon. 10:21 a.m.–5:52 p.m., perhaps with two 1-hr. breaks, Jason downloads images for variations on split image ad.

2/26   Tues. 10:58 a.m.–2.04 p.m. Jason downloads chopper images, finishes ads.

Large-Group Evaluation: Preliminaries

2/27   Jason and Craig present ads at Tip Ball 2—Some ads fairly "tight" desktop publishing, some sketched.

Large-Group Evaluation: Finals

3/6   Split Image Campaign chosen to be developed in POS and other media and presented to client.

Dyadic Elaboration

3/6–3/12   Jason and Craig work on split image storyboard for TV

3/12   Craig leaves company to take job at another agency.

Large-Group Elaboration

3/6–3/26   Jason works intensively with POS specialist and production crew to translate campaign into point-of-sale materials (e.g., shelf units, H-racks). Account Management, PR, Media Buyer, Direct Mail Managers meet and brainstorm integrated marketing for split image campaign. Although Jason does not present in actual pitch, he and most of agency meet to prepare campaign pitch to customer.

[a]Exact times taken from files in Agavez Campaign database.

Figure 14. Craig's chore-reward concept: mow maze to get fishing pole.
Reprinted with permission from Heric Advertising, Agavez Corporation.

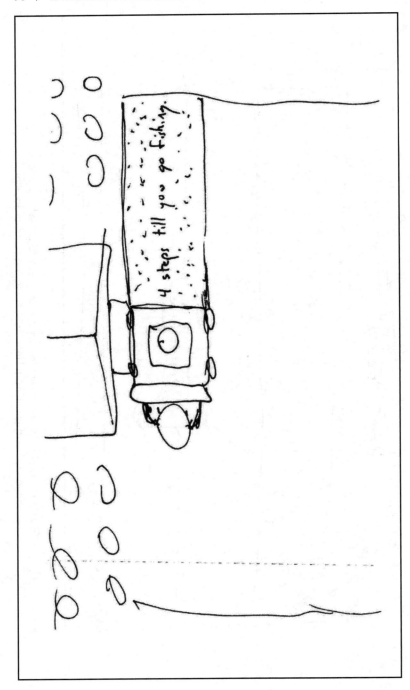

Figure 15. Chore Reward II: Four steps till you go fishing.
Reprinted with permission from Heric Advertising, Agavez Corporation.

spinning hockey player, a golf ball falling into a lake that morphs into a sidewalk puddle, up from which bounces a basketball, and so on. While Jason watched the Olympics that Wednesday night, a visual concept occurred to him, which he sketched on a spiral notepad he kept by the TV:

> The image of a guy that's maybe casting his line out from a boat but below it, matched up perfectly, would be . . . a riding mower. So it gives you—you actually have two separate photos but the way that they're meshed together, it makes one photo. And doing something like that—like a golfer who is getting ready to swing a club but it's the bottom portion is of a push mower. So it's just kind of doing that with different scenarios. You could go on and on.

Another scenario Jason sketched that night was a back view of a person sitting in a chair, watching TV, with the bottom half sitting on a tractor mower (see Figure 16).

Thursday morning, 2/14, Craig and Jason met and explained their previously generated ideas to each other, then decided to try to develop them and others that afternoon in a session that I, having just been given permission to study them, observed.

BRAINSTORMING SESSION

Thursday afternoon, Craig walked three doors down into Jason's office for the brainstorming session. On two walls were metal bulletin boards to which were affixed several ads and comps. Track lighting lit these boards with the only pools of strong light in the room; Jason's large single window framed the brick wall of another building five feet away.

Jason sat at his graphics-powerful Macintosh G-4, which resembled a street rod as much as a computer: decals encircled the screen in a halo of flames. Close by were Pennzoil stickers, speed demon decals, photos of NASCAR stars, and a cutaway view of an engine. Beneath the screen was a speedometer decal, its needle indicating 140 miles per hour.

After quickly telling me a little about their processes and the ideas generated so far, they collaborated for approximately an hour and fifteen minutes. Craig and Jason each contributed nearly the same number of comments—Craig slightly fewer than Jason (140/47.9% vs. 152/52%). Along with discussing the three concepts identified previously, the dyad generated 20 others.

Developing the Split Image Concept

The first concept they worked on was the split image ad, a drawback of which Craig pointed out:

Figure 16. Jason's drawing of split image, TV.
Reprinted with permission from Heric Advertising, Agavez Corporation.

> One thing that's missing in those is . . . when somebody first looks at 'em,
> they need to understand that *this is what you want to be doing* [pointing to the
> fishing] and *this* [pointing to the mower] *is just the dirty means to get to it.*
> [my emphasis]

Here in a flash of insight, Craig distilled the brand promise, "Agavez lawn
mowers get the job done without a fuss so that you can move on to the more
important things in life" into an essential relationship of "means to an end."

Rather than respond, Jason mentioned his own additional insight that had
occurred since their last meeting, suggesting that they add a spiral binding
between the two images to make them look like a flipbook, drawing these on
his images as he talked (see Figures 17 and 18). Doing this, Jason said, "gives it a
natural separation." Craig said it was like the "flipflops you can make monsters
with." Thus, a familiar genre provided a pretext to juxtapose unlike images.

Continuing in his generative insight mode, Craig next brought up another split
image, which attempted to appeal to a demographic missing from the creative
brief: women.

> Craig: I really like the ones about the moms jogging with the baby along.

> Jason: Yeah. The only thing that worried me about that was putting a mower
> next to . . . your child.

> Craig: I don't know, I don't think it would . . .

Figure 18. Jason's golf split image concept. Reprinted with permission from Heric Advertising, Agavez Corporation.

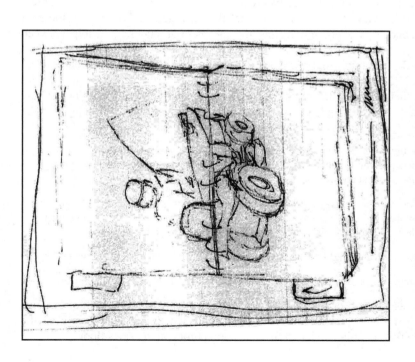

Figure 17. Jason's fishing split image concept. Reprinted with permission from Heric Advertising, Agavez Corporation.

Jason: If you saw it in the campaign, I think it works perfect. But if you saw that in . . .

Craig: Standing in line.

Jason: If a mom flipped it [in the flipbook], she might [shaking his head] "'unh-uh . . .'"

Here Jason moved ahead into a convergent, evaluation mode by pointing out the shortcomings of Craig's approach. Craig next changed the grounds of the debate from emotions and virtue to aesthetics, imagining what something will look like in a new spatial orientation, a trait that neurolinguistic research suggests is a particular strength of males (Kimura, 1999, p. 43).

Craig: I was trying to think if there were any . . . head-on views rather than side views. . . . The mom thing could be head-on.

Jason: Well, that's true. She's pushing the baby.

Brainstorming visually, the copywriter mentioned another head-on split scenario with a grocery cart/mower, but then shifting into evaluation, immediately rejected the version because grocery shopping is more work than reward. An 11-second pause ensued and then he clarified his reason for rejection: "the mower is kind of a means to the end," making this relationship a criterion for evaluation. Continuing his convergent thinking about the rhetorical problem they were solving, Craig told Jason that the only thing missing from the split image concept was communicating the means-to-an-end relationship between the two juxtaposed images.

"But do you think that it's a word thing or . . . something you need to do visually?" Jason asked, initiating discussion of the verbal aspect of the ad after 34 comments about the visual. Words should communicate that idea, Craig responded, and shifting back into a generating or insight mode, he suggested the tag line, "Get it over with." This suggestion met with an 18-second pause.

Jason: [after beginning to invent another tag line that he quickly dismissed, then pausing another 21 seconds]. . . and the whole deal behind saying that . . . what are we saying?

Craig: We're just saying that we understand that it is a *necessary evil.* [my emphasis] That you have to do this thing and it's not—there's nothing glamorous about it. It's just something you've got to do to get on with—

Jason: [evaluating] But that's not really saying anything about our product.

Craig: It's pretty much a parity deal. Everybody is using the same engine.

Here Jason had brought up what would be a key criterion in the Chief Creative Officer's tip-ball evaluation of all campaigns: whether the ad identified the brand so that it could be picked from its competitors on the sales floor.

Perhaps to get more specific about the product, Jason then brought out pictures of his own Agavez tractor mower, saying, "stuff like this can trigger ideas." The image triggered another concept: both now mentioned thinking of using the rabbit and turtle icons on the accelerator of the mower; Craig said they symbolized "getting it done and resting." Jason then suggested that they use the icons to indicate "getting it done quick so you can slow down, . . . the throttle thing."

There then was a 17-second pause followed by Jason uttering a half-sentence on the topic of push mowers, followed by a 20-second pause.

"You've got to admit, that's a beauty," Jason said, showing Craig the picture of his tractor mower again, leading into a discussion of the correct angle for the mower. They then looked at Jason's split images again. The trouble in indicating "mow-then-play" with those images is that they were split horizontally, so a vertical split that would indicate before and after, the traditional time indicator of "action on left occurred earlier than action on right," was not available. They considered doing the images split vertically, halves of the image numbered 1 and 2 to indicate sequence and causation, during which time a 10-second pause ensued, but neither liked the vertical split idea, Jason saying, "I like having the mower down at the bottom because it just seems like it wants to be there at the ground level."

"I think visually it's perfect," Craig agreed. "We've just somehow got to wrap it together."

Drawing as he talked, Jason suggested adding tabs with words to the left side of the mowing/fishing image. This way the ad becomes "the whole . . .

" . . . book," Craig said, completing his collaborator's thought.

Craig, making a critical visual design suggestion that was driven by the visual aspect of writing, recommended putting tabs on the top and bottom instead of side "so we don't have to read a sideways line." Jason drew those tabs on the mowing/TV watching ad.

> Craig: You could have a series of tabs . . . you flip over, and [the bottom half of the image] would be all the models of the mowers. And then up here [pointing to the top half] you could have hunting, fishing, whatever, all the activities.
>
> Jason: Yeah!
>
> Craig: That'd be kind of cool.
>
> Jason: Actually, that could be the POS too. Have dad sit here and flip those. Oh, that's cool, I like that. Very cool.

At this point, Jason began to draw a detailed ink sketch of the flipbook with tabs, spiral binding, and the mower/fisher image (see Figure 19) and the tag, "Get it over with," on the bottom.

> Craig: Definitely will work with POS, too.

Figure 19. Second version of golf flipbook drawing.
Reprinted with permission from Heric Advertising, Agavez Corporation.

Jason: Yeah, it will be great to have that in store. Yeah. (pause)

Craig: Look [pointing to the tabs], you've got all these hobbies listed above . . ."If mowing isn't your passion, what is?"

Jason showed his sketch of the man mowing/fishing to Craig, who said it looked "cool." Jason again brought up the tabs, and Craig recommended a visual solution that he refined as he talked. First, he proposed to have a tab saying "Golf," which could be pulled down and on the backside would be a rider mower; however, he amended that to "pull down 'Golf' and you're pulling down a picture of whatever mower that matches up with the golf. And the[y] . . . would be interchangeable."

Jason said "yeah" in apparent agreement, although to make all the images interchangeable, given the challenges he met later, would have been a staggering and unnecessary feat. Jason then, turning the tables, asked Craig, "What do you think we'd say here and here to get to what you were saying with the copy?"

Craig mumbled something briefly, there was a 14-second pause, and then Neil stopped by, briefly interrupting the process. Resuming after he left, the dyad's convergent thinking again came to the fore.

> Jason: Should we just focus on this and not do anything else?
>
> Craig: I don't think we're going to be able to beat this.
>
> Jason: I like this one. Yeah, let's just do that, that's fine.

After discussing logistical aspects of the problem—the deadline and Jason's being out of town Monday and Tuesday of the next week—Craig resumed elaborating the chore-reward concept with another visual execution of the concept from the front-on angle:

> Craig: I think for the front one somebody, like, skiing and holding on the poles so their hands are in [holding imaginary poles, parallel to ground with tips behind him], almost in that position.
>
> Jason: That could work. Yeah, because it's got that little thing that comes around. So, yeah, that could work.

It appeared that Jason here was referring to the water-ski tow handle, which could be morphed into a lawnmower handle.

Then Craig asked, "Do you mean water skiing? I was thinking snow but water skiing works better, probably."

Craig, however, mentioned the plan of putting the ads in specialty sports magazines and thought the image would work in ski magazines. Jason deflected the evaluative conflict by compromising, asserting that either sport would work. Staying on the topic of head-on shots, Craig again proposed the mother jogger with the baby carriage/mower.

"Uh-huh. I don't have a problem with it."

Jason agreed, "Okay. That's 'cause I'm a parent, man. I've seen the wife's reactions: . . . 'Get them away from there!'"

Diverting the evaluative conflict by changing the subject after a pause, Jason proposed revising the mower/TV viewer of car race ad:

> Jason: What about the—do you think it's a disconnect to show . . . he's wearing a race helmet? Like he's a cup driver. Is that too weird?
>
> Craig: It makes it seem like you're the driver rather than watching.
>
> Jason: Right. Because I was thinking in that one I had with watching the TV, I don't know why, it just doesn't seem to do much. I know a lot of people like to [watch car races], though.

Here strategy, specifically, covering a large demographic group, seemed to override visual interest, convergent thinking again dominating divergent thinking.

> Craig: Yeah, that a huge percent of the people watch TV and that's the whole–and with this target, I imagine that's pretty huge. Well, h**l , any target.
>
> Jason [resuming to a discussion of angles]: Well, you think that works to have him just sitting there with his back to you like this?

Craig approved and suggested a related split image idea: an image of a man in a stadium watching a football game/push mowing. However, bypassing initially occurred, with Jason thinking of someone riding a mower.

> Jason: If you had the shot that was maybe wide angle enough, where everybody is kind of sweeping away, the one person is back, it could almost be the same thing.
>
> Craig: I wonder what he'd be holding onto.
>
> Jason: Well, you probably wouldn't see his hands so it doesn't matter. (pause)
>
> Craig: It's like what else do you push or hold? . . . He's got a drink raised or something and then one arm is kind of down. And on the bottom thing you just have that one arm.
>
> Jason: Oh, that walk-behind mower, that self-propelled. That's a good way to get that through, actually.

Had the two been sketching and showing each other the concepts as well as talking, the bypassing would not have occurred, pointing out the importance of visual communication in mindful verbal-visual collaboration.

After discussing this concept a little more and a long, incubating pause of 45 seconds, Craig revisited the general layout of the ad, suggesting that the tabs hold the name of the mower and the tag, "get it over with." At the top of the page would be the name of the sport discussed. Given that layout, Craig asked if it would need a headline. Jason replied that a line would make the ad work, and he suggested one: "Spend less time in the Bermuda and wearing them." Craig, in silent evaluation, didn't respond, producing a long silence, looking at the floor while Jason looked at the ceiling. Craig then changed the subject, speculating that perhaps the tag wasn't working. Perhaps with the idea of reducing his work, Craig then said they needed to come up with one line that would work across several executions.

Jason then suggested a two-word tab message, "Done that," replacing "Agavez" for the golf half of the flipbook image. He then condensed that to a one-word tag, "Done." Both tabs now put the images in a narrative sequence— "Get it [mowing] over with" followed by "Done" (having fun afterward). An

11-second pause ensued, the calm amidst the mindstorm. "Get by on a little bit," Craig observed. Following up with this notion of brevity, Craig continued, with a flash of insight: "What if . . . it were just, like 'the chore, the reward'? [Because] 'the means [to an end]'—that's too highbrow for this target."

Changing the explicit relationship of the images from one following the other chronologically to cause-effect, Craig had made an important transformation (reminiscent of the kinds of transformations of deep structure in generative-transformational grammar) from the underlying principle of the relationship between product and benefit (means to an end) to the tabs of the mower and recreation images in the flipbook. Demonstrating convergent thinking, he had solved the problem he had mentioned earlier of making the images "wrap together."

> Jason: That's kind of cool.
>
> Craig: And that makes "get it over with" work even better because you put it together with "get it over with" the chore, . . . the reward.
>
> Jason: Yeah, that's cool. I like that.

After this evaluation and a 16-second pause, Jason countered with a facetious inversion, making the recreation the chore and the mower the reward. "I don't think so," Craig responded, convergently sticking to strategy. After a 23-second pause, they discussed camera angles more, then Craig elaborated the copy on the tabs, stating that they could do synonyms for "reward" on the succeeding hybrid images following "chore-reward," synonyms that would tease the reader into viewing the succeeding images.

"That's cool," Jason proclaimed with the highest superlative used at the Agency. Then for 11 seconds they paused, perhaps to bask in their sense of accomplishment in solving their rhetorical problem.

> Craig: Could be the only good campaign.
>
> Jason: It won't go anywhere.
>
> [laughter from both]
>
> Craig [bringing up a Brief criterion of evaluation]: Well, the only redeeming thing is that it could be great POS, and it could be great ads.
>
> Jason: Yeah, even if they don't do the ads [referring to Agavez' preference for POS]. . . . But they have to. They have to. [18-second pause]

Pivots into Many Alternatives

What followed this evaluation of chore-reward were attempts to generate other strong concepts. Only three of the subsequent 100 comments remaining in the session referred to "chore-reward." We can refer to this point in the process as the "pivot point" (comment 187), where invention shifted from the generation, evaluation, and elaboration of one concept into the generation and evaluation of several others. Of the 23 ad concepts, 3 (13%) were discussed only before the pivot point, 3 before and after (13%), and 17 only after the pivot point (73.9%). Thus, Craig and Jason worked pretty hard after the pivot to try to beat the chore/reward ad, but didn't succeed.

But rather than exhibiting freewheeling divergent thinking in developing several concepts, they expended relatively few comments on any concept. Four of the post-pivot ad concepts had just 1 comment devoted to them, 7 more generated between 2 and 4 comments. The most-discussed post-pivot concept generated 15 comments, compared with chore-reward's 178. Clearly, they were a convergent-thinking team, one that made quick decisions and moved on. They evaluated much more quickly than Neil and Jesse, who elaborated several different concepts. Of course, it may have been that Neil and Jesse didn't feel they had as strong a concept as the split image.

The first post-pivot concept was English "crop circles," in which carefully arranged crops seen from the air formed geometric patterns. Jason quickly rejected it because it was a concept that had had a lot of previous exposure. Next, Craig suggested a similar visual concept: a birds-eye view of someone mowing a football field pattern into his lawn. Jason replied, "There's a fine line between corny and . . ." By letting the pause finish his rejection, he softened its impact. Jason then proposed a mower-hero shot, which Craig incorporated on a smaller scale into another visual concept:

> Craig: You'd probably have to do something with an inset shot of the mower on this. But if you . . . take an overhead shot of a lawn . . . the guy is starting to mow, and you . . . do . . . a rat in a maze, a rat with the cheese, or something that's kind of laying over it.
>
> Jason: The overlay thing?
>
> Craig: Yeah.

Writer Craig then proposed another visual execution of the concept, in which a white line was drawn over a lawn in a maze-like pattern that ended at a fishing hole. Jason said "that could be all right," and he asked Craig for the words to drive home the point.

"I don't see that," Craig replied. " I don't know. I want so bad—I *see* a campaign like *that Nike thing,* and it gets me" [my emphasis]. Craig here referred to Nike's "Move," which begins with the consumer in a mundane situation using a product that contributes to the attainment of the desired benefit.

> Jason: Well, it could be cool, I mean, I can see how to do it. I just—
>
> Craig [convergently]: Ahhh—It's a bad idea. (pause)
>
> Jason [in B-movie police officer's voice]: Walk away! Set the gun down, and walk away. (laughs, there follows a 37-second pause)

The artist's humor functioned here to keep the ideas flowing amid the evaluation and rejection of new concepts. Artist Craig here was giving *visual* directions. Also evident in Craig's reference is the intertextual influence of the Nike "Move" TV ad on this team, exemplifying LeFevre's (1987) argument that invention is a social act. This ad later won the 2002 Emmy for Best Commercial. "Move" showed one activity cutting and seemingly morphing into another, beginning with a boy jogging and pivoting, the video cutting to a hockey player pivoting and skating, later, a street basketball player cutting to a pro player, and after depicting a galaxy of elite athletes in action, returning in the last frame to the boy doggedly jogging down the street. Part of the message was starting unglamorously "just do[ing] it," but doing it developed transferable skills to end gloriously. In the chore/reward concept, Craig and Jason took "Move" a step further by actually combining images of activities rather than quick cutting from one activity to another. But film can accomplish nearly the same thing by showing in rapid succession disparate activities with similar forms. "Move" is a causative argument yoked with quick cuts between visually related and sometimes athletically related areas (e.g., using similar movements and the same muscle kinds; i.e., fast-twitch and slow-twitch, and groups). The Agavez ads are comparable because they juxtapose people in a similar body position but doing different activities, such as sitting astride and operating a tractor and a motorcycle, or sitting in a fishing boat/on a tractor.

Both sat looking at the wall during a long pause after Craig had rejected his own maze concept. Jason laughingly gestured, then drew the image/concept of a riding mower towing a boat. Combining product and benefit again, he next proposed a man sitting on his mower in his living room, watching TV. Jason himself quickly dismissed these, however, and a 27-second pause ensued. Jason next described using the tortoise and hare with an inset picture of the mower to create a spread ad across two pages. But Craig, convergently clarifying, asked if spreads were allowed on this campaign, and Jason laughing sheepishly said, "I don't think so."

Craig then suggested a mower pull-cord going across the page. Jason laughingly said it would be cool to have it pull off the page, then suggested a layout with "the page . . . all chewed up." Craig again suggested a layout based on a visual game:

> You know that game where if you match two things up, then you take them away and it reveals a little bit of what's underneath? . . . [two comments later] You see it first, it's just an Agavez logo, and it's a bunch of grass. . . . Then you turn the page and the mower has started to mow and clear out this much. It's revealing—

> Jason: It's revealing like an image of a tractor or something.

> Craig: No, see you've actually got the mower on here which is revealing an image of . . . somebody fishing, something like that.

> Jason: Oh, yeah. That's cool.
>
> Craig: It'd be absurd if we could have that one.

Craig here realized that the POS-intensive budget probably would not allow multiple-page magazine ads. Even though Craig earlier brought up the unlikelihood of multiple-page ads, here we see divergent thinking briefly override convergent thinking. However, Craig did not develop ideas beyond their initial expression that were likely to be unfeasible, unlike Neil and Jesse in the icon situation, who thought they might be a spark to someone else in the large-group collaboration of a tip-ball meeting.

After a phone interruption, Jason returned to the topic of shredded pages, suggesting one that created the image of a tractor mower. Invoking his knowledge of the field to evaluate, Craig said this approach had been tried with a cigarette ad, but the client didn't buy it.

After a 21-second pause as he racked his brain, Jason suggested a pop-up, but a pause indicated that the dyad didn't know *what* to pop up. Suggesting a format was not in this instance generative, though Neil's encouragement of the "split thing" format had been earlier. However, the Nike "Move" ad was on/in the air as an instantiated format. Thus, for social perhaps as well as cognitive reasons, the split image format was more heuristic to the team.

A different format stressing a different medium was next stressed: a "long copy" ad showing a piece of sod and a long message that began "This is the only thing that stands between you and . . . [the recreational benefit]." As the conversation developed, the writer incorporated his previous idea of the rat navigating the maze to get the cheese, suggesting that the copy form the visual design of a maze, again showing how the visual dimension, even of writing, dominated this session. The artist, tracing the idea with his pen in the air, suggested instead that the type follow the pattern of someone cutting the grass, but then said to follow it accurately he would have to flip the type, something that looked weird. Two turns and a 12-second pause later, Craig asked Jason what he thought about "the long-copy ad."

> Jason: I'd love to [do it]. But they would come back and say . . . "these people don't read."
>
> Craig: Yeah. It won't be real long copy.
>
> Jason [laughing]: It will be a short story, not a novel.

After a 33-second pause that further stalled the verbal direction of the session, and then some sketching, Jason suggested another visual scenario, one that generated several related concepts:

> It's just . . . the mower, and about this point, it becomes camouflaged [see Figure 20]. And it's just something to do with . . . , it allows you to do more hunting, or . . . you could do something like that with a boat. Like it gradually becomes like the paint that you'd see on a boat, with the glitter and all that kind of stuff . . . just nice, simple digitals.

Figure 20. Camouflaged mower, roof and golf bag added.
Reprinted with permission from Heric Advertising, Agavez Corporation.

But he wondered how the concept could be used for other activities. To the split paint job, Craig suggested adding a golf bag on the back of the riding mower; the first of several concepts adding props or insignias. Jason enthusiastically said the idea "could work." Moving from riding to push mowers, Jason next suggested and sketched one.

"Here's the engine and . . .[at] the halfway point, maybe it's . . . , like a stock car, painting stickers and all that kind of stuff all over it. . . . It gets the product *up there*" [my emphasis].

The client's preference of showing the product was a criterion or warrant that the artist clearly acknowledged here. However, the copywriter said he just didn't think the concept worked for push mowers. An overhead shot, Jason suggested, would allow the viewer to see more. Craig noncommittally acknowledged this comment.

> Jason: Or maybe [takes his marker and modifies the rear wheel of his push mower sketch (see Figure 21)] this is a racing wheel. You know what I'm saying? Or it's . . . a little slick [rear tire of drag racer].

> Craig: Right.

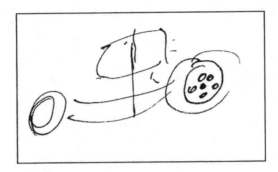

Figure 21. Push mower with slick.
Reprinted with permission from Heric Advertising, Agavez Corporation.

Jason: Just like you were saying with the golf bag. If you stuck a golf bag back here [drawing bag] and maybe it's got the little [draws roof on lawn mower] [see Figure 20]—I don't know. [laughing]

Craig: It's a little corny.

Jason [pushing back on the evaluation]: It is a little corny. But . . . I don't know that it's that bad.

Craig: No, it's not that. But I've certainly learned my lesson. . . . Unless we beat that—[points at split image ad]

Jason: Yeah, you're right.

Craig and Jason here implied that in their experience in the creative system or field, only the best concepts were worth presenting: that only the best concept from each dyad would be developed. The above exchange suggested again the dominant nature of the chore/reward concept: the more Craig and Jason developed the above concept, the more it resembled the chore-reward split image, evolving from just painting the body of the back half of the mower in boat or jeep colors to adding golf paraphernalia and a golf cart roof to the now-golf-cart paint on the tractor mower. However, whereas other creatives might have developed this concept further, writing lines, doing a comp, Craig and Jason evaluated and acted on that assessment, abandoning the concept, again evincing their convergent mindset, keeping their understanding of the creative system central and eliminating excess effort.

After a 54-second pause, Craig, following the trend of variations on a *visual* theme, returned to the head-on view of the woman with the stroller/mower, the return again suggesting that the pair was coming full circle on their invention path:

"You know what, Jason, if you wanted to take the baby out of the stroller, it could be somebody running on a treadmill."

"That's good. That's real good."

Here, the front-angle-shot format constrained Craig's invention to a recreation that would suit such an angle. After a long pause, during which he sketched, Jason returned to the vicinity of the idea of the throttle icons—the hare representing mowing the lawn quickly and the tortoise representing enjoying recreation. He sketched a throttle switch that had the tractor mower instead of the hare as the icon representing "fast," and a NASCAR auto instead of the tortoise (see Figure 22): "Maybe you have the mower and then the thing you wanted, it will get you to do it . . . . [But] that doesn't do anything [Jason laughed, then sighed; then came a 32-second pause.]

Again, the invention principle that followed was variations on an evolving visual theme. During the substantial silence, doing more preparation to bring on another insight, Jason picked up the *Agavez Buyer's Guide,* created by the company doing Agavez' POS, to find ideas. Again displaying their tendency to evaluate, the dyad laughed at its images of uniformly bespectacled, mannequin-like consumers cropping grass:

> Jason [chuckling sarcastically]: They spent a lot of money on their illustrators . . . look at the size of the hands on that guy.
>
> [Laughter. 42-second pause]
>
> Craig [proposing a headline]: What is the *proper* way to cut your lawn?
>
> Jason: [Two turns later, incorporating 11-second and 23-second pauses, reading] Wear safety glasses [chuckles sarcastically]. I can see a lot of people wearing those when they're cutting the grass (70-second pause).

This concept of spoofing a "how-to" ad was reminiscent of Neil and Jesse's "helpful hints" series, which included, at least in passing, "Hang-Gliding for

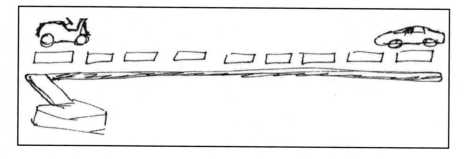

Figure 22. Throttle switch displaying product and benefit.
Reprinted with permission from Heric Advertising, Agavez Corporation.

Beginners." However, where Neil and Jesse developed several executions of this concept, Craig and Jason, after a lengthy pause, moved on to elaborate another project, briefly discussing the camera angle for the maze idea, after which there was a 78-second pause, the second longest of the session.

Jason then said that may be all he had for now, although he next said he liked the visual impact of the pull-cord idea, and Craig said he thought he would try something with long copy. After a 10-second pause, they then began to discuss other clients, and the Agavez session broke up. An analysis of this dyad follows in the next chapter.

CHAPTER 5

Less Divergence than Convergence: Analysis of a Preparation- and Evaluation-Intensive Team's Invention and the End of the Hunt

SUMMARY OF ARTIST-WRITER BRAINSTORMING

To derive the essential composing behaviors of this young, successful team, we now move from composing processes to their analysis, including the factors used to consider veteran dyad Neil and Jesse's composing so that we may later compare their approach with the "young Turks'" composing. As this book is the first detailed study of verbal-visual collaboration, we will focus intensively on the roles of words and visual images in composing verbal-visual persuasive documents, and upon the writer's and artist's roles—roles not always the expected.

Composing Moves Employed in Session

First, let's identify the composing phases recursively engaged by subjects in the study (see Table 2, page 44). These phases are numbered "up the ladder of abstraction," the most abstract being identifying the rhetorical context of the problem but no solution yet; and the least abstract, most tangible phase is completing the advertisement for submission for departmental evaluation. Completing body copy and subheads to support headlines is considered at the same level of abstraction as completing a visual.

Figure 23 shows the progression of composing moves in Craig and Jason's 2/14 brainstorming session.

Craig and Jason did not spend much time on discussing the rhetorical problem and target audience; in fact, the creative brief was not once consulted. Instead they were much more production driven, generating, evaluating, and rejecting or elaborating concepts, headlines, tag lines, and images.

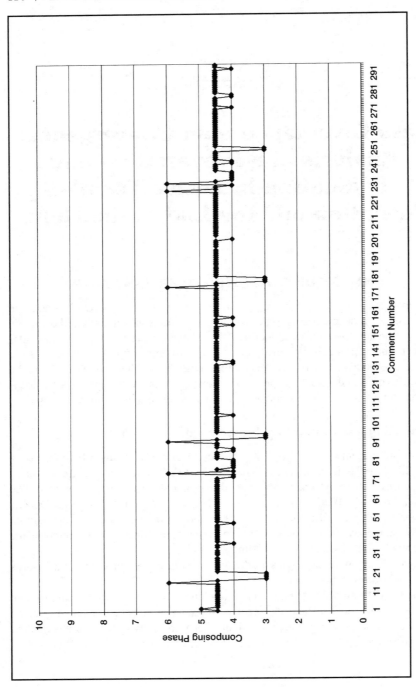

Figure 23. Jason and Craig's composing moves, 2/14 invention session.

Pattern of Concept Generation

Copywriter Craig and artist Jason's collaboration lasted 75 minutes, during which time they discussed 23 concepts, or one concept every 3.26 minutes. The extent that Concept 4 (chore-reward) received attention among the 23 concepts is shown by the line graph in Figure 24. Indeed, for nearly the first two-thirds of the session, chore-reward dominated discussion, and although it was revisited hardly at all in the last third, none of the other concepts was given much time. Since 178 of the comments (62.5%) addressed the successful concept, that left only 37.5% of the comments to cover the 22 other concepts (or an average of 1.71% of the comments per concept, or 4.86 comments/dropped concept, compared with 178 for chore-reward). Of the dropped concepts, only two had any more than 3% of the comments devoted to them: one had 5.3%, the other 10.9%.

As previously noted, of the 23 ad concepts, three (13%) were discussed only before the pivot point (the point at which discussion changed from simply developing the split image campaign to designating it as the campaign they would most likely present [Comment 187]), 3 concepts (13%) were discussed before and after, and 17 only after the pivot point (73.9%). So they worked pretty hard after the pivot to try to beat the chore-reward ad but didn't succeed. But they didn't expend comparatively many comments on any concept. Craig, who had indicated he would do more on the long-copy ad after the invention session, did not.

Was this distribution of their attention because they didn't want to waste time? Could they tell from so few comments the idea wasn't good? Or was it that they knew they had enough? Or was it that the generative chore-reward generated more comments because it was richer? Or all the above? The concepts discussed before the pivot suggest that their knowledge that they had what they perceived to be a winner didn't completely determine the number of comments devoted to a concept: the three concepts discussed before generated four comments between them. Also, one of the three concepts discussed before and after the pivot generated only two comments, but the other two generated the most comments per concept. So it would seem the richness of the concept determined the number of comments spent on it. Looking at the qualitative data, we find that even with chore-reward, some subconcepts (e.g., Jason's attempt at reversing the two for facetious inversion—Cmts. 164–165) were quickly dismissed. Although they gave a nod toward divergence, generating many "ideas of ideas" (inklings), clearly they were convergent thinkers, intent on solving the problem and moving on.

Based on past experience, they assumed that only one good idea of theirs would be selected. This assumption, which largely determined what they developed in this campaign, turned out to be erroneous in this case. Another artist, Des, who worked with two other copywriters, had one campaign selected and the concept of another one used as the basis for large-group collaborative development, large-scale improvisation.

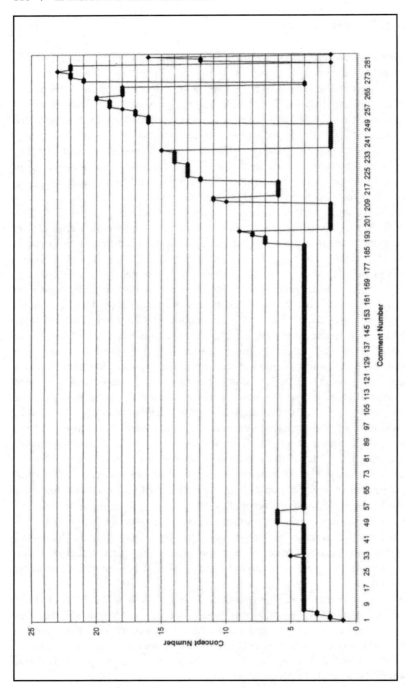

Figure 24. Ad concepts discussed by Jason and Craig, comment by comment: chore-reward (#4) discussed by far the most.

Comparison of Overall Contributions of
Artist and Writer

The copywriter and artist each contributed about the same number of concepts: copywriter Craig generating (11/47.8%) and artist Jason (12/52.2%). As earlier noted, Craig and Jason each contributed nearly the same number of *comments* in the session; Craig slightly fewer (140/47.9%) than Jason (152/52%). Jason had a fairly similar percentage of comments used in the final ad or in conducting the meeting (52.7% vs. Craig's 47.3%). In the dyad, 38.4% of the comments made over the entire session were used in the final ad. Total verbal used and dropped comments were 46.5 (17.2% of total verbal and visual comments). Total visual used and dropped comments were 223.5 (82.8% of total verbal and visual comments; see Figure 25).

The point is that they didn't do a lot with words. Most of the invention session for verbal-visual persuasive documents regarded literally the visual aspects of ad concepts. Of the visual comments, copywriter Craig provided 46.3% and artist Jason, 53.7%; of the fewer verbal comments, Jason provided 47.3% and Craig 52.7%. So the collaboration was not just specialty-specific. Craig suggested over four times as many visual comments as verbal comments (103.5/24.5). In one instance, when the subject changed to verbal when Jason asked what was the

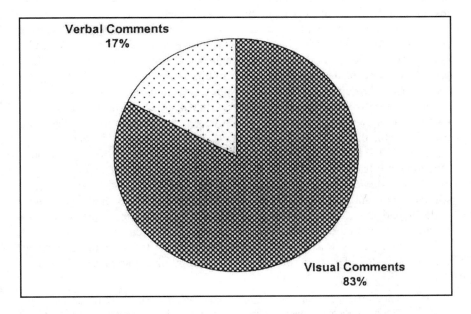

Figure 25. Comments addressing verbal or visual matters in Jason and Craig's 2/14 brainstorming—visual comments most numerous.

headline for the maze concept, Craig said he didn't know. But unlike Neil, he did not return to the Creative Brief to help generate headlines for the visual concepts. Craig worked hard to come up with the words for the split image ad, but his behavior thereafter appears to be due to his convergent mindset—why re-solve a problem already solved?

Collaborative Moves

To further analyze the artist's and writer's interaction, we first look at Craig and Jason's combined totals of each collaborative move, then below compare those numbers against the tallies of visual and the verbal-coded moves to see how the different media occasion different moves. Identified by Burnett (1994) in studying written collaboration, four collaborative "moves" were used by the artist and writer. Two of these moves are more supportive than directive. *Offering prompts*[1] is making neutral comments, reinforcing comments, and questions that elicit elaboration and clarification. These encourage the composer to say more about both plans and inscribed text. *Contributing information* is modifications and elaborations that can be opinions, facts, summaries, suggestions, syntheses, or metacognitive commentary on task, group, or text. A more directive move is *challenging*: asking critical questions, suggesting alternatives, and playing devil's advocate. More supervisory than that was *directing,* giving directions to alter text or plans by deleting, adding, or changing (Burnett, 1994).

The largest percentage of collaborative moves for Jason and Craig is offering prompts (34.6%), interesting because it is clearly a cooperative move. A similar collaborative gesture not counted was laughter in response to the proposed line, graphic, or concept. Jason's contribution in this area was frequent. The laughter served to keep the creative winds in the sails, as it would for a comedian, creating an atmosphere of imaginative play where the dyad could take chances with nascent ideas. We also see this cooperativeness borne out more in that contributing info, the second-most used move, was minutely more frequent than directing (27.7% vs. 27.6%), still substantially back from offering prompts. Directing still had a place, important because of the number of concepts at least mentioned. However, many of these were ideas of ideas. Perhaps challenging was such a distant fourth (10.1%) because there wasn't a lot to challenge in these undeveloped ideas—not much was invested in any of them. Ideas were more frequently dismissed by neglect than by overt condemnation.

Offering prompts was more frequent also because the split image concept was developed relatively thoroughly: of 101 prompting comments, 67.5 (66.8%)

---

[1] The count of offering prompts is approximate and the minimum. Barely distinguishable "yeahs" or "uh-huhs" were not counted because they appeared to be more of a knee-jerk phatic reaction than anything conscious. Other times the two transcribers who transcribed and re-transcribed the tape did not indicate them.

were in the split image ad. By contrast, the difference in distribution of directive comments is less pronounced. The split image ad had 37 verbal-visual directive comments (49.33%), while the other 22 concepts had a total of 38 verbal-visual directive comments. Although there were fewer than 2 directive comments per concept versus 37 verbal-visual directive comments for 1 concept, there were substantially fewer directive than prompting comments regarding the winner (the one the dyad chose to develop, which became one of the three concepts chosen by the Chief Creative Officer to be pitched to the client), suggesting still that successful dyadic verbal-visual concept development may be more consensual than dictatorial.

Comparison of Verbal and Visual Collaborative Moves

To now see in this picture of verbal-visual collaboration whether medium made a difference in the distribution of collaborative moves, we compare the percentage of incidence of each move in the *combined* verbal, visual, concept (in which neither verbal nor visual predominated) and "other" moves against the distribution of collaborative moves within the *verbal* set and the *visual* set of the dyad (see Figure 26).

In three out of four kinds of moves, the verbal and visual distributions were very different. The visual had roughly 150% of the verbal comment percentage of offering prompts, half the verbal percentage of contributing information, roughly three times the challenging, and approximately the same percentage of directing. It appeared that for this dyad, it was easier when collaborating about verbal matters, to contribute facts, observations, or syntheses in words, while when collaborating about visual matters, it was easier to both challenge and offer prompts—encourage and ask for clarification and elaboration. Having identified the general shape of the collaboration, we will now compare it with the dyad's composing the successful split image campaign to see if successful behavior was different.

More Characteristics of Work on Winning Ad

Successful Comments

Of the 178 comments generated about the winning ad, 61.8% (110) were "keepers." So the process was effective but not perfect—who could expect perfection? Keepers addressing the ad were close to equally divided between Craig (46%) and Jason (54%). It was a recursive process. Because of the ad's strongly visual nature, it is not surprising that artist Jason contributed more comments that were used. The ad was discussed mostly regarding visual matters (78/70.9%), with fewer than 1 in 5 used comments (20/18.2%) on the words of the ad. This outcome is not surprising because the words (chore, reward)

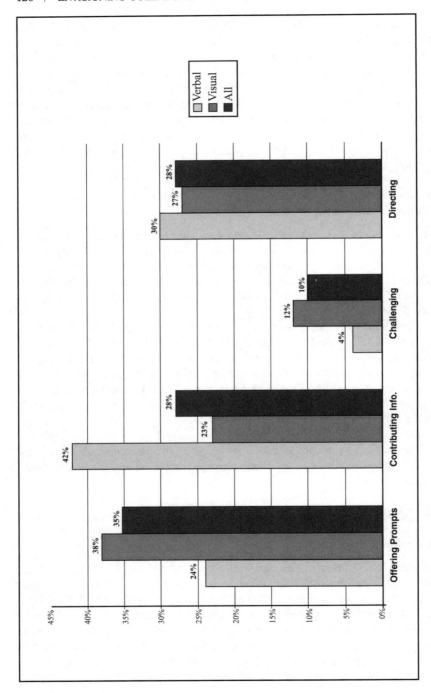

Figure 26. Comparison of verbal and visual collaborative moves, Jason and Craig combined.

remained the same or synonymous across the several visual renditions of the concept that were discussed and produced.

Of the keeper visual comments, Jason made 57.7%, and, perhaps surprisingly, writing specialist Craig contributed 42.3%, close to half of the visual comments (see Figure 27). That contribution constituted close to two thirds of Craig's successful comments (62.3%). Of the successful comments about writing, Craig contributed the majority (60%), but Jason contributed well over a third. These percentages of successful comments reinforce the above conclusion regarding all comments: as with Jesse and Neil, neither Jason nor Craig was confined to his specialized role in their successful exchange. Each invented/designed both verbal text and images. Like Neil, Craig's visual contributions were commenting on layout or images rather than physically producing anything visual beyond a very rough sketch.

One could question how many of the above comments were "uh-huhs" or affirmations of the other's idea rather than other kinds of contributions. Of Jason's 6 offering prompts regarding chore-reward ad verbal matters, none were "yeahs" or "rights," that might just be gestures acknowledging hearing the other person but not giving other input. Of copywriter Craig's 18.5 offering prompts on chore-reward ad visual matters, two were "uh-huhs," and three (27%) were "yeahs." So we find that the comments were mostly unambiguously substantive. Of artist Jason's "keeper" contributions regarding words to the successful campaign, three fourths (6/8) were supportive (offering prompts) rather than directive (2/8). Of writer Craig's visual contributions to the successful campaign, the largest number (23/69.7%) were supportive, unsurprisingly.

Jason was also very supportive in his chore-reward visual comments whose ideas were retained in the final version, with offering prompts his most frequent move (16/35.6%). However, nearly a third of his comments were directing (14/31.1%); nearly a fourth were supportive in a slightly different way: contributing info (24.4%), while challenging was 8.9%. But directing and challenging (18/40%) were less frequent than offering prompts and contributing info (27/60%), thus Jason was more supportive than directive in developing the split image idea. Jason was less directive on the verbal side, only directing (2/25%) and offering prompts (6/75%). The two creatives were offering prompts and contributing information more than directing and challenging even in their specialty (Craig 66.6% vs. 33.3%; Jason 60% vs. 40%; see Figure 28), suggesting a genuine collaborative effort rather than one person dominating the dyad.

Content Contributions of Creatives to the Winning Ad Concept

For the successful split image campaign, Craig came up with the verbal and overall logical principle, while Jason came up with the visual concept. But there was significant adaptation from other sources. Craig distilled the brand promise

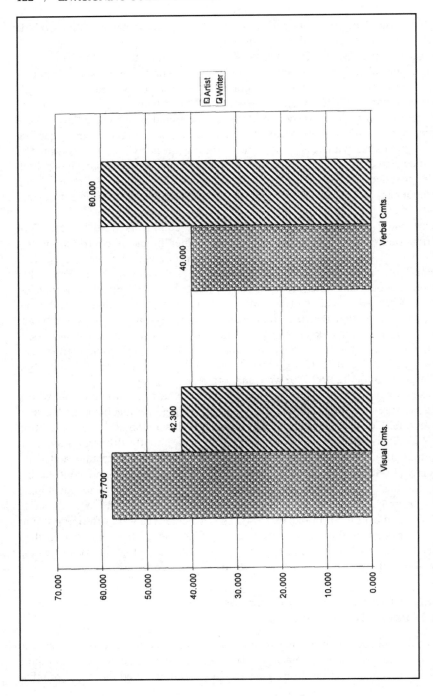

Figure 27. Distribution of successful verbal and visual comments.

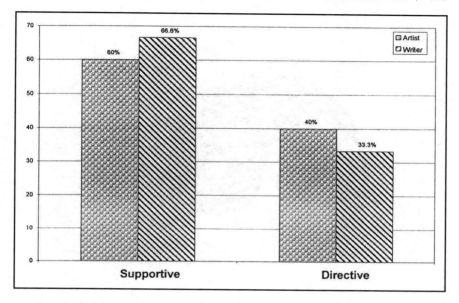

Figure 28. Supportive vs. directive behavior of artist vs. writer when discussing their specialties, successful (split image) campaign.

down to "means to an end," and Jason most likely assimilated the "split thing" in the air—in the Nike commercials in the Winter Olympics and as recommended by Neil—and adapted it to lawn mowing, certainly doing it very different visually but still using the before-after split, creating a yin-yang kind of diagram (see Figures 29 and 30) that visually melded the product and benefit. However, Craig added the "chore" and "reward" labels that replaced TV's time as a method of indicating before and after. So both made critical conceptual contributions to the campaign's success. These creatives seemed to be refiners—people who took an existing visual marvel and transposed it into another medium to meet their different objectives.

In devoting over 60% of their session to the split image campaign, Craig and Jason spent over three times more than Neil and Jesse devoted to any single concept (19.32%). George Jessel said about oratory, "If you don't strike oil after 3 minutes, sit down. Stop boring" (Peter, 1993). Craig and Jason kept boring because they realized they had struck gold.

Characteristics of Unsuccessful Comments

Not every comment was gold, however, and certain behaviors were more characteristic of unsuccessful comments. Craig's unsuccessful comments were

Figure 30. Ying-Yang.

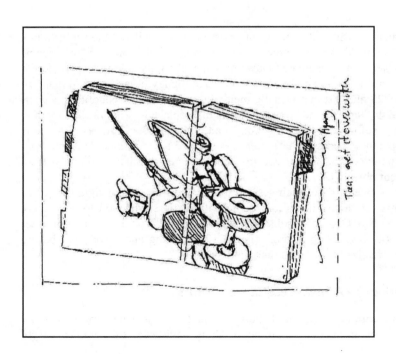

Figure 29. Split image, fishing.
Reprinted with permission
from Heric Advertising
Agavez Corporation.

more visually directive than his successful ones (53.9% of comments directing and challenging vs. 30.3% respectively). When we look at challenging alone, in unsuccessful comments, Craig challenged Jason more in the visual realm than he did in his successful comments; Jason challenged Craig more in the verbal realm than he did in his successful comments. Jason's increase wasn't a lot (from 0% to 7.1%), but Craig's was substantial, changing from 9.1% to 20.6%.

Regarding directing alone, close to twice as many of Craig's directive comments (33) addressed dropped ads compared to Jason's (18). Craig had nearly double the number of dropped directive and challenging comments that Jason had (47.5 vs. 25). And while Craig's larger number of challenging comments (14.5 vs. 7) might be considered a sign of his greater effectiveness because the concepts were later dropped, qualitative data shows Craig challenging to support unsuccessful concepts (e.g., the mother pushing the baby carriage/lawn mower) more frequently (9 vs. 6 comments) than discarding material (e.g., Jason's suggestion to facetiously reverse the chore and the reward tabs). Three of Jason's seven challenging dropped comments were supporting dropped projects. Here again, however, Craig was more directive in that he eliminated a few more concepts. Whether or not he was effective in so doing depends upon the merit of the concept, none of which was developed very far, making it hard to tell.

Used and Dropped Verbal and Visual Comments of Each Author

If we compare writer Craig's used and dropped comments, many more of his successful (used) verbal comments were contributing information (54.2% vs. 32% of his dropped verbal). While he directed in 60% of his dropped verbal comments, he only directed in 25% of his successful verbal comments. The point seems to be that his successful contributions were more collaborative. But since they only consisted in large measure of two words—chore, reward—it's not surprising that directing (generating ideas) was a lower percentage in the successful comments.

Jason offered prompts the most of any of his kept verbal moves (75%/6). He contributed information and also offered prompts the most in the *dropped* verbal moves. Twenty-five percent of his verbal used comments were directing, suggesting some hands-on role in both verbal and visual success. But these did not constitute a large portion of his session activities.

Of the successful visual comments, the artist directed 31.1% of the time. Jason offered prompts in a fairly similar percentage of used and dropped visual comments (the largest percentage of either used or dropped comments, 35.5% and 40.7%, respectively). But of the used visual comments, directing was the second largest percentage of activity, whereas in dropped visual, contributing info was the second-largest percentage of his dropped comments

(28.7%), though directing was still 22.7% of his dropped comments. This suggests that Jason was slightly more successful when he was fully engaged and contributing in directing.

Invention/Arrangement?
Incidence of Visual Cognates and
Rhetorical, Grammatical Elements

To consider verbal-visual collaboration from the vantage point of the product, we will now note how much discussion occurred regarding rhetorical/grammatical elements. We will first consider Kostelnick and Roberts' (1998) visual cognates of these terms (for their definitions, see the previous case). Arrangement (121.5/55.6%) was the most-discussed visual element. As this was a concepting meeting, there was a merging of invention and arrangement, canons that the oral and written classical tradition largely differentiates. On the contrary, arrangement was very heuristic here, dramatizing the elements and rhetorical strategy in the creative brief. An example is Jason's suggestion of the split images, such as the angler sitting in a fishing boat fused with a tractor mower. Arrangement in this case dramatizes and communicates the product and sales strategy by animating it in an original pictorial scenario with actors and action explained by words (sometimes in a character's monologue in Jesse and Neil's cases).

Even with vague, undeveloped ideas, layout was important as a starting point. For example, Jason suggested a print layout showing the product with an attention-getting part of the page "all ripped up" like it had been cut with a lawn mower. The headline would talk about "doing what you want to do." Although this concept was not further developed, it could have been because there was something to comment on—a context had been created, the stage had been built and set. *Like the stage of a theater, layout ideas provide a context for the abstractions of the sales strategy, instantiation.* Unlike the genre found in typical rhetorical studies of arrangement, these concepts were content for the genre of the print ad. They were, in short, something invented. They were also something invented in one genre yet including potential to be instantiated in other genres (e.g., POS) as well.

Looking at the collaborators individually, we find that the artist, like the writer, devoted a majority of his visual comments to arrangement (56.6% vs. 54.5%, respectively; see raw numbers in Figure 31). Clarity was the next most important visual cognate (25% vs. 26.8%, respectively); these clarification comments were collaborative, typically made to confirm that the other understood one's image or visual idea. This definition is slightly different from that of Kostelnick and Roberts, which stipulated the reader as audience; the audience of many of the clarity comments was the other collaborator. But after the originator, this audience served as the initial "reader" of the visual element.

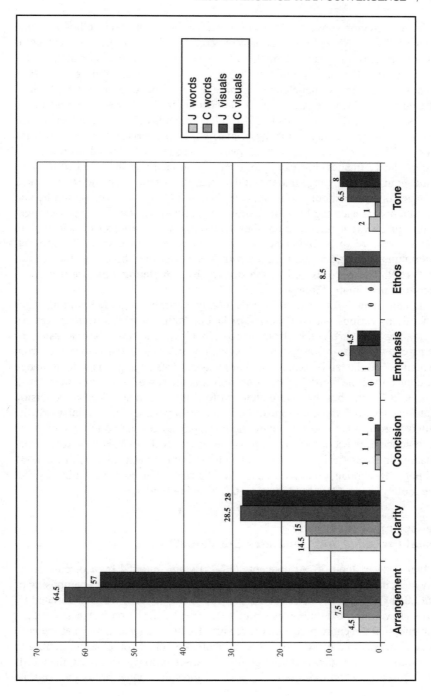

Figure 31. Visual cognate and written rhetorical-grammatical descriptions, 2/14, Jason and Craig.

The art director spoke slightly more frequently about visual ethos than the writer (7.5% vs. 6.7%) and a spatial concern, visual emphasis, but these comments were still less than 6% of the artist's comments. The writer devoted his comments slightly more frequently to tone (7.7%) than did the artist (5.7%), perhaps because this visual element is more directly linked to the writerly voice.

Regarding the team's rhetorical comments about the words in the ad ideas, there isn't a lot to discuss: only 17.5% of all comments in the session were coded for the six verbal elements. Of these, clarity was the largest concern (66% for Jason, 57.1% for Craig). Clarity, however, frequently involved words being used to clarify images. For example, Craig mentioned that they needed to communicate in the split image that the mower was the means to an end. Jason asked if images or words should communicate that, and Craig said words; and he and Jason then suggested tag lines. In a similar situation in strictly writing, we might be replacing a vague reference pronoun with other words more specific to explain what is intended to be indicated, but in this case of verbal-visual composing, an ambiguous image is clarified by words such as the chore and the reward (Cmt. 152). These words deliver the strategy by completing a picture that could otherwise mean many things.

"Arrangement," referring to words nearly entirely, regarded putting lines or words in various parts of the *visual* layout, rather than the *writing* concern of creating structure solely from words. In Craig and Jason's discussion of means-end vs. chore-reward, "tone" related to words and distance/formality from the reader. But the tab on which the word was put was an appendage to an image that contributed the words' tone. Concision was the same—one-word tabs "g[o]t by on a little bit," but they were attached to a striking image. Verbal concision regarding a verbal-visual composition is about how much additional work the written word needs to do to convey the concept, rather than communicating the entire concept as economically as possible in words. Emphasis in verbal-visual collaboration was Craig proposing a headline that emphasized a point made by an image. Redundancy here was used for the sake of impact, possible in small doses solely in print too, but here a verbal-visual redundancy.

Wellspring of Invention: Visual Precedes and Generates the Verbal?

Over 77% of their 23 ad concepts (17.75) were initiated by a discussion of the visual, indicating the centrality of the visual in the verbal-visual composing of print ads by Craig and Jason. However, crucial rhetorical work was initiated by words as well. An example was Craig's statement that the mower was a means to an end, that the chore preceded the reward. He then suggested a visual scenario where a rat was in a maze and had to navigate a winding route before getting to the reward of some cheese. Although the visual scenario was not used, the words were chosen later to drive home the point of the split image campaign. And the words "means to an end" formulated the dyad's central strategy. How well each campaign met this strategy determined whether Craig and Jason chose it to go further. However, except in one instance this general strategy was not something that was used as a line or subhead or tag to generate an individual ad. Individual ads that applied this strategy were more often than not initiated by a visual.

As may be expected given visual initiation of the preponderance of ads, the cognate area with far and away the highest incidence of collaborative moves was arrangement. Craig's biggest arrangement move was visual directing (19.5, 13.9% of his total comments, 6.7% of Craig and Jason's move-coded comments), although he was slightly more cooperative (offering prompts and contributing info) than directive (both directing and challenging) in arrangement (30 vs. 27 comments); Jason was much more cooperative than directive (44 vs. 20.5 comments). But Jason also contributed and developed the visual half of the concept that dominated the meeting. So these cooperative vs. directive numbers don't denote submission or dominance conceptually. One could suggest 100 ideas in 100 comments that were shot down, but one arrangement-directive comment could contribute the winning idea. In Jason and Craig's case, these comments developed into a layout, a concept that dominated.

In this verbal-visual composing process, arrangement dominated invention, on the surface surprising, given arrangement's status as a separate classical canon from invention. Visual dominance is also shown in the statistic that over 82% of the verbal and visual comments made (223.5 comments) addressed the visual. Of the 11 most frequent moves by Craig or Jason, 6 were visual arrangement across a number of moves, the other 5 were visual clarity, and all were visual. All of these findings support the conclusion that the visual was by far the more important in generating ad concepts. Of course not all ideas generated were used. Although nearly all comments ultimately used were visually initiated (98 of 112, 87.5%), most of the comments dropped were visually initiated also (162.5 of 180, 90.3%). These percentages correspond to some degree to the number of visual vs. verbal comments, however (77.3% vs. 16% respectively).

Means of Communication of Comments

While they addressed visual matters, the preponderance of comments were said rather than drawn or written, and this distribution held whether the comments were used or dropped. Nevertheless, drawn comments were essential in the outcome of the successful campaign: Jason with Craig's verbal input developed the flipbook idea by drawing it, and he refined the split image concept by drawing excellent renditions of several variations of the concept in the dyad's brainstorming meeting.

Generative Principles of Verbal-Visual Brainstorming

Others have applied classical rhetorical principles to the analysis of published advertisements. The current study adds to that knowledge by looking at generative principles at work in the *process* of ad creation, including the principles used for ads that were never published. Although, as the research on mindfulness suggests, these principles were not alone sufficient for a successful ad, after Craig took the time to do a thorough analysis of the rhetorical situation, some of these techniques were necessary in the generation of successful ads.

Several principles generated a concept with multiple executions or multiple concepts. The generative principle of *similarity* yoked to *contrast* was used in the largest incidence in the comments involving generative principles of Craig and Jason (47.6%). Using this principle, oxymoronically, Jason yoked the near-opposites (to the audience) of work and leisure, but succeeded because of the similarity of the natural form of the recreation and the yard work.

Although *similarity/contrast* was involved in the most comments involving generative principles, 96 (90.1%) of the 106.5 similarity/contrast comments occurred in the discussion of the split image concept. Similarity/contrast was prolific, however, yielding five executions that were used in the presentation to Agavez (golf, fishing, drag racing, motor biking, hiking), and one other that was presented at a tip-ball meeting.

Causation was the generative principle with the second biggest incidence of comments involving generative principles (32.8%). Both principles work together in the chore/reward concept: the split image visual combines contrast and similarity in that contrasting activities form one continuous yin-yang image. But when Craig added the tab labels indicating mowing as a means to an end—the chore leading to a reward—the concept also communicated a causative argument. The yin-yang combining of the two suggests that neither is complete without the other. The whole man does both mowing and golfing, fishing, drag racing, hiking, or motor biking. The continuous figure suggests closure.

In addition, causative argument was the generative principle used in the highest number of different concepts, in the form of "means to an end," which Craig distilled from the brand promise and used as the central strategy of the session. Ten different concepts were generated from this principle; for example, the rat contemplating the maze he will have to navigate to get the cheese that lies at journey's end, or the man driving the tractor mower that also held a bag of golf clubs and would serve as a golf cart when he finished. The use of this principle most likely is what made the team successful, because causation interrelated the product and the most important benefit to the consumer: one needed to use the mower to get to the recreation.

The only other originating principle the artist and writer employed was *contrast*. Contrast was employed as a visual gimmick: having the ad stand out from other pages of the magazine by having the page shredded like in a paper shredder, but still creating the image of a tractor. The third concept that they generated contrasts the chore and the reward by having, in consecutive pages of an ad, a tractor cut away enough grass from a lawn to reveal the image of somebody fishing. Contrast accounted for 10.3% of comments involving generative principles.

Facetious inversion did not originate a concept, but Jason used it to consider facetiously labeling the mowing as the reward and the recreational activity as the chore. Facetious inversion was used in only 2% of the dyad's comments involving generative principles and was quickly dismissed by Craig; but the principle was also used briefly by the other dyad's art director, Jesse, with similar results. Still, considering the facetious reverse of an existing concept seemed a customary brainstorming technique. Contrast, though, was a presenting or underlying principle in facetious inversion, the visual difference between the chore and the reward, and the verbal/visual contrast between the name (reward) and mowing. Contrast was also central in similarity/contrast and even in causation, where the unpleasantness of the chore must be undertaken to obtain its opposite, the joy of the reward.

Similarity was a mode of concept <u>development</u> for 7% of the comments involving generative principles. Similarity is defined by Corbett as "the likeness of two or more things" and is the principle behind all analogy (1990, p. 103). Craig proposed an overhead shot of a lawn and adjacent landscape, with a white line originating from a person who is starting to mow his lawn. This line follows a lawn mowing circuit but it continues beyond the border of the lawn to end in a fishing hole. Craig said this concept was similar to a child's game, and he appropriated that model to deliver the strategy by analogy, implicitly arguing that playing the mowing game well will win a recreational reward.

Comments involving generative principles constituted 76.7% of the comments in the session. The remaining 23.3% were devoted to procedural comments and to advice on developing the split image layout.

Effectiveness of Verbal-Visual Brainstorming

The previous sections have described the general pattern of verbal-visual collaborative interaction of this dyad. But how well did Craig and Jason's ads address the sometimes-clashing mindsets of the most important audiences? Table 6 shows the distribution of comments that addressed the audiences.

In this invention session, the primary audience is both customer and client. This conclusion is evidenced by the predominance of comments addressing both customer and Agavez interests. It is also evidenced by the preponderance of those joint-audience comments (228.5/275, 83.1%) that addressed the brand promise from the Creative Brief: "Agavez mowers get the job done without a

Table 6. Comments Addressing Audiences by Jason and Craig:
Breakdown of Individual and Combined Totals

	Creative Director	Customer	Customer/ Agavez	Agavez	MegaWorld	Total
Jason	1 (.7%)	6 (4%)	144 (95.4%)			151
Craig	1 (.7%)	8 (5.7%)	131 (93.6%)			140
Combined total	2 (.7%)	14 (4.8%)	275 (94.5%)			291

fuss so you can move on to the more important things in life . . . ," which Craig translated into the lawnmower is a means to an end.

Craig mindfully adhered to the brief when Jason suggested inverting the relationship for fun, enacting a routine that although comic—the golfer speedily duffing to get through the golf to the payoff of mowing the green—was off strategy. The chore/reward fishing ad addressed 17 of the 30 brief attributes, and the chore/reward golf ad, 14/30. Brief attributes most obviously missing from chore/reward were the reasons to believe: the 2-year warranty, Briggs-Stratton engine, and 30 years of experience of the company. However, meeting the key brief criterion of an easy transfer of the concept to POS also made the ad a winner.

With 20-20 hindsight, one might wonder why Jason and Craig didn't stop after they knew they had a winner. But the invention culture of the company at that time stressed developing many ideas to find a good one. Still, the dyad's powerfully developed evaluation phase reflects a convergent thinking associated with a "J" or "judging" Myers-Briggs mentality that is also the mentality of most business managers (Myers & McCaulley, 1985, p. 251).

Their chore-reward split image is an arresting, surrealistic synthesis that intrigues and entertains. The eye is strongly drawn to the central image in the flipbook, and the continuity of the lines make it gestalt, but upon further inspection, it is a surreal image. The completed shapes in the morph makes the image "believable," even though we recognize it as unreal. It intrigues because of its simultaneous wholeness composed by a startling juxtaposition of opposite elements (work and play). Its yin-yang image is a visual oxymoron in the positive sense of that term: an organizing principle that allows us to integrate disparate material that appeals to disparate audiences (the producer and consumer).

CONCEPT DEVELOPMENT AND
TIP-BALL, 2/15–22

Out of town and then working on other projects when they returned, Jason and Craig did not resume work together on the Agavez campaign during this week. Writer Craig's actions during this time, he told me later, were atypical. Normally after a brainstorming session, he would leave, rework the concept alone, and return with something better. However, with this campaign, "I'd go away and think about it, I'd come back and say, 'You know, that was dead on,'" Craig said (TR 401). Jason said the concept was "just a natural because . . . there were so many possibilities [different versions of the concept that worked]" (TR 166). Despite putting all their eggs in one basket, the pair followed their normal behavior of not practicing their presentation of concepts before being evaluated by the large group at the tip-ball meeting.

In fact, demonstrating grace and talent under pressure, just before and then *during* the first, 28-minute tip-ball meeting on 2/22, Jason redrew with felt tip marker on white paper most of the initial rough drawings he had made on lined notebook paper. When their turn came, Craig stood up and announced that they had one idea they liked, "so that's all we're doing," which got a laugh. After stating that the concept would work well in POS, Jason showed the Account Manager and assembled creatives the fishing/tractoring rendition of the flipbook, followed by the golfer/push mower, TV viewer/tractor driver, and female jogger/push mower. Jason then explained that for POS, pairs of stacked mower boxes could be designed so the top box was the reward and the bottom the mower. The visual impact of their concept and POS capabilities impressed Account Manager Steve Douglas and Creative Directors Neil and Jesse, who were running this large-group evaluation and were to choose which campaigns to elaborate further. After the meeting, they selected the campaign as one to develop. Thus, Jason and Craig had been correct so far in their judgment of the split image concept powerfully delivering the rhetorical strategy formulated in the Brief.

Because "people have spent hours pounding . . . out [finished ads] that don't go anywhere," Jason had presented sketches rather than the desktop-published layouts incorporating photographs that most other teams had presented. However, Jason was a drafter who could win against Photoshopped competition. This approach was another wise choice that made the process potentially less wasteful. Now, because Jason felt the absent Chief Creative Officer would also like their selected campaign, he chose to "go to the next step and tighten it up a little more." (TR 168).

2/22–27 TIGHTENING UP

It is beyond the scope of this study of verbal-visual collaboration to discuss all details of Jason's translating and elaborating the concept from a sketch to a "dummy," a client-presentation-quality layout. Nevertheless, an outline of the process can be traced. Immediately after the Friday tip-ball meeting, Jason returned to his office and began downloading images from *ImageStock* and other image databases. The images were of various mowers, people mowing grass, grass and Astroturf, golfers, golf balls, anglers, lures, and the like. He developed the split-image golfer layout throughout the afternoon, and by half-past five, he had a finished layout (see Figure 32), which had evolved from just the flipbook to the flipbook lying diagonally on putting-green-like Astroturf, next to a golf ball. Jason had retrieved this green and ball image from the image bank. Shading gave the flipbook and golf ball the appearance of depth, and the shadow emanating from the golf ball on the putting green image now pointed to the logo of the company. The shading, Jason told me, added not only dimension but also drama. He also made the tabs of the flipbook red and the words white (reverse type) and all capitals, he told me, to create impact and because red was an Agavez color. Jason here surprisingly seemed unaware that all capitals, because of their lack of contrast, are usually less legible than an "up and down" style.

Jason's desktop publishing process was particularly appropriate for the split image concept because as usual he was taking several disparate images and cropping them and arranging them so that they fit together to deliver a new verbal/visual message. In the golf ad, he even combined the upper body of an African American with the legs of a Caucasian because these were the only forms that lined up. Although these images lined up, there was a stratum of sky *beneath* the fairway of the reward page in the split golf/mower image that added a dreamlike quality. To complete this full-blown comprehensive, Jason put gibberish (greeking) where the body copy would go as a placeholder in the design. Jason expected that product benefits and "spec charts" would take its place.

Jason was more synthetic than generative in his computer work, combining available forms. Stock images determining ad messages had become a trend since desktop publishing technology had become available, he told me. Creatives were constrained by the availability of stock images. Sometimes the idea had to be changed because the necessary angle or subject was not available in a stock image. For Jason in the observed case, the precise idea preceded the form rather than started with prefabricated forms, although the general idea seemed to have evolved from the Nike "Move" ad. Combining available images later allowed Jason to closely duplicate one of the hand-drawn pictures.

But not only did the golfer/mower turn out different because of the non-matching background of the bottom half, two other drawings were dropped also after futile attempts to conjoin available images, while new renditions arose from images Jason downloaded from image banks, including a truly "chopped" motorcycle with a push mower replacing its stretched front forks. Jason certainly had not become a "tool of his tools," as Thoreau warned against, but inter-textuality built into his tools had a major influence on this process, structurally embodied in its synthetic concept.

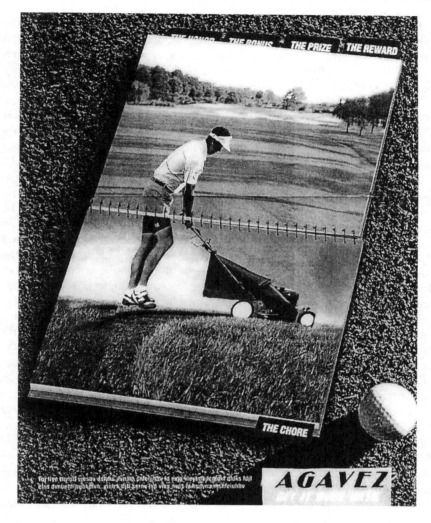

Figure 32. Final layout, golf, split image campaign.

Reprinted with permission:
Photographer: Howard Sokol/Photolibrary.com
Photographer: Roger Holden/Photolibrary.com
Heric Advertising, Agavez Corporation, Photolibrary.com

In the motorcycle ad, the split was vertical with the reward to the left of the chore (counterintuitive in Western arrangement), but Jason changed the layout for the sake of variety. He also put the flipbook of the angler on a weathered fishing dock with a fishing lure next to the book. Drawing the eye, the lure lay next to "The Chore" tab while also pointing down to the Agavez logo.

Words were added in two ways to the tighter versions: first, Craig's tag line "Get it over with" was added below the Agavez logo, a strategic placement because the lower-right quadrant is the second-most visually important quadrant (Baird, Turnbull, & McDonald, 1987, p. 37). Synonyms were also added to the top tabs in the flipbook, so along with "the reward" were "the honor, "the bonus," and "the prize," preparing the reader for other renditions of the concept. Jason told me that he alone did all of the development between the first and second tip-ball meeting, "tightening it up" because he knew the concept would be approved, and he wanted it more ready for the client.

The following Monday, Jason learned that the Chief Creative Officer had not gotten the faxed selections in Chicago, and that he wanted to review all the ads again and decide for himself. To prepare for the new large-group evaluation, Jason spent all of Monday and half of Tuesday downloading images and continuing to prepare his desktop-published comprehensives.

Wednesday afternoon the creatives reassembled with the Chief Creative Officer and Account Manager and his assistant. Jason and Craig were the fourth presenters, and Jason presented new drawings of POS displays that took the meeting's thinking into a new dimension—depth, involving the several surfaces of a 3-D unit. As Figure 33 demonstrates, the elements of an image could even be rearranged by recombining these half-images on a swivel.

The visual impact of their idea impressed Rick Waller, the Chief Creative Officer, who, before rising into administration, had begun as an artist. However, he stressed that although it was a simple but very effective POS piece, it needed to be tied into the Agavez product more centrally. "Remember, this is not about cutting grass, this is about buying an Agavez," he stressed more than once. Neil generously told the dyad that that task could be accomplished in the body copy below the flipbook in the layout. Jason and Craig also presented a sketch of a rack display. These drawings were the only renditions of displays presented in the meeting, and Rick affirmed them indirectly by saying that 50% of the material shown to the client in the pitch should be POS; later, he said, "POS is everything."

By thus addressing many key elements of the brief, Jason and Craig came out ahead, and the tight production quality of the flipbook ads contributed to their campaign being selected by the Chief Creative Officer for further development. Thanks to Jason's two-and-a-half days spent with image banks and Photoshop, the team moved from behind to the fore in producing the most finished ads. After seeing their ads, the Account Manager said the ads would be part of "the sizzle of the show." The team evinced mindfulness in choosing the appropriate

Figure 33. Swivel display, Agavez "split image" campaign.
Reprinted with permission from Heric Advertising, Agavez Corporation.

moment to develop finished work to show—before it was evaluated by a key gatekeeper. Their convergent focus on one campaign and on the brief allowed them time to create effective ideas in not only print but POS, the medium the Chief Creative Officer prioritized as "everything."

Between the semifinals on 2/27 and the finals on 3/6, not a lot was done on the split image print ad. The 2/27 versions were put on paste-up boards. Neil, in his supervisory capacity, was talking to Jason and Craig, stressing that the tag needed to transfer across products and stress the brand and its value position. In explaining, he gave an example of a tag that achieved these goals: "Agavez always works so you don't have to." Jason and Craig translated that into "We never stop working, so you can." They used that tag to replace "Get it over with," words that did not refer to, much less position, the brand. In contributing to this process, Neil helped Jason and Craig edge out the Neil-and-Jesse-created ads, but Neil saw the process as more large-scale collaboration than dyadic competition.

At the final, narrowing-down large-group evaluation on March 6, the split image campaign was one of three chosen to be presented to the client. During the meeting, which included the CEO of the agency, there was no doubt expressed about its candidacy by anyone, and both the Chief Creative Officer and Account Manager affirmed the campaign. Comparing the split image campaign with Neil and Jesse's icons campaign, "Lawns are Our Life, Not Yours," the Chief Creative Officer said there wasn't a strategic difference. But the split image campaign had more visual impact. He said it also showed both the product and the benefit, thus reflecting the brand promise. In a later interview, the Chief Creative Officer said the split image would work very well in retail because it was "so simple."

Other comments in the evaluation meeting were largely devoted to developing the campaign further into POS. As in the previous tip-ball meeting, Jason and Craig presented more POS executions than did Neil and Jesse. In the evaluation meeting, the Chief Creative Officer said to add the reasons to believe—Briggs and Stratton engine and 2-year warranty—to replace the greeking. His advice would help encourage the customer to buy an Agavez rather than just any mower. These were never implemented by Craig.

The reason for this singular lapse of mindfulness was that Craig left the company to take a job at an agency in his home state 6 days after this meeting. Before he left, he and Jason elaborated the split image campaign more, creating the script for a split image TV ad that would be represented on a storyboard at the pitch to Agavez. This ad featured the fisherman/mower rider combination. But instead of print's montage of static images, TV combined footage of boating and mowing so that when the angler turned the wheel in the boat, the boat scene and the mower scene turned. The ad progressively showed more boat and less mowing. The words asked why Agavez mowers were built with the "reasons to believe": Briggs and Stratton engines, two-year warranty, and so on. At the end of these questions, the boat filled the whole screen, and the answer was given: "Because you have better things to do, than worry about your mower" [sic], then the brand and tag: "Agavez: We never stop working. So you can."

The remainder of Jason's time on this campaign was spent collaborating with a POS specialist graphic artist upstairs on the production floor to produce point-of-sale merchandizing for the pitch to the client at the end of the month. To produce the integrated marketing campaign the client required, the rest of the agency now became involved in elaborating the split image campaign. Account, PR, media, and direct mail management met to plan and place media that addressed consumers' demographics, lifestyles, and leisure activities. Market research showed that a substantial percentage of potential consumers both watched and participated in fishing and golf, as well as watched baseball, basketball, and NASCAR.

Demonstrating the imperative of inventing a concept with legs, the media strategy was to work with partners that provided multiple media for message delivery (print, radio, television, online) and that could facilitate promotions. At the national level, the partner chosen was the hunting-and-fishing-specialized *Field & Stream/Outdoor Life*. The media mix included the following:

- Full-page and 1/3-page, full-color print ads
- Radio was planned for 300+ outlets
- TV commercials for the cable OLN (Outdoor Life Network)
- Direct marketing's objective (snail mail and online sales letters) was to increase current owners' repeat purchases. Its chief promotional strategy was "buya geta," offering recreational products with proof of purchase of an Agavez mower. Direct marketing would also update its address list of potential customers. Lists came from warranty registrations; good candidates were customers who had purchased a mower seven or more years ago.
- Outdoor (billboard) ads were planned for expressways
- Online, banners, buttons, and skyscraper ads (ads significantly taller than the 120 × 240-pixel vertical banner)
- An "Agavez Bass Fishing Weekend" promotion was to be pitched in all of the above advertisements
- Ads would be placed on local TV news and cable sports programming. This campaign would be disseminated in 20–25 markets.
- Public relations would be integrated into the campaign, with objectives of local awareness and a tie-in with the split image tag line, "We never stop working so you can." Promotions included a "Race, Hit, Fish Triathlon" [presumably integrating auto racing, golfing, and fishing] and celebrity appearances at MegaWorld. News releases would be used for media relations.

On March 26, 2002, all of these integrated marketing elements were presented in the two-hour pitch to the client. But first came the grand entrance. Twelve-foot tall, four-foot wide sharp, full-color posters, "giant boards," of one Agavez campaign H-rack, topped by a long, bright "Welcome Agavez" banner greeted the Agavez Director of Marketing, their Advertising and Communication Director, and two Agavez product managers as they strode with Heric executives out of the elevators on the sixth floor. In front of this skylight-illumined back-drop, the receptionist, garbed in Agavez red and black, rose from her desk and warmly greeted the party.

After ascending the open, formal staircase behind the receptionist, the group entered the conference room on the seventh floor where they met the rest of the creatives and managers on the pitch team. Awaiting "the reveal," covered up on side walls were the presentation materials, including three of the 8-foot tall H-rack renderings on paste boards. The back wall of the room was dominated by picture windows overlooking an ornate row of 150-year-old office buildings and beyond them a glistening lake. The Agavez entourage was seated near the front of the glass-topped cherry conference table, which took up most of the room.

An introductory segment set up the client for the presentation of the campaigns. First, Heric CEO Jim Montgomery pointed out to the clients that they were a very important piece of business to the agency, implying that servicing their account would be a high priority. Using PowerPoint, the executives next explained that Heric had developed $21 million in annual billing of clients in Agavez' home city (making them the fourth-largest agency in that city just from billings in that city), showing that Heric, though headquartered elsewhere, would be around to look after the customer.

Next, Vice President of Planning Bob Thompson stressed Heric's strategic approach to advertising grounded in consumer attitudes, something the current POS producer lacked. Next, to counter the client perception that Heric didn't do POS, was mention of Heric's other POS work with several national brands. After that, Thompson and Heric Account Manager Steve Douglas discussed the Agavez strategy, going over Agavez' persuasive goals, consumer portrait, and what the brand stands for—the material summarized in the Creative Brief. Heric had presented this strategic material to Agavez before. As Steve Douglas explained to me: "[We] just wanted to reinforce 'Hey, we're the guys who created this for you.' Let you get the positioning. They nodded; it was clear that they understood that we're the ones that got them there" (TR 678).

The split image campaign was the first campaign shown to the client, beginning with revealing POS H-racks that featured stacked boxes with the golfer half the top box and the legs and mower the bottom half. Along with the visual presentation, this campaign was, perhaps surprisingly, presented to Agavez by Neil—operating in his capacity as a creative director and excellent speaker—and by another creative who did not design it. This division of labor often occurred: creatives who generated and produced campaigns were not always the best presenters in the agency or free to prepare; so often, while those who generated and produced put the finishing touches on their ads, others rehearsed and presented these ads in oral pitches to the client.

In the pitch, the pair presented the POS, then the TV storyboard, then the concept-originating print ads on 11 × 17 boards, the opposite order from a normal pitch, so that POS was emphasized. "You could see it immediately connect," the Account Manager recounted later; the four Agavez representatives "really responded to" the split image campaign (TR 679). After the presentation of the other two campaigns, they broke for a catered lunch, then returned for a question-and-answer session and the showing of a second H-rack video. The clients (it was learned later, for they said little during the entire pitch) liked all three campaigns, impressed by the 8-foot tall Photoshop replicas of the H-racks that were revealed campaign by campaign, the great number of clever ads that covered the walls of the entire presentation room, and the 3-D flying animated "tours" of the POS displays that were presented on a video screen. Toward the end of the presentation, Agavez reps said Heric had done a "tremendous amount of work."

Account Manager Steve Douglas stressed that Heric had done this work because they wanted to continue working with Agavez. Heric was the agency that gave Agavez its strategic position, and it wanted to help Agavez expand into other products. Douglas then concluded the pitch by asking Agavez for their business.

Agavez thanked them for their efforts and told them they would have a decision before long, then were given a "leave behind," a book that attractively bound 160 pages of PowerPoint slides, print ads, and POS materials presented in the pitch, and 17 pages of agency bios. Along with the leave behinds, Agavez representatives took some smaller ad boards back to their home office in another state and asked Heric to ship them the larger boards, including POS H-racks, as soon as possible. The Agavez managers at the pitch needed these materials to present to Agavez executives not at the pitch so that a decision could be made. Agavez planned to move quickly because they needed to put out advertising in April, the beginning of the mowing season.

Despite their intentions but perhaps because of the busyness of the season, it took 34 days for Agavez to decide—that Heric Advertising was to be their sole agency. In the end, Heric won the business because, as a rep told the Account Manager, compared with the other agencies' work, the strategy, creative, and media thinking were "ten times better." Heric "blew away the competition" with their creativity and strategic approach (FN 232).

Jason Wells, co-author of one of the winning campaigns, attributed the smoothness of his team's composing process to Account Manager Steve Douglas being "very buttoned down" on strategy, covering it thoroughly from his brief meeting presentation forward (FN 225). Here again we see Jason's convergent thinking: if the problem is correctly articulated, solving it is a pretty straightforward process, a process of honing an answer. Seven teams got the brief presentation, yet Jason's team was one of the few winners because of his arresting, pertinent image that brought together product and benefit, and because Craig distilled the brand promise into the organizing principle of their concept. These elements when properly combined were a powerful argument.

However, MegaWorld could not be depended upon to stack boxes to form split images on the storage racks. Also, the boxes had to have the images on both sides to be able to be stacked in split-image manner, and that was most expensive to the manufacturer. In addition, Agavez perceived that for the international marketing of the product, the surrealistic images on the boxes would be difficult to explain in two other languages. Nonetheless, Agavez really liked the split screen TV, and one of the three decision makers liked the entire split image campaign the best; however, the other two didn't. Recounting the Agavez point of view, Heric Account Manager Steve Douglas said, "Visually, it was a strong campaign for advertising, but [it] didn't necessarily work well for POS." Only one campaign could ultimately be used by Agavez, so "bronze and silver" medalists did not see their ideas produced. Ultimately, POS problems and its inability to be translated into radio killed the split image campaign, but it had greatly helped the agency get the Agavez business (TR 751).

VERBAL-VISUAL COGNITION: ASSIMILATION AND ACCOMMODATION IN THE DYADIC MIND

There were some similarities to and differences from Neil and Jesse's approach in the way the team of Jason and Craig assimilated and accommodated materials. Assimilation is the reshaping of the mental representation of a currently perceived object to fit the existing cognitive structures in the perceiver. Along with assimilation concurrently occurs accommodation, in which the perceiver's cognitive structures (schema) change to accommodate novel aspects of what is being perceived. Layouts or other texts can serve as group schema in group composing (Cross, 2001). As it did with Neil and Jesse, the 3 p.m. Brief Meeting provided novel information (the situation, purpose, and audience of this particular Agavez campaign) that Jason and Craig each assimilated into their preexisting understandings of the rhetorical situation of the Agavez account gleaned from previous tip-ball meetings when Heric had Agavez' non-POS advertising. The Brief Meeting itself triggered one line for Craig that he later discarded. Supervisor Neil also saw the pair in the halls and recommended "the split thing," an open-ended structure for concepts. Writer and artist each had an incubation phase that night on their drives to their homes from work, and then Jason, while watching the advertisements during the Winter Olympics, came up with an initial visual concept. For cognition to occur, as Piaget told us, knowledge structures are necessary; for example, the system of logical categories that the naturalist assimilates his or her perceptions of phenomena into. In the case of Jason and Craig, the morph concept/structure was "in the air," broadcast during the commercial breaks during the Olympics, the Olympic level of advertising, and created by an agency, Weiden and Kennedy, whose "Just Do It" campaign for Nike was considered in advertising circles one of the all-time greats.

Jason appeared to translate subconsciously the Nike video that featured morphing based on principles of contrast/similarity into "the split thing," producing a print yin-yang gestalt in which opposites, in this case before and after, are merged. Assimilating this dynamic "Move" morphing concept into static print eliminated its video properties that had allowed one activity to take up the full screen before the protean conversion into another activity. The resultant split image print layout would become the outward sign of a knowledge structure for the "dyadic mind." This structure continued to change to accommodate key elements of the creative brief, simultaneously turning into, for customers' consumption, an easily assimilated and integrated synthesis. However, Jason's mesmerizing but purely visual initial concept did not deliver the strategy because it did not restrict interpretation of its surreal figures. Words were needed for that.

The same night that Jason drew this split image while watching the Olympics, Craig, at his home, mindfully articulated, among other ideas, mowing from the standpoint of the brand promise: "The chore you have to go through to get the reward." After discussing their ideas when they met the next morning,

February 14, Jason and Craig saw the split image concept as having great potential. When they met again that afternoon to brainstorm, Jason further accommodated the image into the medium by making the split look like a flipbook, giving it a natural reason for being. Craig mindfully scrutinized the brand promise and deduced the implied relationship of product and benefit—that mowing was a means to the end of recreation, assimilating the Agavez strategy into his existing schema/topic of cause-effect. He next accommodated Jason's split image so that it could accept copy by putting tabs on each page. Craig then assimilated his headline onto the tabs by condensing the line into two words to fit the space permitted by the tabs; two words that in their assonance rhymed: "chore" rhyming with the "war" part of "reward," here perhaps Craig's college study of poetry facilitating the rhyme as well as the compression.

This verbal-visual concept was then used to generate several different versions, assimilating stock images to deliver the strategy. Its surreal quality, combining things that are separate in reality, made it even more on strategy: Our world comprises both our everyday reality and our "separate" imaginative life as we operate in the everyday; the split image campaign delivers the strategy by combining work and play, attaching dream and fantasy to the everyday work world to create an absolute reality or "surreality" (Encyclopedia Britannica Micropedia IX, 1974, 692/2). Surreality allowed the use of the product and the reception of a benefit to be literally joined at the hip—transforming the lawn mower into the angler, biker, or golfer. Previously, the "Move" commercial, through a series of quick cuts, had allowed a similar joining or transformation of the amateur exerciser using the product to the elite athlete, and the chore of practice into the reward of elite performance in the professional and Olympic-level event; in both, the product is a part of the means to the end of elite performance.

The surreal schema of the split image permitted combining the disparate. The Internet image bank intertext facilitated this by providing parts of the picture that line up but are incongruous conceptually, even more so (in the case of the subterranean sky stratum) than initially conceptualized when drawn on paper. So the Internet contributed some of the startling "imag-ination" (image innovation) of this work.

Once Jason and Craig had come up with the concept and decided to produce it (insight and evaluation phases), its final phase—elaboration—caused more assimilation and accommodation. Jason's pencil sketches had not filled in a backdrop for the flipbook beyond drawing a wavy line below the flipbook to indicate a headline and the client's logo. Jason initially put the flipbook on top of ½"-tall grass for a backdrop. However, figure-ground contrast was weak: to an extent, the book blended into the long grass. So Jason discarded this backdrop because it did not assimilate well. He next found an image of putting green grass with a golf ball casting a long shadow resting atop it. He assimilated this backdrop, inverting the golf ball image so that the shadow pointed the right direction, layering the flipbook on top of it. He accommodated the layout by putting shadows around the book to make the light look similar to the golf ball's long shadow in the backdrop. Doing so also allowed the flipbook figure to stand out from the grassy "ground" better. The assimilated golf ball's shadow added extra emphasis by creating a wide, dark line connecting the client's logo to the golf ball, suggesting the connection between the product and fun.

This split image ad had powerful persuasive impact, and not simply because it aroused curiosity by oxymoronically yoking the seeming opposites of work and play. Such a yoking did not seem bizarre, producing a chimera. Perhaps why such a yoking works is, as McLuhan notes, games (and perhaps by *extension* recreation) are extensions of popular response to workaday stress (1964, p. 208). So the workday stress of the chore produces the reaction that is the game; again a cause-effect situation, a reason why this yin and yang form a larger unity.

The next chapter will compare this collaborative process of the young Turks with that of veterans Neil and Jesse to conclude our inquiry into verbal-visual collaboration in a creative system.

CHAPTER 6

Collaboration En*visioned*

We have focused very specifically on dyadic collaboration to answer the calls from the disciplines of technical communication, college composition, and business communication for detailed research on verbal-visual composing. To conclude our analysis, we return to the beginning: the research questions. The first and overarching question is "What is the nature of verbal-visual dyadic collaboration in an advertising system of creativity?" What we have witnessed is a narrative tracing a cross-section of verbal-visual collaborative composing, from the surrounding economic and field conditions (e.g., Olympics TV ads), to the client, vendor, and customer contributions and constraints, to the agency managerial influence (CEO, Account Manager, Chief Creative Officer, Creative Director), to the dyadic collaborations, to individual processes at night that in Jason and Craig's cases prepared them to collaborate the next day. This is verbal-visual collaborative composing in a social context. Such detailed research in our case includes the following subquestions:

- To what degree is the composing visual? Verbal?
  - In ad concepts?
  - In discussion topics?
  - In intradyadic communication?
- How do the verbal, visual, and verbal-visual rhetorical elements of arrange-ment, clarity, concision, emphasis, ethos, and tone factor into the composing processes and products?
- What is verbal-visual dyadic invention?
  - What are commonalities in the sequences of invention?
  - What is the function of pauses?
  - What is kept? What is discarded?
  - What kind of audience analysis was used?
  - Were any transferable principles of verbal-visual invention used?

- How is power handled among collaborators?
  - To what degree are collaborators supportive? Assertive?
  - How is conflict managed?
- How mindful and productive are the dyad and the large group in decisions that involved the dyads?
- How do the findings of this first extensive study compare with existing models of verbal-visual collaboration and creativity (e.g., Csikszentmihalyi, 1996; Mirel et al., 1995)?
- How do artists and writers who come from very different communicative traditions and mental models create a common text representation that assimilates and accommodates rhetorical elements effectively?

For the processes observed, the answers to these questions and others follow in this chapter, often achieved in summarizing the statistics from the cases and comparing the dyads. The research questions generated by these answers and suggestions for teaching verbal-visual collaborative composing complete the study.

INITIAL VERBAL-VISUAL INVENTION PREDOMINANTLY CONCERNED WITH VISUAL

An essential finding in the analysis of two dyads' initial brainstorming of campaigns is that verbal-visual invention was predominantly concerned with visual matters. Over 82% of the verbal and visual comments made in Jason and Craig's brainstorming meeting (223.5 comments) addressed the visual. For Neil and Jesse, 74.7% of the comments addressed visual matters.

Dominance of Visually Initiated Concepts in Initial Invention

An interesting contrast is the difference in the artists and writers' generations of verbally or visually originated concepts. Writer Craig contributed over a third (33.8%) of the dyad's visually originated concepts, while artist Jason contributed only 4.8% of the dyad's verbally originated concepts. Moreover, 54.5% of Craig's concepts were visually originated, but only 2.1% of Jason's concepts were verbally initiated. On the other team, the visual contributions of the writer were more striking: writer Neil contributed 72.2% of the concepts that began with an image or scenario, but on the other hand, artist Jesse contributed over half (53.3%) of the verbally originated concepts. Neil and Jesse, though, generated nearly twice as many visually originated concepts (7.9) as verbally originated concepts (4.1). Of the concepts Neil generated, the percentage that he began by mentioning a visual image was 82.3%, while 39% of Jesse's concepts began by his mentioning a headline or other words. Little over a third of Jesse's verbally originated concept material (37.5%) was developed by the dyad for the tip-ball session, and about the same percentage of Neil's visually originated concept material was used (38.5%). But because Neil was more prolific, comparing the previous percentages can be misleading: Neil contributed 2.5 successful visually originating concepts, but the amount of successful verbally originating concept material of artist Jesse was 0.6.

Of the 12 complete concepts they generated, Neil and Jesse chose to develop twice as many visually initiated concepts (4/2) for tip-ball presentations. Only one concept of the 35 generated by both teams was approved beyond the tip-ball meetings, the chore-reward or split image concept. Artist Jason visually initiated that concept in his dyad, although Neil had earlier recommended the visual approach.

Prevalence of Visual Topics in Rhetorical Elements Discussed in Initial Invention

Of the 11 most frequent moves by Craig or Jason, six were visual arrangement across a number of moves, the other five were visual clarity, and all were visual. For Neil and Jesse, when we look at the cognate area with the highest incidence of a particular collaborative move, we find they made by far the most comments directing each other about visual arrangement—23 for Jesse (21.7% of his comments, 10% of Jesse and Neil's total comments), 21.5 for Neil (17.6% of Neil's comments, 9.4% of Neil and Jesse's total comments). Furthermore, in Jason and Craig's verbal-visual composing process, arrangement dominated invention, on the surface surprising, given the arrangement's status as a separate classical canon from invention. Fahnestalk, however, (2001, p. 33) noted that the canon of arrangement "has always been invaded by its stronger neighbors, the first and third canons [invention and style]." Dragga and Gong note that arrangement and invention occur simultaneously; however, they considered layout itself a part of the canon of delivery (1989, p. 56). From the examples given, their theory appears to be based on an examination of multiple-page technical documents, news stories, and promotional brochures. Composing processes were not examined. But the concepts for one-page ads that creatives generated for the Agavez campaign were largely visual scenarios that instantiated the sales strategy. More than a superstructure, the scenarios of these verbal-visual documents were much if not most of the content, clearly something invented. In the verbal-visual composing processes of mostly single-page ads and POS observed in the current study, arrangement (predominantly layout) governed invention.

In addition to the above statistics, writers challenged the artists more (averaging 6.3 of the dyad's comments compared with 1.35 of the dyad's comments) respectively in the other's domain. These numbers show that the visual thinking of the writers was much more extensive and developable than the verbal thinking of the artists. Perhaps we have this result because the visual is a more direct, *more primary way of conceptualizing verbal-visual documents* for both artists and writers in collaboration. This visually intensive way of thinking may start with our acquisition of language—we initially acquire language by pointing to objects and naming them (Tiano & Keep, 2008). Neil, in an individual protocol experiment in which he created ads for a magazine (Cross, 2008), commented on visual topics in only 25% of his comments on images and words. However, when collaborating with an artist who could render his ideas, Neil discussed visual topics 75% of the time. Such writers inhibit a substantial amount of visual thinking they are unable to fully express and render because of their limitations as graphic designers and artists. So when they collaborate with artists, they can more fully realize their concepts. Writers could draw well enough with stick men, Jason told me, that he could understand the concept (FN 225).

We could argue that the zone of proximal development was at work in stimulating that visual thinking: students in groups of more knowledgeable peers have been found to become more adept at the skills and strategies they were practicing (Hillocks, 1995, p. 72). However, note that the artists did not do nearly as much verbal thinking in their writer-artist pairs as the writers did visual thinking. For quite a while, developments in semiotics, cognitive psychology, and neurophysiology have made clear linkages between visual thought and composition, suggesting "the act of writing involves more visual thinking than we recognized in traditional composition classes" (Costanzo, 1986, p. 86). A recent study shows at the abstract planning stage we engage visual memory when composing sentences, when conceptual representations generate not only words but also images. This study as well replicates research showing visual working memory engaged in generating concrete nouns for definitions (Kellogg, Olive, & Piolat, 2007, p. 107; Sadoski, Kealy, & Gomez, 1997). It may be that for writers, their visual competence (in a generative transformational grammar sense) is much higher than their visual performance. Thus the zone of proximal development could increase the visual performance of the writer more than the verbal performance of the artist. Eventually, with students' and professionals' full access to desktop publishing through such programs as Microsoft Office Publisher, it may be that our print communication of all genres will include many more visual components and thus fully realize our thinking. The above findings also lend more support to the contention that it is not by chance that we denote original thinking as in*sight* and *imag*ination, though we more frequently denote this thinking with words, suggesting the major contribution of both the verbal and the visual.

Channels of Communication of Comments

How were these verbal and visual topics communicated in initial brainstorming? During their invention sessions, both dyads communicated to a degree with drawing and writing as well as talking. Craig and Jason had many fewer written and drawn comments—nearly 95% were just said—but they were further along. At home the night before their collaborative invention, while watching the

Olympics, Jason had drawn the split images that became their winning concept. The drawing done during the meeting was also crucial: the flipbook with the tabs format put the surrealistic joined images into a believable context, and the visual concept was the necessary foundation for Craig to integrate the images into the rhetorical strategy with his "chore, reward" catchphrase put on the tabs.

By contrast, Neil and Jesse each or both drew while making 26.1% of their comments. Looking at the drawings shows that Jason and Craig were much farther along and thinking convergently. Where Jesse's sketches were images rather than layouts, Jason's in-meeting sketches for the split image campaign were framed by rectangles, suggesting ad layouts and providing gestalt visual closure, a continuous, unbroken contour that created visual impact. Jason had several versions of a strong visual concept at the onset of the brainstorming session, so less visual experimentation was done during the meeting. And in a short meeting earlier that day, Jason and Craig had worked with those images Jason had drawn the night before while watching the Olympics.

Jason and Craig were not only further along visually but also strategically because Craig had transformed the rhetorical strategy into an organizing principle: cause-effect. Each member of the team also contributed a larger percentage of used verbal comments. Where Neil and Jesse each contributed 2.6% of the total dyadic comments as successful verbal comments, that is, words that were used in the versions presented in the tip-ball meetings, Jason and Craig contributed 2.7% and 4.1% respectively. The low percentages of words, however, could be explained by Neil's doing the copy lines in a separate session that afternoon, while Craig just had to use one word for each tab in the flipbook chore-reward campaign, and Jason and Craig never developed any of the other concepts sufficiently to generate headlines, subheads, or body copy.

Jesse and Neil had more inscribed comments (drawn and/or written, or both along with said) retained in the ads that went forward. They clearly "thought with a pencil" some of the time, developing the several concepts they brought to tight for the tip-ball meeting. For both dyads, drawing was critical in moving the project forward because it provided a common text representation. Moreover, layout served as an external schema in which to assimilate both words and pictures.

Writer/Artist?

Regardless of what they imply regarding the communication of ad concepts, within the dyads, all of these findings support the conclusion that the visual was by far the more important in *generating* ad concepts. If, when they have the opportunity to have their visions rendered, writers and artists both think and talk mostly about visual matters in inventing ads, then their drafting or executing is much more different than is the visual conceptual thinking each does in invention. It may also be that writers would communicate more visually than they do now in solely written compositions if they had the technique or collaborators to do so. In any case, when we investigated a verbal-visual variety of collaboration, not only does the concept of authorship change from that of the romantic writer working alone in the garret, but also *our very concept of writer and artist change as these roles overlap and to a degree merge.*

RHETORICAL ELEMENTS IN VERBAL-VISUAL COMPOSING

Given the propensity of writers in this study to participate in visual composing when collaborating with artists, we need to consider how writers can do that most effectively in our verbal-visual age. As Foss (2004) notes, "as rhetorical theory opens up to visual rhetoric, it opens up to possibilities for more relevant, inclusive, and holistic views of contemporary symbol use."

The Verbal-Visual Interrelation of Rhetorical Elements Addressed in Dyadic Composing

The predominance of visual topics in the collaborative dialogue, however, does not indicate that the *writing* generated was insignificant, because meaning in the dyads' print ads is produced by the *co-occurrence* of verbal and visual information, as Baumgarten has told us about the medium of cinema (2005). To understand the effect of verbal-visual print ads and the properties and parameters within which writers and artists composed them, it is necessary to isolate the verbal and visual components and then, most important, consider their interrelation. Applying a common terminology to both verbal and visual features helps us understand how words and design elements in the document produced work rhetorically, individually and together. This study has reported the incidence in verbal-visual brainstorming of six rhetorical dimensions of written communication that have corresponding visual elements, identified by Kostelnick and Roberts: arrangement, emphasis, clarity, conciseness, tone, and ethos (1998). To further consider some of these elements, I now examine Williams' (2007) discussion elements of verbal style, such as cohesion, and apply them to the visual realm. The next section defines these elements and discusses how the creatives used these elements verbally and visually to communicate Heric's rhetorical strategy for Agavez.

Arrangement

Written arrangement is the disposition of verbal materials. Visually, arrangement is ordering materials to reveal their structure—their hierarchy of information and the like (Kostelnick & Roberts, 1998). Because of the brevity of verbal information in the print ads—one-sentence or even two-word (chore-reward) headlines and one-paragraph body copy—there was not much attention paid to verbal arrangement, such as paragraphing, outlining, and so on. There was some discussion of subgenres, like long-copy ads. Regarding purely visual matters, creatives discussed where to put objects; for example, whether to put a racing helmet on a man sitting on a tractor mower in his den, watching a NASCAR race.

The words often referred to the image directly; for example, Craig, envisioning copy laid out to trace the path of a lawn mower winding its way about a lawn. Positioned over the visual, the copy explains it: "This [referring to the lawn] is the only thing that stands between you and going fishing." The pictures aid and complete the text, and vice versa. So in verbal-visual compositions, arrangement is no longer the words' position regarding other words or design elements in relation to themselves, but rather the words in relation to the images. Thus verbal-visual arrangement is typically the interdependent deployment of verbal and visual signs.

One way of defining this interdependence is "cohesion." Williams (2007) notes that sentences should begin with old information and end with new information. Because the image is typically seen first in verbal-visual text (Wysocki & Lynch, 2007, p. 301), the verbal line needs to have a reference, even if indirect, to the visual (the old information), then a connection with the new information, be it the product or whatever else. The ads Jesse and Neil generated for the pitch were less verbally-visually coherent than Craig and Jason's. The "Another Satisfied Agavez Owner" ad visually minimized the mower—the topic of the ad—to permit a juxtapositional approach (Schriver, 1996) in which words and images have an underlying connection but do not overtly cohere. However, by minimizing the image of the mower, they minimized the identity and importance of the product. Looking at the icons ads, we see that the line doesn't mention the mower directly. "Lawns are our life, not yours" stresses lawns where the image stresses the golf ball. It is not as direct or cohesive: the reader has to think about it more. With regard to the mower-hero ad, "Honey weren't we going shopping for shoes today?" and the subhead "You'd rather be doing anything than cutting grass," both headline and subhead do not refer to the mower image in any direct way. The tag, in smaller, thinner type (poor figure-ground contrast for something that needs to be emphasized), says "Agavez makes life easier," but that is not directly referring to the point of preferring doing anything but mowing. Again, there is the opposite of verbal-visual cohesion because the line does not begin with the dominant visual image, instead it is all new information.

Clarity

Addressing verbal and visual elements, Kostelnick and Roberts note that "clarity strategies help the receiver to decode the message, to understand it quickly and completely, and when necessary to react without ambivalence" (1998, p. 17). In the split image ad, clarity caused words and image to be grouped in the same dominant visual. Moreover, the reason for adding words to the split image was clarity, according to Craig, to show the mower was the means to the end of recreation. When Craig put "the chore" and "the reward" on the respective tabs of the mower and the recreation, he related the chimera to the strategy. The visual clarified by narrowing the meaning of the words down from "any chore" and "any reward," while the words narrowed the meaning of the curiously juxtaposed images to relate them to the strategy. Each serves the other as a semantic link to the strategy. One serves as a node while the other a link (see Figures 34 and 35). The link is the reason the node is related to the strategy.

To be the most clear when combining words, we typically start with a more easily graspable short unit, which introduces a more complex and difficult unit (Williams, 2007). Could this principle transfer in any way to verbal-visual communication? With the split image ad, the simple words did not initiate the message because people see the puzzling, nonveridical image first. But the tabbed words along with the tag, "Get it over with," succinctly explain the images and serve as preamble for the more complicated central argument in the body copy and tag that, because of its engine and warranty, the Agavez is the tool to get the chore over with. One function of the visual in this case is to draw attention and establish the context in which the mower sales pitch makes sense to the target

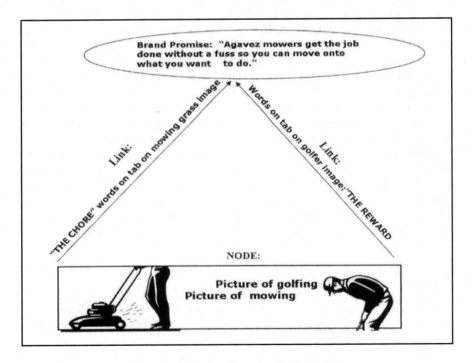

Figure 34. Words relate visuals to strategy.

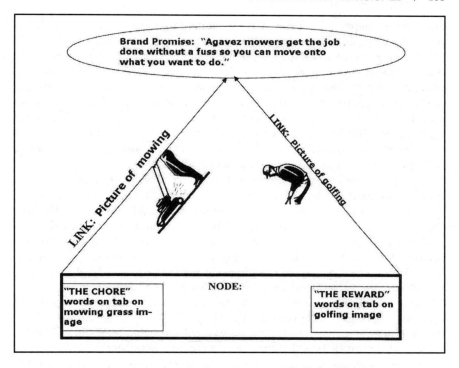

Figure 35. Images relate words to strategy.

audience. Another function is a tacit argument that, as McQuarrie and Mick (2003) note is "not the sort of direct assertion . . . that stimulate[s] counterargument" (p. 216). The arguments are, first, that golf is earned through chores such as mowing lawns. The second is that Agavez will help you get the job over with. This verbal-visual argument is bare-bones but provides enough identification with at least a central tendency of customer values (mowing, a chore that we get over and move on to what we want to do more) to prepare the reader for the "reasons to believe" and the full argument. So clarity in verbal-visual persuasion, though necessary to identify the product and claim, may be more influential when more subtle and gradual, because numerous studies have shown that people actively avoid processing advertising (Phillips, 2003).

Another way to enhance clarity in written prose, Williams tells us, is to align major characters with subjects, and actions with verbs. Regarding verbal-visual communication, is there a lack of clarity when the image topic is not the subject and the action in the image is not the verb of the headline? Neil and Jesse's ads are much more indirect because they don't do that. Whereas Craig and Jason's depicted actions are also in linguistic subsets of subjects/nouns—chore and reward—mowing is for most a chore, golfing for most a treat or reward. The point is the words do relate the character and the action, where Neil's words "Honey, weren't we going shopping for shoes today?" are juxtapositional—they don't relate on the surface, and you have to put the verbal and visual into relation yourself. That may have enthymemic value for those who solve the riddle, but it requires the viewer to have the patience and intelligence to accomplish the task. As the Director of Market Research said, it is "a lot to get your head around" (TR 714). But whatever is dominant in the ad, word or line, needs to be rapidly understood; as the Chief Creative Officer told me, "You better be able to capture them in a real quick moment" (TR 422).

A sometimes severe impediment to verbal clarity, vague reference can also be a verbal-visual problem, as Craig told me. Putting "it" or another pronoun in a headline with another word as an antecedent can backfire when people think the antecedent is in the visual image. When communicating in a verbal-visual medium, the writer is adding another dimension to her or his communication and needs to coordinate the rendering of the concept both in old and new dimensions. The self-referential quality of much writing is undone when visual images are added in any of the verbal-visual relationships mentioned above.

Vague visual reference was also a problem. On the presentation versions of the icons ads, instead of, in Toulmin's parlance (2004), data supporting the claim, the artist had greeking. These reasons would have helped the Chief Creative Officer and client believe that there was a winning argument made by the ad. Greeking may encourage a form-content split, where layout is mostly considered from an aesthetic rather than semantic viewpoint.

The creatives also worked to make sure that visual elements did not obscure the name of the brand and mower, so that the client's mower would be selected at the store and so that the reader would connect the product with any equity in the brand—its positive reputation.

In the end, problems of clarity were the reason the split image campaign was also finally rejected, although it was one of three that earned the agency the Agavez business. Agavez sold mowers to consumers not only in English-speaking but also in French- and Spanish-speaking parts of the world, and the client and the ad agency ultimately found it would be too difficult to translate the image of "a guy mowing his lawn on a motorcycle," as one Heric account manager put it, referring to the split image of the biker/mower. Here, at least in the eyes of the managers involved, surrealism, although creating visual sizzle, interfered with the purpose of selling the mower.

Concision

Williams defines concision as "compression" that involves (a) deleting meaningless words, (b) eliminating words that repeat the meanings of other words, (c) deleting words implied by other words, (d) replacing a phrase for a word, and

(e) changing negatives to affirmatives. I often tell my students that verbal concision is a balancing act between the poles of the laconic and the prolix, either pole causing obscurity.

Kostelnick and Roberts (1998) define visual concision as referring to "the visual bulk and intricacy of design." It means not "as minimal as possible" but appropriately succinct for the situation (p. 19). Jesse engaged this principle in explaining his design of the icon ads. Most current magazines, he told me, are busy—visually cluttered. The trouble with too many things going on visually is "people don't know where to look. Unconsciously, you just want to look away—it . . . repels you." When the reader is flipping through busy magazines, a spare, clean page might pique someone's interest, Jesse said. So visual compression, such as that found in the spare portraits of Richard Avedon, creates visual impact, reinforcing verbal compression.

At Heric, visual design could force verbal compression. Craig mentioned an art director he worked with who would give him 10 characters of space to fill, creating the newspaper headline writer's dilemma of fitting the topic of 24 column inches of copy into 10 characters. Here visual constraints yielded verbal concision. Stylistic continuity could be an added reason for compression: Jesse felt that simple, uncluttered pictures needed the same kind of words.

The degree of concision can be affected by the different kinds of relationships between words and images. Including juxtaposition, Schriver has identified five such verbal-visual relationships. In redundancy, words and image each convey the same information. Of course, redundancy is largely frowned upon in writing, but some redundancy is built into the English language (e.g., "now" used in a sentence in the present tense). Regarding the merit of verbal-visual redundancy, this approach is the least concise and is decreasingly used in advertising; however, some people are more auditory/word learners and some are more visual learners, so some verbal-visual redundancy may be useful to accommodate these divergent learning styles. The higher the learning curve, it would seem, the more useful are clear redundant verbal-visual messages, because they communicate to both our verbal and visual processing centers of the brain.

The rest of the verbal-visual relationships are more symbiotic. Complementary relationships, in which words and pictures have different content that combine into one clear concept, can be concise. One such example is Craig and Jason's split image ads. In supplementary verbal-visual relationships, one mode dominates (relates the main idea) and the other "reinforces, elaborates, or instantiates the points made." Depending on the amount of overlap, such designs could be concise or more redundant. Neil and Jesse's golf ball icon supplemented by "Lawns are our life, not yours" exhibited such a relationship, a relationship that was somewhat laconic.

Juxtapositional relationships are "characterized by different content in the words and pictures, in which the key ideas are created by a clash or a semantic tension between the ideas in each mode; the idea cannot be inferred without both modes being present simultaneously" (p. 413). This approach is the most laconic, dangerously obscure in some cases. However, it can be the most intriguing when we have felt a sense of an answer but have to think about it, and our thoughts are rewarded. Semiotic theory shows, as McQuarrie and Mick (2003) note, that "any sign structure that resists immediate decoding but signals the path toward ultimate resolution of this problem is inherently pleasurable" (p. 208). The lawn mower-hero ads use this mode. The jaunty mower visual clashes with the excuses, in words, not to mow. Perhaps they are resolved by the tag—"Agavez makes life easier." However, the tag's subtlety and vagueness might make the ad frustrating or irritating (McQuarrie & Mick, 2003, p. 208). And, depending on one's perspective and the ad, it either gets a laugh because of male (Mars)-female (Venus) differences or offends because it stereotypes, or a little of both.

Verbal-visual concision issues prompted debate in Neil and Jesse's brainstorming the "Another Satisfied Agavez Owner" concept, a concept that turns upon the contrast between the headline and the recreational visual. From the words of the "Another Satisfied . . ." ad, whose topic is the satisfaction of owning a mower, we expect to see mowing foregrounded, but instead see a man doing a clown dive, reeling in a deep-sea fish, and so on. Adding an explanatory subhead, "He's working hard," proposed by Neil, was rejected by Jesse, who said, "It just ends in the shot; . . . you have to lead them on" (TR 17). This discussion illustrates a tendency in advertising away from verbal-visual redundancy. Research showing that the amount of copy anchoring images decreased from 1954 to 1999 speculates that consumers are becoming more competent readers of verbal-visual texts. Creatives today often risk viewers not getting the point of the ad because other ads that anchor images with text decrease pleasure (Phillips, 2000). Verbal concision in a verbal-visual ad thus regards how much additional work the written word needs to do to convey the concept, rather than communicating the entire concept as economically as possible in words. Ultimately, Neil "ended in the shot," as Jesse suggested, because, as Neil told me in a later discussion, "That's sort of an old rule. . . . I'm not saying it's not meant to be broken. But . . . gag . . . a gag, it's too much. It's like [imitating a viewer] 'Okay, I get it, I get it.'" Clearly, the rules of joke writing were applied here across two media. Although Neil noted the goal was not sheer entertainment, but rather persuasion, the writer still didn't want to give the viewer "too many elbows to the ribs" (TR 186).

However, the words "another satisfied Agavez owner" and the picture of recreation were too minimal, and Neil added another visual (of an Agavez tractor) at the bottom, and the tag line "you've got more important things to worry about" under the logo to "drive it home with the strategic thing" (TR 18). But the next day the ad was still somewhat obscure to Neil. He later changed the tag line to "Agavez makes life easier," a tag that was even less explanatory but that applied to all the power tools Agavez made, in accord with the creative brief. At the second tip-ball meeting the Chief Creative Officer suggested changing the tag again, to "We spend a lot of time on these mowers so you don't have to." Feeling that suggestion was too long for a tag, Neil condensed the tag to "We always work so you don't have to," then, becoming more linguistically concise by eliminating the negative phrasing, he condensed it to "We always work so you can play" (TR 62). "Play" clearly refers to the dominant image of diving, biking, or other sports in the ad, while the antecedent of the subject of the sentence refers to the mower and the prominent logo at the bottom of the ad. This new phrasing is more accurate because one still has to work—do the mowing when the mower functions. In this development, we see some increase in verbal-visual clarity while not sacrificing verbal-visual concision.

A lack of coherence among elements, however, still made the ad somewhat hard to process. Perhaps the connections would have been made solid with the body copy that was, although indicated by greeking, never written. Neil knew early on the connections were missing and needed: as he told me before changing the tag the first time, he needed to communicate that "he's already cut his lawn and he's out there doing (the sport in the picture)." This information would not be redundant—gagging the gag—interfering with concision, but instead necessary to unify the verbal and visual elements. Because he was also developing four other concepts, Neil was not able in the time available to tie together loose semantic ends.

As a result, with five discrete visual elements, including different boxes for the headline and logo with tag, the "Satisfied" ad is disunified. By comparison, the split image ad, despite splicing disparate images of product and recreation, is visually integrated because of its chimera's continuous visual lines and its four words of headline incorporated as tabs on the flipbook. Thus a visual and contextual logic is provided for the proximity—in this case of word and image—that as Arnheim (2004, p. 388) notes provides a perceptual link.[1] The artist also integrated appeals by using recreational elements to emphasize the client's logo. For example, in the golfing split image ad, the shadow coming off the golf ball points directly to the Agavez logo (TR 240). This technique of connecting image and text in an invisible line is the perceptual tie of "alignment" identified by gestalt psychology (Schriver, 1997, p. 313). This integration evinces maximum verbal-visual concision. It also evinces verbal-visual closure, because verbal and visual signs integrate into a larger, fully articulated message.

Verbal-visual concision is reduction of word and image to get maximum impact and meaning for all signs, thus interrelated with emphasis. It is a lack of redundancy between linguistic and visual, but clarity still must result, thus it is also interrelated especially with clarity. It is, as Williams said about words, removing the inessentials (here across both media) so that the essentials become salient.

---

[1] Arnheim here drew on the work of gestalt psychology (e.g., Koffka, 1935, pp. 164–165).

Emphasis

Nevertheless, once the cutting is done, some essentials are more essential than others. How can we create a verbal-visual emphasis? First, let's look at how the brain selects what to focus upon. Cognition, simply defined as "knowing," comprises knowledge of at least two kinds: (a) perception, or knowledge via seeing or awareness; and (b) conception, knowledge via thinking and judgment (Lindemann, 2001, p. 87). The visual typically piques our interest first in a verbal-visual ad (McQuarrie & Mick, 2003, p. 216), perhaps in part because we have been interpreting visuals longer than we have been interpreting words. As Innis notes, "Langer, Pierce and Dewey show us that our first experiential encounters are not with 'objects' that have meanings that fit over them as an interpretive overlay, but with intrinsically meaningful wholes" (2007, p. 6). Visual memory also is stronger than verbal memory (McQuarrie & Mick, 2003, p. 217), again suggesting the power of the visual. Dual-coding theory indicates that images can be encoded both symbolically and analogically, creating more associations than merely words in memory (Mazzocco & Brock, 2006, p. 65; Paivio, 1986). Vivid mental images can also confer the status of reality, adding plausibility and compellingness to what would be otherwise vague or implausible arguments (Markham & Hynes, 1993). The compellingness may be explained by the findings of experimental research showing that attention and emotion cannot be separated (Bolls, 2008). As Langer tells us, art gives form to feelings (129), a reason advertising uses artistic techniques to arouse interest.[2] Gestalt psychology notes, however, that some visual forms are stronger than others, forms such as the circle or triangle that have visual closure—a continuous, unbroken contour. These figures are not dominated by their contexts easily: "Strong figures resist change or disintegration under poor viewing conditions or variations in the viewer's attention" (Schriver, 1997, p. 316). Strong visual objects, as Langer's work asserts, affect our consciousness: "The distinctively human ambient . . . is a symbolic or symbolically transformed ambient, with both endosomatic and exosomatic dimensions" (Innis, 2007, p. 10). Langer notes that forms can "impregnate" intuition and perception (Innis, 2007, p. 13). Regarding the subconscious pull of strong images, Owsley (1972) went so far as to say that the strong visual image controlled one's experience of an environment. Perhaps this is much of the power of the idol upon the idolater. Forms, constituting what McLuhan (1964) calls the "unconscious depth messages of ads" (p. 205), can create great visual impact or emphasis.

Along with forms, certain positions on the page as well as in syntax contribute to emphasis, what Kostelnick and Roberts define as "prominence or intensity of

---

[2] Langer (1957) notes that the feelings aroused cannot be named. They have "import," not meaning (p. 127). However, in a verbal-visual advertisement, forms and their import can be used to get attention, and then words can tie the visual forms into the sales strategy.

expression" (1998, p. 19). Regarding syntax, Williams tells us to put the most important material in the first and last words of a sentence, places of maximum emphasis. The first part should take the topic, put as simply and concisely as possible, while the end can significantly increase both complexity and word length (2007, p. 108). Of course, the number of words devoted to something in print also typically indicates importance. From a visual standpoint, researchers have suggested that, all else being equal, the top left and bottom right quadrants have greater visual impact than others (Locker, 2006, p. 133), and that the optical center of the page—where the eye goes first—is, as Moen notes, "slightly above and to the left or right of the mathematical center" (2000, p. 39). Thus, in any given page, the above areas will automatically be emphasized. The trick is to control what is emphasized, as Kostelnick and Roberts tell us (1998, p. 16); they also note that size, darkness, contrast, and other design elements can create visual emphasis.

Verbal-visual emphasis thus involves not only the position but also the amount of verbiage and visual space devoted to a topic and their interrelated salience. In the juxtapositional verbal-visual relationship, emphasis is largely attained by the semantic contrast of headline and image, yet this cognitive dissonance is relieved by the discussion of the product in the body copy. In a supplementary verbal-visual relationship, emphasis shaped the icons ads and their outcome in the Agavez campaign. Initially in the golf ball ad, the headline, "Lawns are our life. Not yours." was dwarfed, like the mower, by the huge golf ball on the windowsill. Jesse, however, quickly increased the point size of the headline and logo, increasing the emphasis even more on recreation because the line explains what would otherwise be seen as a poorly cropped image that obscured most of the lawnmower, yet left wheels and handle seemingly sprouting out of the golf ball. After the Chief Creative Officer told the dyad to "romance the product," the golf ball shrank, and the mower moved more into the open. However, campaign strategy conflicted with visual design in the final version. Because the client loved to see the product in its ads, Jesse experimented with making the golf ball and mower equal sized in the final version. But design principles told him (e.g., see Lester, 1995, p. 172) a good picture needed "one dominant visual. If you have them both giving the same impact, . . . it's not going to grab me." In verbal-visual emphasis, the concept is stressed by both word and image. The headline "Lawns are our life, not yours" determined whether mowing or recreation would dominate, and the headline deemphasized the product of the client, the gatekeeper audience. Because the icons concept did not integrate the partially conflicting needs of key audiences, design principles that emphasized this message that extolled the benefit by diminishing the product made rejection certain.

On the other hand, the product was emphasized in the mower-hero ads from the start, but headlines in large type of the advancing color gold, such as "Honey, weren't we going shopping for shoes today?" and the subhead, "You'd rather be doing anything but cutting grass," disparaged mowing and, indirectly, the product. Although the logo and tag, "Agavez makes life easier," began to explain the dominant presence of the mower, the lack of coherent, mutual verbal-visual emphasis or of an evident underlying juxtapositional unity made the ad less effective. By contrast, the words "chore" and "reward" on the tabs of images of mower and recreation respectively in the flipbook, framing a strong, startling closed figure, evinced unified, complementary verbal-visual emphasis, an emphasis made greater by design unity that created closure. Verbal closure is a "sense of ending" (Keep, McLaughlin, & Paramar, 2008). What *chore* and *reward* added to the visually closed image was a sense of explanation of the surrealistic chimera, an ending to our interpretative journey of seeing and thinking. As Lindemann notes (2001, p. 87), "seeing" (perception) and "thinking" (conception) impose an artificial distinction on processes that must work together in cognition. Verbal-visual closure, involving both processes of cognition, is words completing the meaning of the visually salient or dominant image. The image must be salient enough to get us to read words that interpret the image in a way that communicates the purpose or intention of the composer. In most cases, completion along with closure is most persuasive. With completion, the dissonance of thought and feeling evoked by the image is resolved by the words regarding the product, service, or charity advertised. Verbal-visual closure and completion create the greatest emphasis.

Ethos

Two aspects of our rhetorical understanding of ethos pertain to this investigation of verbal-visual composing: the use of words, images, and layouts to reflect the brand identity of the client, and the use of verbal and visual signs to reflect the integrity of the client. Of course, these two elements overlap, but separating them for this discussion allows us a consideration in greater depth. Let us first examine the verbal-visual conveyance of integrity. Williams defines linguistic, stylistic ethos as writing to as one would wish to be written to. Specifically, one should be candid, trustworthy, accessible. Visual accessibility is also crucial: Kostelnick and Roberts (1998) say that the visual needs to anticipate the readers' needs, and to look professional by being well made, to cultivate a sense of character or credibility (347).

From these definitions, we can derive a definition of ethos constituting Quintilian's genuineness of character rather than Aristotle's definition of the *appearance* of character. Verbal-visual ethos would not include surreptitiously discounting the reader's needs by being inaccessible, aloof, or deceitful. Instead, both in the verbal and the visual elements, one should be candid, accessible, trustworthy. So a picture of a product with false and misleading claims about it in the copy would be an example of poor verbal-visual ethos. A misleading visual depiction of the product with the logo of the company would be another example of poor verbal-visual ethos. The mower-hero ads were close to the border in this regard because the gorgeous shots of the mower were done with a special camera and lighting that made it look better than it would when the customer unpacked the box. Verbally, the tag, "Agavez makes life easier," was in some instances truer than others: in *Consumer Reports'* evaluation of ease of use, Agavez mowers were "good," the middle rating. In general, the mowers were solidly competitive among others in the evaluations.[3]

The ethos concern of meeting the consumers' perceived needs was considered in the episode when Craig suggested the split image of a mother pushing a mower and a baby carriage. Jason objected to the ad because, based on his wife's response to children near his mower, he felt that for mothers, the images of babies and lawn mowers did not mix. In representing their mowers this way, Agavez would appear at best flippant and irresponsible.

Creating a professional image was foregrounded when Jason mentioned a low-budget buyer's guide done by another company for Agavez, which featured wooden-looking, punctilious models wearing safety glasses while mowing. Jason mocked the appearance of the cover, while Craig sarcastically proposed the line, "What is the perfect way to mow your lawn?" Here the grandiose words belied the cheap document production quality, yet complemented the punctilious image, creating a lack of credibility intended in this parody of a competitor.

Identifying and distinguishing the product among its competitors is a critical role of verbal-visual ethos in advertising. Brand identity is the "configuration of words, images, ideas and associations that form a consumer's aggregate perception of a brand" (Upshaw, 1995, p. 12, cited by Barker & Stutts, 1999, p. 219). Creating a memorable identity for the client so that its reputation and products can be positioned favorably in the viewer's mind was the creatives' task. By putting the red color of the brand (the lawnmower was painted black and red) on the "chore, reward" tabs to stress brand identity, Jason and Craig engaged ethos. The color signifying the mower, combined with the words, suggest (with varying degrees of ethos, depending upon the model) much of the brand promise: "Agavez gets the job done without a fuss so that you can move onto the more important things in life."

Verbal-visual ethos was also engaged when the artists included the logo or brand signature. This unique representation of the company includes elements in at least two media. The verbal identity is the brand name and other linguistic components, including the tag line. The visual identity is the customary colors, formats, distinctive font, and any symbols of the brand signature (Delineate, 2007b). All dyadic teams participating in the pitch used the Agavez brand signature, which included its name in a distinctive font and an accompanying graphic

---

[3] *Consumer Reports* was never mentioned in all of the discussions I witnessed at Heric for 3 months. Yet because the client had competitive ratings, they might have been used to help sell the product.

symbol, comparable to the "swoosh" insignia that accompanies the verbal identity in the Nike logo. In many layouts, however, the name of the company was white instead of either black or red because the grass caused poor figure-ground differentiation from the company colors. However, the winning campaign that the client ultimately used did put "Agavez" in black in the logo. Their logo's distinctive type is another example of using the visual to reinforce the verbal, and both to reinforce brand identity to position the product favorably in the reader's mind through words with a distinctive visual shape.

Since ethos is in part a reflection of the professionalism of the image/text, it also is enhanced by strong verbal-visual cohesion, coherence, concision, and emphasis. Strengths in these areas created for the split image campaign a strong verbal-visual ethos, which enhances brand equity, the asset value to the company of the brand (Delineate, 2007a). A competent, professional image reinforces and enhances the favorable aspects of the reputation of the company that encourage both consumers and shareholders to buy.

Tone

Tone factored into several verbal-visual processes and products of the creatives. The standard rhetorical definition for verbal tone is the composer's attitude toward the subject as revealed by word choice. Visual tone is defined in a comparable manner by Kostelnick and Roberts, although referring to visual elements. They note we can create a range of visual voices through use of typefaces, italics and boldface, space, and other elements of design (1998, p. 20).

Visual tone was used to support linguistic tone in Jesse's choice of type font for the "Helpful Guide" ads. Coupled with a script font for the headline was a font resembling American Typewriter, used for the instructions because it was prevalent in the 1960s in "helpful" instructions in consumer catalogs. The fonts he chose were intended to be "kitschy," conveying "a retro kind of goofiness" that reinforced quirky verbal instructions such as, for golf, "If you are, however, unsuccessful . . . just smack the heck out of it."

Images can also support the overall effect because they contrast with the tone of the accompanying words. The surreal chimera of mower and golfer is intriguing, like a Magritte painting (e.g., "Le Modele Rouge") or one of his advertise-ments ("Image a la Maison Verte"), because the continuity and accuracy of form momentarily tricks the eye into perceiving the impossible image as normal. Craig's straightforward words "chore" and "reward" make the surrealistic image stand out by contrast because they don't distract, but the words also integrate the two disparate images conceptually, making the document clever rather than garbled, and "cool," as Craig and Jason both described it. In the creatives' offices, in the tip-ball meetings, and in the president's office, "cool" was the highest rating for approval of the aesthetics of the advertisement. "Cool" meant the communication was well constructed, catchy, fun, intriguing, stylish, of high status. How words and images could achieve this depended: as the Chief Creative Officer said, "sometimes you play off the picture; . . . you might have a humorous visual and a dead serious line. So it isn't in tone that they have to be connected, but in an idea they have to be connected" (TR 421).

"Cool" is charisma, and as Geertz notes, charisma is a "sign of being near the heart of things" (1983, p. 123). To determine the heart of the matter for their consumer audience, Heric did qualitative market research. This research indicated that the Agavez buyers see themselves as "work[ing] hard for their money." "Chore" and "reward" connect with that work ethic. Because the consumers' highest educational attainment was high school or some college courses, the straightforward words were well chosen. The words were also well chosen for their assonance, which creates a rhyme that makes them catchy. Another belief "near the heart of things" for the consumer was that recreation mattered. The visual, though surreal, still connected the product to the desire of the heart of the audience, literally joining product use and recreation at the hip in a *trompe l'oeil*.

Seeing and focusing on "features of perceived images engage us in calling up information we have stored through prior experience and can now recall and recount verbally," as Heath notes (2000, p. 122). This work of the "visual brain" incorporates highly specialized cells that process color, motion, and the like, which interact with each other in a parallel processing system of perception (Chao & Martin, 1999; Heath, 2000; Zeki, 1999). Cognitive studies of verbal-visual persuasion note that once attention is gained, beyond getting attention, more in-depth processing occurs in elaboration—when the ad is "linked to other cognitive structures or sign complexes already present in the mind of the consumer. . . . The greater the number of these linkages, the more central the structures to which the ad is linked, and the larger and more complex these structures, the greater is the elaboration" (McQuarrie & Mick, 2003, p. 206). The greater the elaboration, the greater the chance the ad will be retained (p. 208). Moreover, the greater the positive elaboration, the greater the persuasion, if persuasion is made possible by identification, as Burke has told us (1962). Identification includes "shared . . . experiences, objects, and goals" (Kenney, 2004, p. 333). Visual rhetoric, like its verbal sibling, relies upon identification to persuade (Hope, 2004, p. 155). Joining the customer's desired experiences and goals with the product in a visually attractive manner would help the customer psychologically see the product as part of the customer's identity.

In the split image ad, the straightforward tone of the words is reinforced by the sharp denotativeness of each of the two half-images, but also contrasts whimsically with the chimera of the mower/golfer, mower/boater, mower/biker. The Magritte-like beautifully colored and proportioned merger of product and thing desired (recreation) adds to the "cool" appeal, the mesmerizing, magical quality of the ad. The novelty of displacement of visual elements from their usual interpretive contexts intrigues the reader also, as Foss noted (1993, p. 216). Readers inquire further to resolve their cognitive dissonance. Burke (1962) said that prose style was a mesmerizing "incantation" (pp. 40–42). Visual dazzle but not glitz, produced by a strong combination of displacement, gestalt values and colors, was a key component of verbal-visual tone in this case, the "sizzle" of the dazzle emphasized by the contrasting solidity of the steak/plain words on the tabs. The plain words also serve to some degree as the "straight man," setting up the visual "gag man." On the other hand, the assonance of the words "chore" and "reward" adds rhythmic to visual impact.

In verbal-visual tone, the words and images can also convey the *same* attitude. The succinct words and simplified, iconic visual elements in the icons ads worked together to suggest the priority of recreation. This continuity is likely one reason why the campaign was a semifinalist. On the other hand, the tone of the lines, "Honey, weren't we going shopping for shoes today? You'd rather be doing anything than cutting grass"—waggishly disparaging mowing—contrast with the jaunty, light-painted mower; but this tone does not play off the image. The contrasting attitudes of words and image are not connected by an idea, such as "Agavez gets it over with fast and cheap so you can have more fun." The tag, "Agavez makes life easier," starts in a direction of a connecting argument, but *how* the mower does this never replaced the greeking that held a place for these reasons to believe. Consequently, the ad does not work; the tones don't oppose one another to create synthesis or irony. Even surrealism had unifying substrata, for example, of the subconscious (Bohn, 2002, p. 170). In a juxtapositional verbal-visual relationship, a clash, unexpected synthesis, or tension creates the larger message from the disparate parts (Schriver, 1997, p. 422). But in the mower-hero ad, the image and words do not, in Hagan's terminology (2007), "collaborate" to produce cross-modal meaning that contradicts, clarifies, or challenges the ordinary meaning of the words or image alone (p. 54). Instead, words and images just diverge.

Differences in Use of Rhetorical Elements by Different Dyads

Let us now consider further how these elements were entailed in the dyadic composing *processes*. As I previously noted, when we look at the cognate area with the highest incidence of a particular collaborative move, we find Neil and Jesse made by far the most comments directing each other about visual arrangement—23 for Jesse (20.8% of his comments, 9.6% of Jesse and Neil's total comments), 21.5 for Neil (17.6% of Neil's comments, 9.4% of Neil and Jesse's total comments).

Neil and Jesse's devotion to this area was one of several major differences between the dyads (see Figure 36). Neil and Jesse devoted over a third more of their comments to visual arrangement, although directing—visual arrangement was still the second-largest category for Jason and Craig as well. However, in all of their high-frequency comment categories regarding arrangement, Jason and

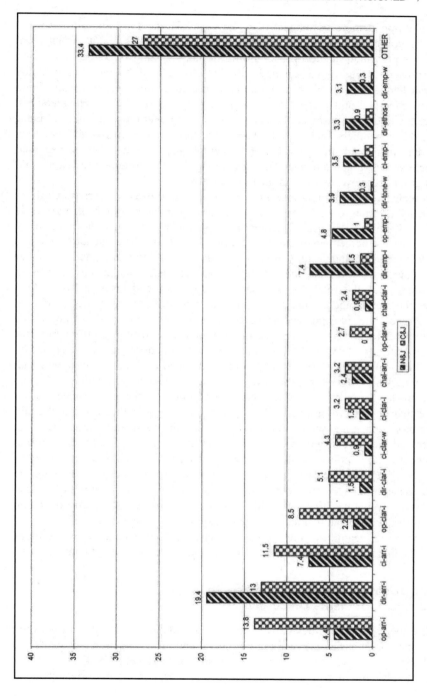

Figure 36. Comparison of dyads' collaborative styles, rhetorical elements, and media—in percentages.

Craig dropped more comments than they used in the final ad. But Neil and Jesse incorporated over 71% of their directive comments about arrangement into ads presented at the tip-ball. From the net-swishing basketball obscuring the mower to the Agavez-owning satisfied clown diver to the excuse-ridden mower-hero ads to the pie chart with the fat slice of fishing, and others, Neil and Jesse developed and presented many more scenarios in the tip-ball meetings. Since their concepts stressed the value of recreation over mowing, in accordance with the consumers interviewed, Jesse and Neil also emphasized more than did the other dyad. In trying to achieve emphasis, Jesse and Neil's discussed camera angles, graph dimensions, and wording that foregrounded recreation and backgrounded mowing, even in the mower-hero ads.

In their largest comment category, Jason and Craig offered nearly three times as many prompts on the topic of visual arrangement as did Neil and Jessie (13.8/4.4%). Craig and Jason offered prompts regarding visual clarity at nearly four times the percentage of Neil and Jesse (8.5/2.2%). The evidence here again shows that Craig and Jason were not only more supportive and passive—rather than *developing* multiple ideas (because of the higher incidence of offering prompts)—but also more focused upon clarity. Craig and Jason had over three times the percentage of directing comments regarding visual clarity (5.1% vs. 1.5%) and twice the percentage of contributing information regarding visual clarity (3.2% vs. 1.5%), over four times as much contributing information for verbal clarity (4.3% vs. 0.9%), prompted each other substantially more regarding the clarity of words (2.7% vs. 0%), and challenged each other more on visual clarity (2.4% vs. 0.9%). And in nearly every clarity category in which comments were made (5 out of 6), the comments contributed to the final, successful ad more than they were dropped. These percentages suggest that Jason and Craig were more concerned with precision. Examining the comments shows that most addressed the split image ads. One comment of Craig's clarified brainstorming procedure at that point: "Visually it's perfect; we've just got to wrap it together somehow." Other comments expressed the cause-effect concept in drawing the chimeras and in succinctly communicating the verbal message on the tabs, such as Craig's "What if .`. . it were . . . like 'the chore,' 'the reward'?" Jason and Craig got further with the ad that they devoted most of their comments to in the session, generating its headlines (however brief), whereas Neil generated his headlines after the initial brainstorming session. Comments addressing clarity helped.

Comparison of Artists and Writers in Rhetorical Elements Discussed

Are there commonalities between the writers of the two dyads and between the artists? Comparing the two writers' verbal and visual rhetorical elements, we find that Craig and Neil both stressed visual arrangement (19.4% vs. 16.4% respectively), but then diverged on their second-most popular rhetorical element, visual clarity for Craig, and visual emphasis for Neil. Craig's visual clarity comments frequently were getting across his opinion to his collaborator and determining the intent of his collaborator's visual comments. He was very careful to communicate effectively—to both listen closely and respond precisely. However, Neil's comments were chiefly about the layout, adding details to the image or changing it to emphasize the concept. Neil's emphasizing comments were more directive; Craig's comments regarding emphasis were mostly contributing information about an advertisement similar to one Jason had suggested.

On the word side (the smaller percentage of each writer's activity), Craig's largest percentage of comments (4.8%) were devoted to clarity, among other things getting to communicating strategy directly in "the chore, the reward." Neil's comments about word matters were most frequently about emphasis (3.1%), ethos (3.1%) and tone (3.5%). Emphasis and ethos referred often to the reasons to believe that the lawn mower would deliver the brand promise, "Agavez gets the job done so that you can move on to other things." Still, these reasons to believe were not put in the comps presented to the tip-ball meeting, diminishing the ads' arguments because the claims were unsupported by facts. A lack of follow-up prevented full actualization of the idea.

Artists Jesse and Jason each also commented by far the most on visual arrangement (17.2% and 22.1% respectively), unsurprising given their purpose of brainstorming ads. Visual clarity was the next largest percentage of Jason's comments (9.8%), reflecting Craig's devotion to that area as well. And visual emphasis was Jesse's second-largest percentage (7.9%), again reflecting the similar distribution of comments of his collaborator. The dyads clearly were heedfully interrelating in this way.

In the verbal medium, artist Jason stressed clarity (5%), the clarity reflecting Craig's similar concern. Jesse made relatively few comments regarding words, but his largest percentages addressed emphasis (2.6%) and ethos (2.6%), the same chief word concerns Neil addressed. But where Neil stressed the reasons to believe, Jesse deemphasized them, particularly when the image was a hero shot of the lawnmower. An example was his suggested headline, "It's got whatever horsepower, as if you cared," addressing part of the brief and the Account Manager's sentiments that the customer "hates mowing." Jesse and Neil's conflict reflected the clashing interests of the client and the customer, a problem Craig had overcome by appealing to the common ground of the two constituencies: the need for the mower to attain the reward of fun.

COMPARISON OF SEQUENCES OF INVENTION IN ARTIST-WRITER TEAMS

Having determined the kind and incidence of verbal-visual rhetorical elements that their composing processes addressed, let us compare other elements of the two dyads' composing processes. Neil and Jesse composed 60% of the time

(45 minutes) that Jason and Craig brainstormed (75 minutes). Jason and Craig had also already had a previous brainstorming session earlier that morning, though brief and generating little content. Neil and Jesse took two more work sessions to come up with concepts they felt were ready to develop for tip-ball.

When we compare the composing moves during the brainstorming session of each of the dyads, we find a major distinction in the amount of on-site preparation done. It is necessary to first review these different moves made, moving numerically from least to most general (see Table 2).

Unlike Neil and Jessie, Craig and Jason did not spend as much time discussing the rhetorical problem, situation, and target audiences, the creative brief not once consulted (see Figure 37). Instead, Craig had focused on the brand promise and translated that into "the product as means to an end." In this way Craig and Jason were like the chess masters in Chase and Simon's study (1973), who focus only on the eight or so pieces that matter most in the middle of a chess match (as cited in Anderson, 2007, pp. 66–67). Because of their narrowed task representation and early success in invention, Craig and Jason were much more production driven—generating, evaluating, and rejecting or elaborating concepts, headlines, tag lines, and images, perhaps because they found a suitable idea quickly and used it as a yardstick to eliminate others quickly. They were much less recursive than the other dyad, their process resembling more the linear composing process of an engineer that Selzer identified (2004, p. 323).

Neil and Jesse, on the other hand, did more preparation recursively throughout the session, consulting the brief when they ran out of ideas. They also looked at all the various parts of the brief rather than focusing on the brand promise (see Figure 38).

Neil and Jesse considered different POS pieces for different environments, while Jason and Craig did most of their POS later: they didn't address POS much until they had a "spot-on" concept, but they made sure that the concept they developed had POS potential. In addressing POS amidst concept generating, Neil and Jesse did not focus on solving the problem of simultaneously addressing the disparate audiences of client and customer. They got ahead of themselves a bit. On the other hand, they did address the real retail situation. For example, they briefly considered but dropped adding fake boxes to the inventory on the shelves. These boxes would advertise the lawnmower in the sporting goods or other leisure activity sections. However, Neil vetoed the idea because the retailer MegaWorld would not allow it. Although Craig and Jason's concept was selected to be one of three presented to the client, it did not make the client's final cut because of the split image boxes proposed: one box depicting the bottom half of the man mowing lawns, one box depicting the top of the man golfing. Drawing on long experience with the retailer, the client reasoned that MegaWorld employees would never keep the boxes stacked as desired after the initial setup by an outside team. So it was wise to consider the client-retailer needs. But one also had to placate the internal audience at Heric and the client and consumer; it was difficult

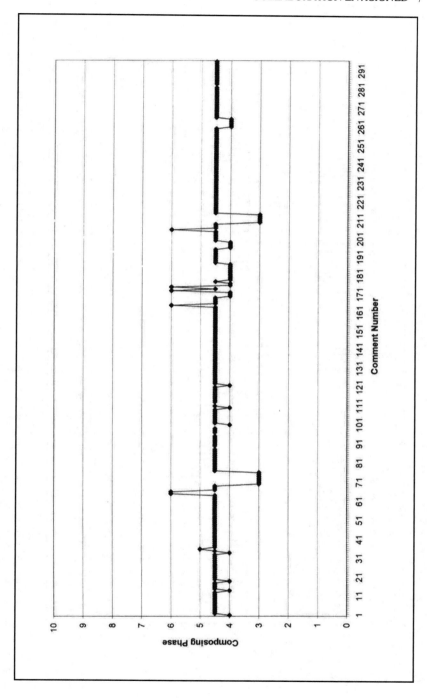

Figure 37. Craig and Jason's composing moves 2/14: brief never consulted.

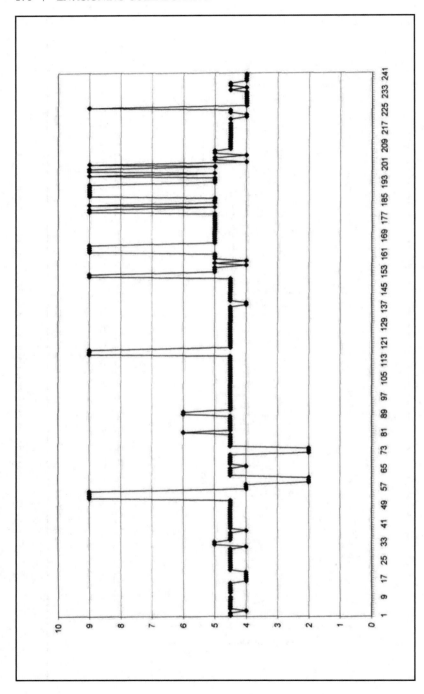

Figure 38. Neil and Jesse's composing moves 2/14: brief increasingly consulted to generate ideas.

for creatives to do it all. Separate studies of writers and of visual artists show that how someone represents the problem to be solved is a significant part of what makes the person creative; successful writers and artists are solving a different problem than less-successful composers (Flower & Hayes, 1994, p. 73). Although not completely different, the problems solved by the two dyads were scarcely alike.

COMPARISON OF COLLABORATION STYLES: ASSERTIVE VS. SUPPORTIVE

How did the artists and writers in the dyads manage the collaboration? Was each person more supportive (offering prompts and contributing information) or assertive (challenging and directing)? Did anyone dominate? Neil and Jesse had a much higher number of assertive comments on average per concept than did Jason and Craig: 7.62 assertive comments per new concept vs. 3.26. Of Neil and Jesse's comments, 59% were assertive, compared with 37.6% of Jason and Craig's. Offering prompts was clearly much more of Craig and Jason's approach than Neil and Jesse's. Jason offered nearly twice as many prompts as Jesse (19.5% of his dyad vs. 10.5%), and Craig nearly tripled the number of Neil's prompts (15.1% of his dyad vs. 5.7%).

Copywriter Neil's largest number of visual comments fell into the category of directing (19%), whereas writer Craig's was offering prompts (13%). Craig had roughly half the percentage of directive comments as Neil, who had a little over a fourth of the offering prompt visual comments of Craig. Neil was also substantially more directive verbally than Craig (6.8% vs. 3.6%). The artists had the same visual move preferences as their teammates, although less pronounced. Jason offered prompts 15.9% of the time, almost twice as often as Jesse (8.7%). Jesse directed in 16.2% of his comments, as opposed to Jason's 10.6%. One might have suspected that the dyads would have one director and one prompt offerer each; that would seem a better ecology. But Jason and Craig *generated* more concepts, requiring supportiveness to allow birth. Neil and Jesse *developed* more concepts, so they needed to direct the development. In word development, we again see Jason being much more supportive (5.8% sppt. vs. 1.3% asrt.), while Jesse was more assertive (3% sppt. vs. 6.3% asrt.).

Thus, the differences are much more along dyadic lines than functional roles. Because assertive comments were content comments, this incidence would be expected since Neil and Jesse presented numerous ads in the tip-ball, but Jason and Craig only one concept. Still, Jason and Craig made the largest number of assertive comments (challenging and directing) on any single concept: the chore-reward had 60 assertive comments, whereas 23 assertive comments were the largest concentration for Neil and Jesse in the failed tree-cloud concept. These results thus do not indicate that Jason and Craig were more supportive in their winning concept, though they may have been in others that they did not feel would go anywhere. The point seems to be that the more commitment, the more the feeling you're on a roll creatively, the more assertive you get.

DYADIC SELF-EVALUATION

Comparison of Dropped Comments by the Dyads

We find that the comments that the dyads ultimately decided not to use in advertisements presented in the evaluation meeting reflected their different approaches outlined above. Artist Jesse more than doubled the percentage of dropped directives of artist Jason. Neil had over 33% more dropped directives than Craig. This outcome implies that Neil and Jesse did more wasted directing, even by their own criteria. Jason and Craig were more supportive in a way discussed below.

The difference in dropped challenging comments between the two groups isn't much: 8.8% Neil and Jesse challenging vs. 7.4% Jason and Craig. Jesse, in the few times he challenged, once stopped the rehashing of an ad they had done in a previous campaign, but otherwise did not challenge to dismiss ineffective concepts. Neil did challenge to dismiss some dropped ideas: he said using two pie charts to show the priorities of recreation over mowing was too busy, that the shot of a person wearing golf shoes running a tractor mower was "kind of 'so what,'" dismissed by faint acknowledgment the facetious inversion idea— was silent after his "uh-huh." He also dismissed two seemingly infeasible POS ideas. Thus Neal was more potent in his challenges, one of the ways he was more dominant in the dyad.

This brings us to differences in dropped supportive vs. assertive comments between the two. When we look at the dropped assertive comments, we find that Neil and Jesse's percentage is 41.2%, a hefty percentage of their total comments, while Jason and Craig's is substantially less at 24.8%. But in supportive dropped comments, Jason and Craig lead (36.8% vs. 27.6%). These comments supported the invention of numerous slightly developed, abandoned concepts.

Comparing writers with artists produces additional patterns of behavior. Writers had substantially more dropped directive comments (29.4% of writers' total comments vs. 18.9% of artists' total comments). Craig's dropped comments addressed concepts (long copy creating a visual maze) and details of the visuals (e.g., a person at a football game having a stadium cup, in the top half of a split ad). Jason's were the same. Jesse and Neil's, along with the above topics, occasionally were headlines.

Did the artists or writers offer more supportive dropped comments? While the writers made more directive dropped comments, the artists led dropped supportive comments, 20% to 12.8% for the writers. More challenges from the artists might have resulted in more quality material.

Comparison of Dyad's Percentages of Dropped vs. Used Comments: Efficiency of Comments

Although they produced a "finalist" and were longstanding national- and international-award-winning creatives, because Neil and Jesse did not produce an ad that was shown to the client, one could say that all of their comments were unsuccessful in this particular instance. However, it is also instructive to look at how many of their comments addressed ads they ultimately presented at the tip-ball. This number tells us how efficient their process was by their own expert judgment. The percentages we find indicate that there may be substantial room for increased efficiency in dyadic verbal-visual invention regarding ads.

Neil and Jesse had a very similar percentage of retained comments that each contributed to the team (14.5% and 14%, respectively). Craig and Jason's percentages were a little higher and more diverse (18.2% and 20.2%, respectively). Neil and Jesse were clearly more of a divergent- rather than convergent-thinking-dominant dyad, keeping alternatives open by developing several concepts instead of one and by suggesting things initially in the brainstorming session they later cut.

Regarding dropped comments contributed during the session, Neil and Jesse had a higher percentage (38.9% vs. 32.6%, respectively) vs. Craig and Jason (29.8% vs. 31.8%, respectively), showing their divergent rather than convergent character, at least in what they initially brainstormed. Neil, although a dominant force in many ways, also had the largest percentage of discards. Was that because Jason and Craig paused more before they spoke? Did they edit their oral contributions more before saying them?

THE PAUSE THAT REFRESHES AND OTHER VARIETIES: COMPARISON OF PAUSES IN THE DYADIC COMPOSING PROCESSES

Because the lengths of the sessions of the dyads were substantially different, for the sake of comparison, the frequency of pauses was calculated rather than just the total number of pauses. Pauses were defined as no speaking for over 9 seconds. Neil and Jesse paused on average every 2.64 minutes, while Jason and Craig's average was once every 2.5 minutes, so Jason and Craig paused 9.5% more frequently. However, Neil and Jesse paused longer and perhaps mulled over more what they would say next in those instances, an average of 36.25 seconds per pause, as opposed to 27 seconds per pause for Jason and Craig.

Neil and Jesse paused 17 times compared with Jason and Craig's 30, about 57% of the latter's number. This percentage is similar to Neil and Jesse's percentage of Jason and Craig's minutes in session 45/75, that is, 60%. So the relative number of pauses wasn't much different. It thus does not appear on the surface that Jason and Craig had fewer dropped comments because they thought silently more and edited themselves more before they spoke. What each dyad used pauses for, however, was much different (see Figure 39).

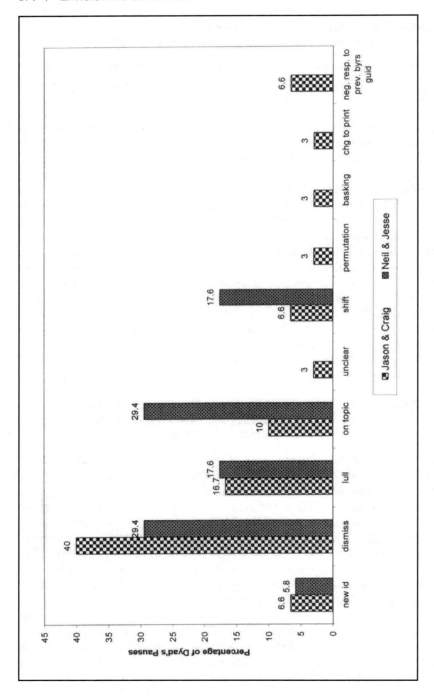

Figure 39. Comparison of pause functions, Neil and Jesse, Jason and Craig. 2/14.

To dismiss a just-mentioned concept, Jason and Craig used the pause slightly more than 25% more often (fully 40% of all their pauses). Here, the dyad would be discussing the idea, then one would not respond, so the idea died. Sometimes one would disapprove of the concept, and the pause would be the "period" punctuating the verdict. Their need to dismiss was much greater because they had nearly twice as many concepts (23/13) and only developed one of their 23 (4.3%), as opposed to Jesse and Neal developing 7 of 13 (53.8%). However, Jason and Craig could have used rejection, even squelching to dismiss concepts; advantages of the justified pause are proposer saves face, and dismisser avoids risk of argument and defeat due to poorly articulated comments, especially in one's own field.

Such dismissing pauses were also crucial for Neil and Jesse, along with thinking silently while continuing to develop a topic. These two categories were their most frequent use of pauses (29.4% each). One might expect a high incidence of pausing amidst concept development because the dyad developed over half of their ideas. Developing the ideas required more constrained, rigorous thinking than did generating preliminary premise after preliminary premise. Still, because Jason and Craig developed one topic much further than any other topic of the two sessions was developed, along with one other on-topic pause, they had two on-topic pauses while developing the split image campaign. One occurred just before Craig suggested "chore, reward" for the tabs, clearly a pregnant, incubative pause.

Other relatively large sources of Jesse and Neil's pauses (for each category, 17.6% of their pauses) were a lull in which they could not generate an idea, and pauses before the topic shifted to a previous topic or different subject. For Craig and Jason, the lull was also a major source of pauses—the second-most frequent. We could expect this lull because Jason and Craig were uncertain whether they should invent any more after they developed the chore-reward concept, because they thought only one strong concept of theirs would be used. However, the dyad told me before they started that I might be observing them while they stared at the floor for extended periods—they typically had some long pauses in their collaborations.

We can see where the pauses fell in the following line graphs (see Figures 40 and 41). The x-axis is the comment number in its sequence.[4] In Jason and Craig's first 193 comments, in the main the comments spent developing the chore-reward concept, there were 14 pauses; in the concluding 104 comments, there were 16 pauses. So although the last part of the session was a little more than half as long (54%) as the first part, it had 114% of the number of pauses in

---

[4] Comment number was chosen rather than time because comment number shows semantically where the pause fell: how many thought units were between each pause. Although a cell is demarked "pause," the pause is actually after the marked cell. This arrangement keeps the comment numbers accurate.

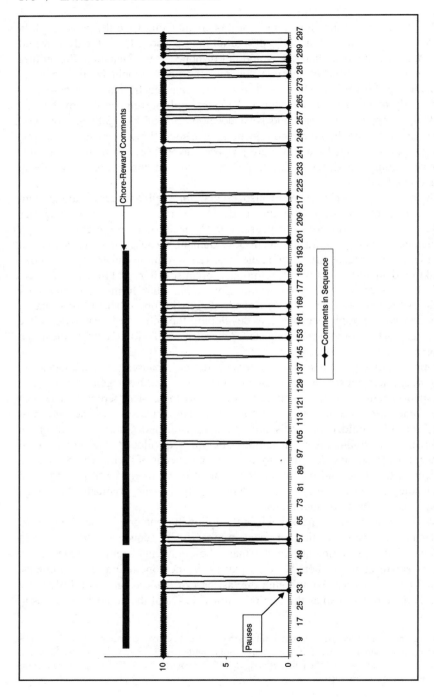

Figure 40. Location of pauses in sequence of comments: Craig and Jason, 2/14.

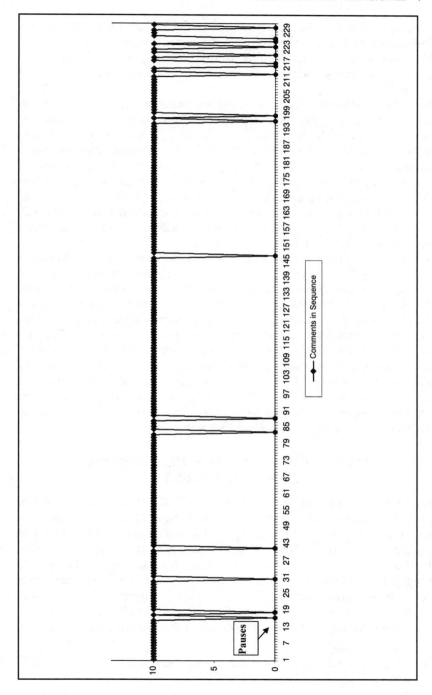

Figure 41. Location of pauses in sequence of comments: Neil and Jesse, 2/14.

the first part. So the pauses were more concentrated where the dyad generated different concepts, less frequent when they developed one good idea.

With Neil and Jesse, nearly half the pauses (7/17, 47%) occurred in the last 8.7% of the comments, so in essence, they paused the most when the winds of invention died down.

An analogy was useful to Hayes in describing pauses during a writing protocol: "Occasionally, the porpoise [book says purpose] reveals itself by breaking the surface of the sea. Its brief surfacings are like the glimpses of the underlying mental processes, which the protocol affords us. Between surfacings, the mental processes run silent, run deep" (Hayes, 1989, p. 81). In our case, given the abundant dialogue of the creatives, focusing upon their pauses during collaboration is more like observing a diving duck that occasionally dives under the water to fish for the prey/idea. Other times, the duck dives underwater to cool off, the equivalent of the lull. Sometimes it "ducks" under to avoid conflict (being eaten): that is the dismissal pause—saving face.

Dismissal pauses explain a seeming contradiction in the composing pattern of Jason and Craig. It is counterintuitive that the offering prompts and contributing information champions would also be the elaboration and evaluation champions. One would think the more assertive dyad would be more evaluative. But Jason and Craig just let the concepts go, they did not overtly reject many. After the pivot, they had a yardstick (the split image concept), and it wasn't difficult for them to apply it. The rules of the system of creativity as they understood them were that you could only win in one good campaign. So they were very judging afterwards. They came up with many other ideas, but dismissal pauses frequently followed because as the concepts initially appeared, they did not measure up. This behavior underscores Jason and Craig's evaluativeness. They were directive on the split-image ad but not on inferior concepts.

DYADS' CONFLICT MANAGEMENT BEYOND DISMISSAL PAUSES

Regarding overt conflict, there were not large differences in the amount of conflict in the two dyads: Neil and Jesse challenged in 11.8% of their total dyadic comments; Jason and Craig, 10.1%. The older dyad's increased conflict dispels the hypothesis that Neil and Jesse's long professional association with each other had led to complacency.[5] Burnett (1991) found that writing groups that engaged in constructive conflict were more productive than those that didn't; however, this outcome was not the case with our subjects in this instance. When we consider conflict differences between functional roles, we find the artists challenged substantially less (3.9%, 3.8%) than the writers (7.9%, 6.3%);

---

[5] See Weick and Roberts' (1993) discussion of development of group mind vs. development of group.

given the higher incidence of visual comments, this difference may well be, as noted above, because writers thought more visually than artists did verbally.

Beyond resolving conflicts in their interaction, was there any difference in the way the dyads resolved conflicting interests of key audiences of the campaign? By looking for commonalities and addressing them, Jason and Craig were applying a win-win conflict-resolution strategy. On the other hand, by trying to appeal partially to the conflicting interests of the two audiences, Neil and Jesse applied a compromise approach. Surrealism allows the win-win conflict style to be applied regarding the clashing interests of customer and client because the authors could show the client's product (mower) and customer's recreation (top half of teeing golfer and fairway of the golf course). From a visual standpoint, joining the formal lines tricks the eye and mind into closure (in gestalt sense) initially. After perception has occurred, reason engages, showing the impossibility of the combination, but the cultural and advertising visual tradition of surrealism (particularly of Escher, and Magritte for both former and latter) provides both a schema and a visual *raison d'être* (Toulmin's warrant, 2004) that allows us to accommodate the message delivered by this otherwise bizarre image.[6]

On the other hand, Neil and Jesse's conflict style of compromise/negotiation did not work because there was no visual integration of the opposing images of recreation and work. When Jesse brought out the mower more from behind the golf ball, the result was visual busyness. The superiority of Jason and Craig's split image is its visual integration. It would appear, then, in verbal-visual compositions, that visual integration is just as important as any other kind of conceptual integration (e.g., verbal, verbal-visual, semantic). One of the most successful popular artists, Norman Rockwell, used symbols of diverse American audiences and avoided details that would have alienated any audience. In this way, he fostered audience identification with his work (Kenney, 2004, p. 333). The split image is both formally integrated and culturally integrated because of the cultural tradition of surrealism that in the 1960s entered the popular culture through popular and commercial art such as album covers. Jesse did not use an artistic tradition that gave him integrative visual license. In fact, a pop art tradition—exemplified in Warhol's Campbell's Soup can icons—was used that stressed modernist design rules of avoiding busy images and of having a dominant visual, blocking his attempt to appeal to both customer and client in a more complex image. Although he knew that the client and Chief Creative Officer wanted to show the mower, amid other pressing obligations, he ignored this knowledge.

Ultimately, Jason and Craig's solution for integrating the disparate audience interests did not prevail either. The inability to guarantee a split image formed by

---

[6] A more recent rendition of the "split ad" genre can be seen in the 2007 Gore-Tex multi-million dollar global marketing campaign in which humans meld seamlessly into animals.

adjoining boxes, along with the avant-garde shockingness of surrealism contributed to the client's eliminating the split image in the final cut. The client was not sure Spanish and French language speakers would understand the chimerical image. It is not certain whether Agavez decision makers were aware that Spain and France are where surrealism began and flourished. But whether the client was aware of this or not, the client's perception and belief is what determined whether this creative work was published.

EFFICIENT PRINCIPLES OF CONCEPT INVENTION: VERBAL-VISUAL TOPOI

Beyond incubative pauses, focusing on the brand promise, and "thinking with a pencil," what were productive techniques of generating verbal-visual concepts? After viewing and analyzing the particulars of the collaborative processes of the artist-and-writer teams, we found several principles employed, most of which are topoi (topics or sites of invention) of classical rhetoric. As Corbett notes, "the human mind . . . does think about particular things, but its constant tendency is to rise above the particulars and to abstract, to generalize, to classify, to analyze, and to synthesize. The topics represented the system that the classical rhetoricians built upon this tendency of the human mind" (1990, p. 95).

Of course, a premature enactment of these principles, before thorough scrutiny of the rhetorical situation and determination of applicability of its elements, is not effective, even if the principles themselves are excellent tools. However, despite their premature application due to a combination of circumstances, such principles are worth studying in order to teach or practice verbal-visual composing successfully, just as chess players benefit from studying the sequences of moves of chess masters. Neil and Jesse extensively used the classical rhetorical topic of contrast, contrasting the benefit and product in over half of their ads, including the icon campaign. Contrast was used to get attention, that is, "selecting something to process" (McQuarrie & Mick, 2003, p. 203). Contrast was used in both verbally and visually initiated ads. Sometimes the contrast was between the words and the picture ("Another Satisfied Agavez Owner"), sometimes the contrast was between two things in the picture. The attention gained by the contrast, however, sometimes worked against the campaigns because of the product and benefit's disparity. The humorous and visual emphasis on recreation distracted the reader from the product. Jason and Craig used contrast exclusively in a little over a tenth of their ads, mainly to create attention in visual pyrotechnics such as shredded pages. Similarity, another classical topic, was used to spell and point out analogous relationships for a little over 7% of Jason and Craig's comments. Given the prominence of contrast and similarity as generative principles for over 2,300 years, it is not surprising that over three-fourths (75.8%) of generative comments employed these principles.

At 17% of the total generative principle comments, causation was the last prominent principle, although only Jason and Craig used it. But it combined with the split image (similarity-contrast) to generate the only winning concept of the dyads. Causation, related by the words on the tabs and the split image in a complementary relationship, lucidly conveyed the brand strategy by showing the product as means to the desired end of the benefit. The least-used principles were obversion and facetious obversion. Facetious obversion, or reverse psychology, accounted for 4% of the total comments. This approach to persuasion is also old if not ancient, dating at least to Tom Sawyer's whitewashing of the board fence and Br'er Rabbit's pleas not to be thrown into the briar patch. Obversion (the other side of the coin) was a technique Neil used frequently in general, although it accounted for 2% of the total generative principle comments.

We can add to these topoi articulated in discursive language a *layout* principle that also serves as a topic or site of invention: what Neil called "the split thing." The chimerical fusion of opposites is a visual pattern and tradition that can be used in attention-getting ways to juxtapose seeming opposites to dramatize an underlying relationship between the two. When we combine the comments of both dyads, we find this fusion of similarity/contrast the largest category (40.6%). The surreal appearance of products of this principle seemed to cause these professionals to use it extensively. Just as our dreams may juxtapose out-of-context objects in a world that feels real, the continuous visual lines visually integrate disparate objects in ways that startle and pique curiosity, thus motivating the viewer to read the words selling the product. It is no surprise that surrealistic images have been widely used in ad campaigns.

All of the generative principles of verbal-visual invention employed by Jason and Craig would be found in two classical common topics, as Corbett arrays them (1990, p. 97), comparison (similarity and difference) and relationship (cause and effect). One would expect that the creatives would use common topics because these limited number of argumentative principles are suitable for any occasion or kind of speech (Corbett, 1990, p. 24), rather than specialized topics useful for only one kind of discourse. The current study shows that these common topics not only transcend the boundaries of discourse types (e.g., epideictic, deliberative, and forensic) but also the specialized limitations of visual, spoken, and written media.

For Neil and Jesse, in addition to the 201 comments involving generative principles, there were 28 (13.9%) other comments devoted to elaboration or procedural or other support matters. Comments involving generative principles dominated the meeting. By contrast, for Craig and Jason, comments involving generative principles constituted 76.7% of the comments in the session. The remaining 23.3% were devoted to procedural comments or to elaboration—advice on developing the split image layout. Here we see that while Neil and Jesse spent most of their session in generation, Craig and Jason moved beyond invention into drafting in the Flower-Hayes (1981) composing process model. In the Csikszentmihalyi creative process model, Jason and Craig moved more from insight through evaluation into elaboration. Neil and Jesse moved from insight back into preparation, looking at the brief several times. Because Jason and Craig integrated the disparate audiences and purposes in their rhetorical problem, they were able to anchor visual concepts in the strategy more quickly. Because of convergent-dominant thinking, they quickly dispensed with less-immediately effective concepts and developed their cometary winner.

AUDIENCE ANALYSIS BY DYADS, ARTISTS, AND WRITERS

Another way the dyads' approaches contrasted regarded audience. As Figure 42 shows, though separated in the visual for the sake of comparison by individual role, each dyad stressed a different audience configuration. There was much more similarity within the dyad in terms of audience addressed than there was between the two artists and the two writers.

Where Neil used schema (organizing principles such as similarity, contrast, etc.) to generate ideas to try to meet the strategy, Craig translated strategy *into* an organizing principle: "means to an end," then invented ads that used/illustrated that principle. This more focused, integrated invention subsequently allowed the dyad to have a more convergent than divergent process. On the other hand, Jesse and Neil trusted more in the large-group component of the creative system and strove to include viable ideas that might be further developed by others. In their dedication to alternatives and resistance of closure, as well as their inability in this case to come up with a clear winner, they were less frequently decisive in their evaluation stage. It may be that a convergent-dominant mentality is best for dyads composing alone. But for dyads who feed into large-group collaboration, a divergent-dominant mentality fosters more input from more people. Depending upon who are in the dyads and the large groups, either approach could be best.

MINDFULNESS IN THE COLLABORATIVE EFFORTS

Regardless of their decision-making approach, the most successful teams are those that stay mindful, heedfully interrelating regarding a common, mindful, accurate[7] task representation (Asch, 1952; Cross, 2001; Weick & Roberts, 1993; Weick & Sutcliffe, 2006). If the creative brief, which was largely responsible for the task representation in the processes we are examining, is composed accurately, it would appear that a team—whether the large group or dyad—that adhered most closely to the brief would be most successful. But adherence may

---

[7] Perfect objectivity is an unattainable ideal, but through careful analysis of data, using appropriate methods, we can be closer to it and thus have a better opportunity to be more effective.

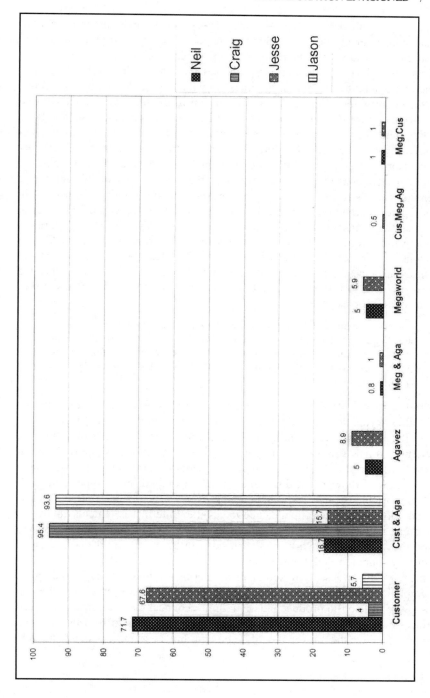

Figure 42. Comparison of audience preferences by artist, writer.

not be easy, particularly if the brief includes numerous and sometimes contradictory consumer attitudes and client preferences that must be then translated
verbally and visually into a concise, coherent, persuasive message.

How mindful were the composing processes and some of the resultant products
of the two dyadic teams, and in their case to what degree did the brief facilitate
heedful interrelation? The brief [8] was clear and in the main very effective, but
there were a few discrepancies between the brief as presented in the Brief
Meeting and the qualitative research, seemingly because the research itself
reported somewhat conflicting attitudes. Although the research reported prospective consumers seeing grass cutting as a "comfortable escape," it also suggested
that prospective consumers just wanted to get the job over with and forget it. The
latter view was stressed in the oral presentation of the written brief where, in
the struggle to come up with a coherent strategy from this contradictory data,
it was said the consumers "hate to mow their lawns." Also, the Brief Meeting's
stressing John Goodman's character in *Roseanne* as representative of the Agavez
owner helped to exclude women as an audience in at least one ad in a campaign.

These instances, like Jesse and Neil not showing the mower, evinced a
typical problem in instantiating and articulating either text goals or text itself,
as Flower and Hayes note:

> The best instantiation of a goal or the best representation in prose is the
> one that is sensitive to the largest number of constraints. But when the
> competition among these constraints is too fierce or attention is too
> limited, writers may simply ignore some of what they know. Instantiation is
> a choice. (1984, p. 155)

Mindful of the brief and of the other research, Neil and Jesse experienced
difficulties trying to focus on the capacity of the product—on functionality,
simplicity, price, features—and to focus on the recreation activities the consumer
would move on to afterwards to forget the mowing. Also, brief-supported contradictions arose in the dyad's disparaging mowing yet providing hero or beauty
shots of the lawnmower. The disparaging headline in loud yellow type contradicts
the "comfortable escape" view of mowing even as the candy-apple-red, laser-
painted, mower-dominant image encourages it. While these elements contradict
each other, they also reflect the conflicting attitudes of various customers. Such a
mixed message did not work in what needed to be a unified ad that presented
a mutually supportive relationship between product and benefit.

This relationship Jesse and Neil planned to bring out in other ads, including the
bar graph, icon, and line graph. There, although Neil and Jesse stressed the benefit
but showed little or no product and often didn't connect the relationship between
product and benefit, the greeking used to place hold was to be filled in with
reasons to believe the mower should be bought; however, they were not filled in

---

[8] See the brief in Chapter 2.

for the presentation. Thus, Neil in his copy, was not so much erroneous as he was incomplete. Because his message was less direct ("Lawns are our life, not yours. Agavez makes life easier"), that incompleteness was a fatal flaw: the visual stresses the benefit, and the visual is already stronger than the verbal. Evidence or data in Toulmin's (2004) parlance (e.g., 2-year warranty, Briggs and Stratton engine) was needed to support Neil and Jesse's claim that Agavez made life easier (presumably, by getting mowing over quickly), resolving the seeming opposition of mower-product and recreation benefit.

To be sure, in the other dyad, Craig called lawn mowing a "necessary evil," a sentiment reflected in the tag, "Get it over with." But mowing was more central because it was necessary to get to the fun. Craig was more concerned with the relationship between the topics of mowers and recreation, with the links instead of just concerned the nodes, as can be seen in the cognitive map below (Figure 43).

During the collaboration, Craig seemed to see the job of copywriter as clarifying the relationship between mowers and fun. When Jason whimsically suggested inverting the relationship, Craig firmly held to this idea, mindfully adhering to the brief and his resolution of conflicting consumer attitudes. Furthermore,

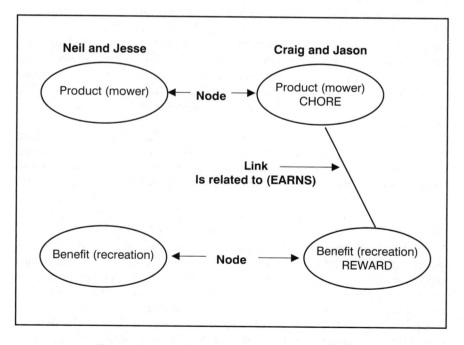

Figure 43. Linked nodes relate product to benefit;
unlinked nodes do not.

in uniting product and recreation visually, Jason and Craig communicate the "mowing as comfortable escape" perception of some customers. While one's legs propelled the mower into the grass, one's mind could be on the golf course. Thus the split image appealed to a greater number of audience attitudes than did either Neil and Jesse or the brief and its explanatory meeting. Jason and Craig in focusing on commonalities, pulled together more elements of the rhetorical situation. Neil and Jesse either based their composing routines on conflicting elements or were unable to complete intended more comprehensive arguments by the deadline.

Verbal-Visual Mindfulness

In the chore/reward ads, the unity begins in the image with the continuity of the lines, which create a closed, dominant figure—a "good gestalt" (Schriver, 1997, p. 316)—but upon further inspection, a surreal image that startles because of its wholeness composed by the juxtaposition of seemingly opposing elements (work and play). It is a verbal-visual oxymoron in the positive sense of that term, more than just mishmash because of the tabbed words "chore" and "reward." Classical rhetoric tells us the verbal figure of oxymoron, if apt and fresh, startles by joining contradictions, displaying in its creator the ability to see similarities, what Aristotle felt was a special sign of genius (Corbett, 1990, p. 456). The similarities found between the contradictory elements of work and play are that in the ethic of the "hard-working" audience described in the brief: work earns play such as golf, chores bring their reward. Both are central, interrelated elements of a life. The chore-reward concept provides an organizing principle that integrates normally contradictory material that appeals to disparate audiences of the ad.

Initially, the figure is an oxymoron and has that effect. But when we unpack it, it is also a typified story of a chore followed by a reward. In its compression, it is elliptical, like the classical scheme of omission, ellipsis. As Kress (2006) has noted, the questions we ask visual narratives are "what else is there?" (We fill in the ellipsis.) and "what is the relation of things?" (We determine cause-effect.). So this ad entails questions that the reader answers, enhancing reader pleasure, which is immediately associated with the product.

In this case of verbal-visual collaboration, mindfulness takes into account all aspects, including the client's desired position of the mower and the visual aspects; there is visual positioning that is tied centrally to psychological positioning. Successful psychological positioning is to have the consumer remember the product with the attributes the target market believes are desirable. As Jason noted the day after the chore-reward concept was invented, "What we're showing in that [layout] that we like better: you got your product there, and you get to see an instant reward or benefit to having a product" (TR 81). This visual presence was very important. As noted above, imagination comes from the word "image." Our mind thinks and creates in images as much as words. If we put the mower out of the way visually, we're positioning the mower out of the readers' mind. This isn't going to allow the consumer to remember the product in a marketplace crowded with competitors. Perelman and Olbrechts-Tyteca note (1971, pp. 116–118) that presence (the extent to which a favorable object or concept is foremost in the consciousness of the audience members) leads to greater persuasiveness. This concept comes from studies of visual perception by Piaget, particularly suggesting the importance of visual presence.

Mindfulness in design thus includes displaying (a) all the key components together (b) in the right relationship—verbal relationship and visual relationship. Part of design in this case is remembering the purpose of trying to sell a product. In the Agavez case, that meant talking about the activities but making sure the audiences saw the mower, saw that it had what the consumer wanted on it, and saw a readily identifiable brand.

In print ad design, mindfulness is also inventing concepts as print ads that can be "blown out" into messages in different media for an integrated marketing campaign. In such a campaign, many or all possible media are used. The kind of conceptual thinking needed is similar to that of Ellul's description of the propagandist's approach in this regard, although Ellul does not consider advertising propaganda: because one medium is better able to deliver one aspect of the message and another, another, all must be used. "The propagandist," Ellul notes, "uses a keyboard and creates a symphony" (1965, p. 10). Mindfulness involves considering how the overall message will be delivered by multiple media. Some of the public relations managers at Heric complained that PR had not been factored into the mix early enough. Decisions need to be made regarding which part of the message goes in which medium, and which constituencies in the audience each medium reaches. For more details on the construction of multiple media campaigns, see Cross (1994c).

Was the task representation for the dyads (the creative brief) an effective preparation? It was to Jason and Craig, who identified the commonalities amidst the disparities. Craig and Jason did not look at the brief during the meeting. They had internalized it and added to it in determining the link between audiences. Perhaps the problem to the creatives who followed the brief more literally was in the wording "more important things in life" than mowing. Although lawn mowing is not sufficient for the good life for lawn owners, it is necessary, so it is vitally important. The Brief Meeting presentation also encouraged Neil and Jesse's response because it was stated that potential customers hate mowing their lawns, an opinion expressed in the qualitative research that conflicted with the mowing-as-a-comfortable-escape attitude mentioned elsewhere by the same research.

Looking at all dyads that pitched ads in the Agavez tip-balls, one finds that complete adherence to the brief did not necessarily spell success. After including all ads created in the preparation for the Agavez pitch (71 ads) and sorting by brief attributes appealed to, I found only little more than half of the winners (54.5%) were in the top 11 of ads with most brief attributes. (I chose the top 11 because 11 ads won.) Meeting the highest quantity of brief attributes was not the greatest determining factor. The winners, however, differed from the average in incidence of certain audience attributes: 100% of winners delivered the brand promise as opposed to 77.5% of the entire field and 73.33% of the losers. Where 94.5% of the ads of the winners showed the mower (partial showings got less than whole credit), 61.33% of the losing ads did so, and 66.47% of the entire field. Over half of the winners included the 2-year warranty (55%), while few of the losers did (10%). Half of the winners mentioned the Briggs and Stratton engine, compared with 6.7% of the losers. To the judges, clearly describing the product and presenting it as the effective means to an end, as well as perceived POS capability, mattered much more than covering all audience attributes described in the brief.

Mindfulness thus was not found only within the parameters of the brief. The Chief Creative Officer's "Neighbors" ad to an extent transgressed the client's goals, expressed in the brief, in showing Agavez as less expensive than another mower of its same class. But at the time, Agavez was relatively inexpensive, and that was a stronger selling point than claims of quality without exception in some of the other ads: One can't get mowing over with if the machine is recalled to repair a defect (as Agavez and nearly all other mowers including many more expensive were during that era) or if it breaks. As one of the three campaigns pitched to the client, the "Neighbors" campaign still gave the client the option of using a convincing, completely accurate selling point, even against Agavez' wishes.

Was Craig's inclusion of the woman mower the result of inattentiveness, since the brief stipulated a predominantly male audience and the Brief Meeting stressed the character best representing the target audience was John Goodman? Craig's inclusion acknowledged that the customer could be single, single mother, or other lawn mowing female homeowners. Even if the single mothers' average income was at that point $7,000 below the target household income, including marginalized audiences, alerting them about a product that they could afford better than others was ethical as long as the product was dependable. Also, as Jason pointed out, mixing power mowing and children in the way Craig advocated was not advisable from an ethical or emotional perspective. For all reliable products, given the good quality and low price of most Agavez mowers, including sometimes-marginalized audiences was advisable, as the split image golf ad did by including an African American subject, if surrealistically, on Caucasian legs.

Of course, the brief should not be deviated from except where it is not the best plan. In most ways, the Agavez brief written by the Account Manager was an excellent plan. It clearly stated reasons to believe, giving evidence for many claims made. It clearly discussed the client's marketing and media strategy, emphasizing the client's wish to integrate POS into the brand strategy and to work with an agency that did excellent in-store advertising. It stressed the client's perception that Heric's primary weakness was an inability to do in-store integrated POS. It concisely relayed demographic information about the customers, including age range, whether they owned a home or not, education, household income range, general vocations. It painted a detailed psychographic portrait of the biggest customer, addressing values, attitudes, lawn mowing habits, and recreational priorities.

It also associated product with some higher priorities of the customer in a cause-effect relationship (Agavez lawn mowers get the job done without a fuss so you can move on to the more important things in life. . .). Although not in all cases, this claim of reliability was still in nearly all cases true and was backed by the best warranty in the business.

Heric won the Agavez account with this brief. But the most mindful creatives supplemented it. This independent judgment is needed for complete mindfulness to avoid the danger of groupthink, a thought pattern of "self-censorship of deviations, doubts, and counterarguments" (Janis, 1982, p. 175; cited in Weick & Roberts, 1993).[9] For example, one might rigidly adhere to an unethical plan— an action that, although condoned by the group, does not fairly address its environment. One may argue that ethical concerns are impractical or optional, but as was noted at the Association for Business Communication International Convention,[10] Enron proved that ethics is not pointless ruminating on bromides. Ethics can keep people out of jail, an eminently practical concern. Mindfulness thus needs to address ethos, in Quintilian's sense of the good/ethical person speaking well; one must attend to ethical issues of the task in the moment, as well as the emotional dimension (e.g., audience reaction) and the logic of the task. Mindfulness in collaboration is not just coordinated, focused thought and activity, but coordinated, *ethical* thought that effectively responds to all relevant dimensions of its context.

One aspect of the entire context is the natural environment. The Agavez mowers, like all things produced by human beings, had strengths and weaknesses. On the one hand, they had the best warranty in the business and long-lived engines. On the other hand, their "dirt cheap" mower—just one model of the numerous kinds of mowers they sold—was considered "disposable" and might not last more than the warranty. Like many manufacturers, Agavez was under tremendous pressure to sell at the low prices of big box discount retailers to meet

---

[9] Groupthink is disputed by Aldag and Fuller (1993), Fuller and Aldag (1998), and some others. Other researchers believe the concept has even wider applicability (e.g., Baron, 2005). But all conclude there is not enough research to prove or disprove it. Elements of the U.S. government decision process involving "Iraqi weapons of mass destruction" suggests ongoing applicability.

[10] Author unidentifiable after search of conference notes and query to Bizcom, The Association for Business Communication list serve.

the low price points dictated by these retailers. Particularly stressed could be the "opening price point," loss leader products that open the door to the line of products of the brand. Many manufacturers responded by devaluing the brand, decreasing quality (e.g., lowering the fiber count in t-shirts) to also be able to decrease price. But the Agavez mowers nearly entirely had fair-to-excellent ratings in *Consumer Reports*. And the rhetorical strategy was also "green" in that it promoted utility but not an "outdoing the Joneses with a designer mower" mentality that was promoted by high-end mowers. The advertising agency did not address green issues directly, but the brief's reasons to believe and the no-nonsense portrayal of the task the product discouraged overconsumption.

Although risky, it would have been beneficial to the agency to mention to the client the value of improving quality on their lowest-end mower to not only do the right thing but also be able to strengthen the ethical and in many cases commercial appeal of the product. Also, more product interrogation (De Pelsmaker et al., 2001, p. 271), for example, being cognizant of the *Consumer Reports* ratings of the products, would have been nearly entirely a strategic advantage as well as an ethical advantage for the creatives we have scrutinized. They would have been aware of more of Agavez' strengths compared with other mowers and would have reduced the possibility of misleading claims.

Mindfulness addresses the management of the large-group composing process in another way as well. As Hutchins notes, "When the labor that is distributed is cognitive labor, the system involves the distribution of two kinds of work: the cognition that is the task and the cognition that governs the coordination of the elements of the task" (1995, p. 176). After establishing the rhetorical problem to be solved, managers allocate the resources—human and otherwise—to solve it. If the creatives on the project are given so much work in a short time frame that it repeatedly shortens their needed sleep, this demand interferes with their morale, and in a larger sense, human rights. It also interferes with their cognition while doing the task. Although the Chief Creative Officer wanted to "blow out" all campaigns, to create a myriad of three-dimensional POS pieces, the Account Manager wisely convinced him to rescind the order and limit the POS pieces to something doable (two-dimensional representations) by the deadline. As it was, a video artist and a graphic artist each got an hour's sleep the night before the pitch. One day of nearly 24-hour labor, however, was much better than seven. And they got time off afterwards. Clearly, just through fostering an environment conducive to mindfulness, the cognition that governs the coordination of elements of the task can have a major impact on the cognition involved in doing the tasks. Mindfulness requires a mind unimpaired by sleep deprivation.

DYADIC vs. LARGE-GROUP PRODUCTIVITY

When we compare the concepts per minute generated by each of the dyads, the quantitative information is belied by the qualitative. Craig and Jason averaged generating a concept every 3.26 minutes, while Neil and Jesse averaged a concept every 3.75 minutes. However, as we have seen, 178 of Jason and Craig's comments (62.5%) regarding concepts addressed the successful split image concept; that left only 37.5% of the concept comments to cover the 22 other concepts (or an average of 1.71% of the comments per concept, compared with 62.5% for chore/reward). Of the dropped concepts, only two had any more than 3% of the comments devoted to them: one had 5.3%, the other 10.9%. The dyad spent most of the session developing what they believed was their best concept, betting their time, as it were, on their outstanding horse. Neil and Jesse were slightly slower in generating concepts, but no concept received more than 20% of the dyad's comments. At first glance, it would appear their approach was to enter five horses into this race and to spend time grooming each for its run for the roses.

However, remember that Neil and Jesse saw the competitive-sounding tip-ball meetings as more collaborative than competitive. They proposed more ideas with the hopes that even if they were not chosen they might help another concept coalesce or that someone might sharpen one of their ideas. Even though none of their ideas were chosen, Neil and Jesse were asked to take over another dyad's Agavez concept (one of two that it had generated that were chosen) and develop it to the degree of completion necessary to be successfully presented to the client. Also, Neil gave Craig and Jason the root tag line they ended up using: "Agavez never stops working so you don't have to" became "We never stop working so you can." Jesse was one of the pair that made the oral presentation of the "Neighbors" campaign to the client. Moreover, Neil, who on the day of the Brief Meeting had recommended that Jason and Craig try "the split thing," co-presented the split image campaign to Agavez. So Jesse and Neil's collaborative, improvisational attitude and job functions allowed them to maintain a central, productive role in the larger collaborative process that ultimately produced the material the client saw and bought.

CONTRIBUTION OF THE STUDY TO EXISTING MODELS OF VERBAL-VISUAL COLLABORATION

Neither Neil and Jesse's nor Jason and Craig's collaborative approach fit the three models Mirel and colleagues (1995) posited as a starting-point taxonomy based on their own verbal-visual composing. They suggested Morgan's three-model view of collaboration (1991), in which (a) writers create material that they give to artists who then complete the project; (b) writer and artist each compose drafts, then get together and integrate material; or (c) writer and artist compose together. Mirel and colleagues, however, noted that little research existed on the topic to verify any model (1995, p. 260).

Different from the models proposed above was what the Heric dyads did (typical processes for them), beginning with attending a brief meeting conducted by an account manager for the campaign, there gaining input from other account executives, media buyers, public relations specialists, and other creatives. We also saw the individual generation of lines and images, and dyadic generation of concepts. After the concept was approved, others in the agency began to develop it in radio, TV, direct mail, online, and event/promotion media. What this process adds to Mirel and colleagues's initial conception is a fluctuation between large-scale, dyadic, and solo composing, and a transposition of the verbal-visual concept into several media other than print for staging a multiple-media campaign. This system of creativity, although not necessarily including the tip-ball format, is commonly found in advertising agencies.

Both dyads' composing processes repeat the standard pattern of creativity identified in advertising by Young in 1944, more recently summarized for 10 other fields as *preparation-incubation-insight-evaluation-elaboration* (Csikszentmihalyi, 1996). Working on the Agavez campaign before and attending the Brief Meeting provided preparation, and the intervening afternoon and night provided incubation for Neil and Jesse. Jason and Craig *prepared* in the Brief Meeting and *incubated* on the way home, engaging the brain's capacity for parallel processing. *Insight*-generation of elements of their most successful campaign (triggered perhaps by domain immersion) occurred the night of the Brief Meeting. Both watched the Olympics, during which the Nike "Move" ad was shown. In watching Olympics ads, the two creatives were preparing by immersing themselves in the domain—the exemplary examples of their discipline. The morphing of the "Move" ad may have inspired the surreal combining of product and benefit in Jason's print images. Nike's association of the product (shoes and athletic garb across at least eight of the sports featured) with the goals of athletic competition, achievement, and grace may have, along with the brief, influenced Craig's distillation of the relationship of the product as means to an end.

More *incubation* (in pauses) and *insight* occurred the next day during brainstorming meetings where several other concepts were generated and the separate elements of the split image campaign were edited and coalesced into the chore-reward concept. In the second of these brainstorming meetings, they also *evaluated* most concepts.

Dyadic composing promoted individual self-reflexivity, helping creatives become more objective about their own work. For example, Craig was able to discard his "rat in a maze" and "camouflaged tractor" concepts after he proposed them to Jason, and he and Jason elaborated them. This process gave Craig the perspective to see these ideas weren't feasible. After this second brainstorming meeting, they *elaborated* the split image campaign to prepare for the large-scale *evaluation* of the Chief Creative Officer with input from managers and other creatives at the tip-ball meeting, then the *evaluation* and *elaboration* of the client.

For Neil and Jesse, *incubation* in pauses and *insight* occurred in the brainstorming meeting and Neil's fleshing out the lines. *Evaluation* occurred regarding some concepts (though with fewer than Jason and Craig's) in their brainstorming meeting. Moreover, *evaluation* was the function of both the subsequent meetings with Jesse and the tip-ball meetings with the large group, and then the *elaboration* of the selected materials followed and the final large-scale *evaluation*, resulting in the rejection of the icons campaign, but Neil and Jesse's *elaboration* of "Neighbors, Why Pay More."

To consider for this new model the functions of the individual, dyad, and the large group in these processes, we find that *preparation* was substantially large-group via the Brief Meeting in Neil and Jesse's case and nearly completely large group in Jason and Craig's. *Incubation* was individual, and insight was also solo in Jason and Craig's case to a degree, with each of them generating key elements at home. *Insight* was dyadic as well when Jason and Craig combined words and image by developing the flipbook layout. For Neil and Jesse, *insight* was dyadic for most of the layouts and concepts, but Neil generated the lines individually. Preliminary *evaluation* was dyadic, as the groups chose what to present. Like Jason, Neil was able to get the objectivity to evaluate his own concept once after Jesse started to develop it: the group thus allowed the individual to become self-reflexive. These processes suggest that advertising composing fits Csikszentmihalyi's model, including the domain as he defined it.

In the *evaluation* phase, the criteria of the domain or discipline (in this case the practice of advertising) became apparent as well as the criteria of the field (the political/economic system of organization(s), who finance these kind of creative works—the agency, client, distributor, and customer). Fields serve as filters to help us choose amid the flood of information of what to pay attention to (Csikszentmihalyi, 1996, p. 42). In the convergent-thinking-dominant dyad, the perceived field became prevalent early on: Jason and Craig knew they needed to present just one campaign, and so they had little patience with anything that did not surpass what their understanding of the domain and field told them was a strong concept. However, for Neil and Jesse, the divergent-thinking-dominant dyad, the tip-ball group was seen not so much as gatekeepers as additional collaborators. In a sense, by originating numerous alternatives but connecting with the large group for their final development and evaluation, Jesse and Neil act as sectors of a larger mind that finishes the group thought process.

The disparate collaborative approaches of the two dyads may have been driven more by job functions than by sensibilities. Jason and Craig's responsibility and accountability largely ended after the dyadic level—in the execution of the task. And they were measured by whether their work was produced. As Craig said, the tip-ball meetings made everyone more secretive and possessive of their ideas than they were at some agencies. Another creative said that Heric had been more interdyadically collaborative in the invention stage before the establishment of the tip-ball meetings. Neil still "bounced things off people" sometimes before the tip-ball, but said, "you can get into trouble because they're working on it too." Along with dyadic competition, however, Jesse and Neil's responsibility also extended to coordinating the efforts of others executing the task—they were not only responsible for the outcome of their dyad but also substantially for the outcome of the large group. This coordination responsibility initially extended in the first tip-ball meeting to both creator and filter.

However, for both dyads, final evaluation at Heric was by the Chief Creative Officer, with input from the large group, occurring at the tip-ball meetings. After the dyads' preliminary development of concepts for presentation at the tip-ball meetings, elaboration was large-group as many nonwinning creatives as well as the production staff were conscripted to "blow out" the ads from print layouts into POS advertising and to present the winning campaigns in the successful pitch. Neil and Jesse resumed their managerial roles by co-presenting campaigns to the client in the pitch. Neil, who had recommended that Jason and Craig try "the split thing," and who had with Jesse tried the approach himself unsuccessfully, ended up presenting Jason and Craig's winning rendition. Neil thus was more successful in his managerial cognition than his task cognition.

A key element of acceptance in the system of creativity was that although the material presented was verbal-visual, it was also presented and sold to evaluators *orally*. In fact, Desmond Renfield, the artist of the team that came up with two of the three winning ideas presented to the client and who did the artwork for the ad that was ultimately used by the client, said that oral presentation was 50% of whether the client bought the campaign or not. Account Manager Steven Douglas said that it was 90%. Regarding the Agavez campaign, this state of affairs created a situation for Des of no little irony: In a previous presentation his brilliant but blunt, forceful style had struck the client as disrespectful and overbearing. Agavez told Heric's account manager to "keep that Canadian [expletive deleted] away from us." A wag at Heric suggested (although, unsurprisingly, not to Des) that when Agavez arrived for the presentation, the most effective use of Des would be opening the doors of the clients' automobiles for them and parking their cars. Although Des did not do valet parking that day, following the clients' request, he was, along with the researcher, kept out of sight during the winning pitch. Clearly, the pitch was a place where, in Ong's words, media "interfaced" (Ong, 1979) with orality directly in providing a rhetorical context for the print verbal-visual messages that followed, enhancing the reading and viewing experience of the client, and then closing the sale. As Devon Peterson, Associate Account Manager, put it in an interview,

> Geoff: Could you just take the ads in and give them to them and walk out of the room? Or just send them to them in the mail?
>
> Devon: Yeah, we could have if we really didn't care about winning.
>
> Geoff: So what does the oral presentation do to give you the win?
>
> Devon: It's where you stand there and you look them in the eye and say, "This is what we believe. . . ."
>
> Geoff: How is that better than putting it in writing?

Devon: Because . . . we want them to trust us. We want to have that relationship because we want them as a partner. So . . . they need to see us right there with them, talking to them. (TR 661)

Verbal-visual products thus were, of course, necessary but not sufficient to secure their publication. The pitch was not only about the ethos of verbal-visual products but also about the ethos of those involved in the process of composing them—about maintaining a trusted relationship with the financer and co-author of the messages.

The Fate of the Tip-Ball Model

The highly improvisational mode of dyadic-large-group-collaborative inter-action described in this study of Heric's winning all of the Agavez business changed 3 years later. Although they had been a key selling point to clients because all creatives were involved in the client's campaign, tip-balls were abolished, a move one creative said was welcomed by all creatives. He said that requiring 10 dyads to work on campaigns when only 3 were accepted ended up requiring much unpaid overtime from creatives. This employee said that the Chief Creative Officer put off choosing the campaigns, forcing teams to spend the whole weekend tweaking campaigns. When creatives repeatedly got in that situation, this employee said, they didn't put in their best work but only "face time." Even though the date of the pitch was set back by Agavez, several aspects of the Heric campaign preparation fit this pattern: the number of dyads involved; the extra tip-ball meeting and consequent continued tweaking of cam-paigns (albeit due to material that was reported lost in the mail); the need of the Account Manager to stop the POS production staff from having to render everything in 3-D (a problem, however, the Chief Creative Officer said was due to miscommunication); the near all-nighters put in by two graphic artists; and the Sunday-before-the-pitch dry-run meeting that involved all of the integrated marketing team, including the CEO and Vice President of Research.

The tip-ball approach, operating on the "numerous ideas produce one good one" principle, made mindfulness more difficult because of the number of concepts involved. In real time, in the second tip-ball meeting, Chief Creative Officer Rick Waller had to pick the finalists from 71 entries, possibly producing information overload for him and some half-developed ideas from creatives. The idea was also to improvise—conduct large-scale brainstorming—in tip-ball meetings. That was good and bad when Rick Waller thought outside of the brief to do the honest Neighbors campaign, although he was off strategy. The point is that it is hard to not react in a routinized fashion (using the most sensible appeal without heed to the strategy) if one is thinking on one's feet in front of 30 subordinates and superiors. A creative told me that the Chief Creative Officer was known to take over and change one campaign in each tip-ball.

Even if that were true, Rick was giving his creative input, and he had been enormously successful.

And Heric won by overwhelming the other four competitors in terms of both quality and depth. They also presented Agavez with one completely "non-spin" campaign to choose if they desired. It would appear that if the account were of sufficient size to remunerate all fairly, and if there were time enough to do nearly all of the work during reasonably normal working hours, the tip-ball approach would be effective. This condition appears, however, to be a "big if." But cutting the number of dyads participating to five might allow some productive competition as well as dyadic and large-group collaboration.

One might think that if each dyad worked on a different account, there would be more interdyadic collaboration. But giving credit due could still create the problems alluded to by Neil above. For example, Creative A gives Creative B an idea for his account, and that idea scores big for Creative B, allowing Creative B to keep the account and stay employed and get a bonus. However, Creative B gives Creative A a weak idea, and Creative A loses her account and is laid off. In the tip-balls, the original work of the dyads is presented: contributions are clearer—claims can be staked. However, contributions need to be identified from the final mix, and that can be difficult. For example, while collaborating with visual artist Des, Malcolm Adderly wrote the slogan (tag line) that was ultimately used by the client—and was in use several years later, even after Agavez had been bought again. However, Adderly, who was Assistant Chief Creative Director, had to leave the Agavez team to work on other Heric projects, and it did not appear that he was given full credit for this contribution at the end of the campaign. As he put it when I asked, "I know I did it. And I still get paid to do so. Whether ten years from now someone says 'Malcolm wrote that line,' I don't care about that. As long as we can sell something that sells product, and the client is happy with the work, and it's the best for the agency . . . it's enough" (TR 777). His spirit was truly collaborative; it is one of the chief challenges of collaborative endeavors to make the reward structure support such effective approaches.

The creative I spoke to recommended instead that the Chief Creative Officer award accounts to each dyad but spend more time learning what made individual creatives tick and motivate them with things that mattered to them (e.g., money, praise, public recognition, more responsibility, promotion). He also recommended a technique used by a previous director: give each creative an opportunity to do one of the best assignments offered that year. He then saved the creative's work and entered it in Advertising Federation competitions. The creative was motivated to do his or her very best to do well in the competitions. As Rothenberg noted, "Without [credit for their contributions], creatives cannot win the awards that gain them the recognition that boosts their value" (1995, p. 201). Clearly, the best collaborative approach involves more than the most effective communication network and skills: it also includes effective motivation.

THE ROLES OF CONCEPTS AND LAYOUT IN GROUP
ASSIMILATION AND ACCOMMODATION

We can further examine the role of task cognition in verbal-visual composing by reviewing additional findings from the previous two chapters. Group verbal-visual composing involved the cognitive processes of assimilation and accommodation identified in individuals by Piaget (1971) and developed to describe collaborative behavior (Cross, 2001). The individual mind assimilates information into an existing conceptual framework, changing that information to some degree to fit this framework, and the mind modifies that framework to accommodate the new information. Individuals in collaboration still individually assimilate and accommodate, but to succeed must do so in coordination in ways suggested above. Individual, dyadic, and large-group collaboration is typically involved in the verbal-visual composing in advertising. How did assimilation and accommodation occur across such a system of creativity?

The Agavez campaign began with the Account Manager assimilating new information from the client regarding Agavez' plan to consolidate one agency's POS and Heric's print, TV, radio, direct mail, and outdoor advertising roles into integrated advertising by one agency. The Account Manager assimilated these new needs into his existing knowledge of the Agavez product and customer. In so doing the Account Manager composed the creative brief, which outlined the situation, purpose, and audience attributes for the new Agavez campaign. One part of the situation was to create a tag that worked across all Agavez products. Argument elements were also included in the brief: the brand promise, or in Toulmin's parlance (2004), the claim (Agavez gets it done so you can move on to more enjoyable things); and data (2-year warranty, Briggs and Stratton engine). The brand promise was well constructed because it put the product and benefit in a relationship where the benefit relied upon the product. The intended ethos of the product, or brand personality, was also stipulated: "smart, yet simple and no-nonsense." Finally, the Account Manager named most of the different media in which the campaign would be expressed: print, radio, relationship marketing (e-mail typically), and POS that had to work within the tight restrictions of chief retailer MegaWorld.

The brief thus established the campaign's problem space, root argument, and conditions of signification (the different media employed offered specific expressive options and restrictions). However, not all market research was assimilated into the brief—seeing mowing as a comfortable escape, a contradictory attitude yet present with other attitudes in the market research, was ignored, as it was in the summary statements of the market research report itself. That omission, however, did contain a benefit: the consumer depicted had a consistent mindset that could be addressed by copywriters who were working on several accounts and who were already greatly challenged to create constructs that translated into a medium in which the agency was not perceived to be strong—POS—and to create tag line slogans that not only sold lawn mowers but also all the other products that Agavez made. The oversimplification may have had a more constructive than destructive effect by helping creatives avoid cognitive overload. Although the predominant audience was thoroughly addressed, not all significant potential audiences were included in the Brief Meeting either, and stressing John Goodman as customer further excluded these audiences. On the other hand, if all that the excluded audiences could afford were the entry-level mower, that exclusion would be more ethical than not.

This formulation of situation, purpose, audience, media, ethos and core argument was assimilated at the Creative Brief Meeting by the creative dyads, who accommodated their extant understandings from previous Agavez campaigns to any new material. After this preparation, Neil and Jesse each slept on it, going through a period of incubation that night. When they got together to collaborate at 9 the next morning, they each sketched partial and abbreviated layouts to help them assimilate the new information and new assignment provided by the brief. They tried to create a concept involving a split image: a tractor/golf cart, also mowers with parts that look like golf balls or tees; it is likely Neil got this idea from the Olympics "Move" commercial. Neil and Jesse came up with collective preliminary visual concepts, many for which Neil then went off and generated insightful lines. In writing, he also accommodated old material to the new rhetorical situation, turning an old, unused tag line into a headline and unused radio ads into the "helpful guide" print ad concepts. Then in their evaluation meeting the next day, he and Jesse selected (assimilated) the best lines and the new "helpful guide" idea into the collective print concepts. The sharp, polished words helped make the originally fuzzy concepts distinct as Jesse next accommodated the visual concepts to the words in comprehensive layouts that Neil reviewed. When Neil noted at the next dyadic meeting that the fishing and hunting graph and chart layouts didn't communicate well, Jesse chose a basketball picture that did, and Neil accommodated the line to it. During this elaborating process, layout—however partial or abbreviated initially—provided a common text representation so that writer and artist could coordinate their activity together and apart and contribute heedfully, both verbally and visually (within the limitations of their audience analysis and memories), to their collective design.

Typically, the key elements of Neil and Jesse's concepts accumulated and integrated gradually from rough sketch to finished lines to finished layout, rather than being worked out in a thumbnail sketch in the brainstorming meeting, as occurred with the other dyad. Unfortunately, some remained in the internal text representation rather than making it into the text.

From the conceptual framework of the Brief Meeting, Craig and Jason came up with the word and visual components respectively for the chore-reward ads at home that night. Craig envisioned a rat going through a maze to get cheese, the chore necessary before the reward. Most likely continuing to assimilate outside influences, Jason sketched his split image idea on paper while watching the Winter Olympics, which featured new ads from the most respected agencies in America, including "Move," an ad that later won an Emmy for best primetime commercial. Jason may have subconsciously assimilated and transposed that ad's conglomeration of quick cuts of action flowing into similar but unrelated action into the print venue's conglomeration of continuous but seemingly unrelated static images. Or he may have been following Neil's recommendation to do "the split thing." Or both, or neither. Regardless, he came up with an arresting series of images combining product and benefit.

The following morning, Jason and Craig met to coordinate their different thinking into joint ads. This coordination is often achieved in verbal-visual composing, as it was here, through the construction of physical, developable representations of constructs—layouts. Craig's concept of the rat striving for the cheese was not strong visually—most likely, representing the customer/man as a mouse would not win the hearts of customer or client, but the concept was strong verbally because it showed product and benefit in a necessary relationship that appealed to the values of the hard working customer. On the other hand, Jason's split images were nonexistent verbally but strong visually. In working on Jason's split images in the flipbook format, Craig added his notion of the mower as the means to an end, of the chore leading to the reward. As this notion was assimilated into the split image concept, Jason accommodated the split image by creating the flipbook with tabs for the words that communicated the chore-reward relationship.

When their concept had been developed in layout, the dyad took it to the tip-ball meeting, where it was accepted and internalized by the large group. It is important to distinguish here the concept from the various instantiations of it in different media. The concept was storyboarded by Jason and Craig to draft a TV ad. After Craig left, Jason and a POS team accommodated the concept into numerous kinds of point-of-sale merchandizing, including an H-rack, end-aisle display, shelf talkers, ceiling danglers, floor stickers, and the like. They also created prototypes of billboard ads from the concept. Preliminary plans were also made for use of the concept in radio, online, direct mail, and promotions. The concept assimilated the audience needs of the different media and accommodated itself to the conditions of signification as far as it could. However, it ultimately was rejected because it would not communicate itself in the POS situation of randomly stacked boxes and also because the client perceived its surreal-appearing message would not be easily assimilated by foreign audiences.

After their finalist ads were rejected in the second tip-ball meeting, Neil and Jesse were given a concept developed by someone else. This concept (the neighbor's lawn looks great, my lawn looks great, but I have money left over for fun) assimilated a new headline provided by the Chief Creative Officer ("What are you going to do with the money you save by buying an Agavez?"), and it assimilated all the new visual images and POS ideas Neil and Jesse came up with.

From what happened above, several things become apparent regarding verbal-visual collaborative equilibrium, the process of assimilation and accommodation. The intertext appeared an important factor in verbal-visual invention. Porter noted that intertextuality in a discourse community is "the bits and pieces of Text which writers or speakers borrow and sew together to create new discourse" (1986, p. 34). In the verbal-visual medium, the passed-along part can include the organizing principle, the layout principle of the image, which serves as a schema. How was this intertext communicated? Members of a specific profession are one of three "discourse communities" that Miller and Selzer (1985) speculated strongly influenced workplace communication, an influence Csikszentmihalyi (1996) labeled "the domain." To discern advertising's state of the art, advertising creatives routinely watch the Olympics and Super Bowl. This study suggests how a visual concept and a product-benefit relationship (Nike's means to an end) may be assimilated through a professional domain (or discourse community) to influence invention in another medium. We also see how the intertext of Internet image banks such as gettyimages.com and indexstock.com cause creatives to assimilate unplanned elements to the work, such as the stratum of sky above the mowed lawn and below the golf course, and the combination of African American head, torso, and hips with Caucasian legs in the golf split image. We see how the *imag*-ination of the work may be influenced, assimilating and accommodating intertext; but the successful art director must still discern what combinations best support the rhetorical strategy and must have the technical ability to make those elements visually coalesce.

The complex, iterative writer-artist teamwork involved in assimilating rhetorical/design elements and making them coalesce verbal-visually is enabled by layout. Even for vague, undeveloped ideas in the dyadic brainstorming sessions, layout was an important starting point. For example, the split image began as a drawing combining men mowing and recreating, with the rationale missing. Although this concept was incomplete, it could be developed because there was something to comment on—a context had been created, the stage had been set. Layout's tangibility helps verbal-visual collaborators develop promising concepts precisely by avoiding the bypassing that occurred when Jason and Craig (not sketching at this point) discussed skiing, but one thought the topic was snow skiing while the other thought water skiing.

Nevertheless, the successful layout requires a concept able to assimilate and accommodate the audiences, purpose, situation, different creatives' take on the concept, and different media (e.g., POS) that have different conditions of signification. For example, in television, the split image ad became a joining of two ongoing worlds—two separate movies of boating and mowing. In POS, the third dimension allowed rotating the images on the turntable piece, and the boxes provided natural separation of the two parts of the image but also the problems of being appropriately stacked. The *picture* of the flipbook became an actual flipbook that served as a buyers guide on a display rack of mowers. The sign became the thing, and with that transformation came new needs to accommodate. Different media can have different rhetorical emphases that must be accommodated as well: TV and print are about the brand, the Chief Creative Officer told me, but POS is about the product. The purpose of the former is to get one into the store; the purpose of the latter is to close the sale. Of course, these purposes were not entirely discrete because Agavez wanted its POS to communicate the brand strategy. But the concept must work with the emphases of different media to be effective.

For the purpose of discussion, I say the *concept* has to assimilate and accommodate these things, but the idea is still a construct, of course, not a brain. The successful concept as ideation (not layout) is a way of thinking that enables some minds to contribute to it, stop working on it, and others to start, as we can transfer software from one PC to another. It also may assimilate elements that predate it but are relevant to the campaign, like the old tag line, "Lawns are our life. Not yours." that Neil transformed into a headline for the icons campaign. It may assimilate elements that are invented afterwards for other concepts that fail but have salvageable parts that one can appropriate.

Thus, an adequate concept is an idea of sufficient applicability that it allows a group of creatives to develop it through both individual and collective assimilation and accommodation. A successful concept such as the split image is a knowledge structure for its composers that facilitates certain verbal-visual interrelations suitable to the situation, purpose, and audience; it allows us to integrate disparate material into a verbal-visual argument for the product. The split image was generative because it could assimilate several recreations in different versions and accommodate itself to them, splitting vertically, for example, when a motorcyclist image called for it.

The concept is an idea that is reified in its physical representation: the layout. Layout fosters writers and artists working together, needed due to the limitations of short-term memory and the limitations of our abilities to communicate visual/verbal ideas only orally. But the concept/layout (concept embodied, materialized in layout) is, in a McLuhanesque way, an extension of the brain because it reifies thought and allows it to be reviewed and worked on collectively; it becomes a collective text representation, a mediator that keeps group members on the same page. It is also an institutional memory of the work that allows other minds to engage in it after one team leaves. The concept/layout is not only a mediator but also ultimately a product.[11]

Bridging the interior, esoteric worlds of professional writer and professional artist is equally challenging for collaborators. Although the brief and Brief Meeting oriented the dyads strategically regarding the rhetorical situation, at the

---

[11] In *Forming the Collective Mind* (Cross, 2001; e.g., pp. 170–175), I illustrated how an outsider's written text was converted to serve this function.

tactical, hands-on level, what brought the creatives trained in the very different media of writing and graphics together was layout. Layout allows writers to think more broadly across the verbal-visual continuum of communication about how to realize their purpose for their audience in the situation at hand. It allowed Craig to shed a weak visual concept and integrate his words into a more successful image. In essence, it allowed both members of the dyad to think collectively, then to reify a collective assimilation and accommodation as a powerful verbal-visual message. Bakhtin noted that the uttered word is the shared territory of both the individual and the culture, displaying characteristics of both (Bakhtin, 1981, p. 272; Himley, 1991, p. 4). Layout is shared territory of the word (verbal medium and its culture) and the visual image (medium and culture), unifying both in its foregrounding of the visual aspects of each, perhaps in so doing reminding us of the need of not only visual but also semantic continuity. In verbal-visual collaboration layout is also the shared territory of the artist and writer, a site/means of composing together.

QUESTIONS FOR FURTHER RESEARCH

To what extent are the verbal-visual invention processes described here generalizable? Kostelnick (1989) has shown that a too-strict establishment of a process model of architectural design was ultimately rejected by architects because it was inaccurate and constrictive. Certainly, such a reductive model is counterproductive for any kind of composing. But numerous empirical studies have shown that some procedural knowledge—both general and task-specific— is necessary to compose written text effectively (Hillocks, 1995, e.g., p. 215). Kostelnick called for more than one model of the process, applicable for different composing situations. My study does not reveal *the* collaborative verbal-visual composing process, but it does reveal collaborative verbal-visual composing processes—particularly invention processes—that can provide procedural knowledge applicable across a range of activities; how wide the range, future studies need to delineate, along with the following questions:

1. To what degree do visual topics dominate in other verbal-visual collaborations? In collaborations between writers and experts in other media, such as radio, TV, Internet? Do other protocols and qualitative studies support that writers inhibit much visual thinking that they are unable to fully express and render because of their limitations as graphic designers and artists? When they collaborate with artists, do they more fully realize their verbal-visual concepts? After they collaborate with artists, do they, following Vygotsky's process of learning (1978, pp. 56–57), internalize more of the visual thinking and engage it independently of the artist? Neil had worked with Jesse for 20 years, and yet his visual thinking

reduced markedly when he composed alone. The question is whether visual thinking was not so much developed in working with artists as that it was engaged.

2. Connors (1993) used the canon of delivery to analyze the format and conventions of submitted academic journal article manuscripts. Involved in the production of these elements was layout. Dragga and Gong (1989) note in their theory of verbal-visual editing based on multiple-page documents, that arrangement occurs simultaneously with invention, but layout is a part of delivery. The current study of composing processes of mostly one-page advertisements and POS shows layout to be central to invention. We need further research of composing single and multi-page verbal visual documents to determine the typical initiation of layout and its effectiveness so initiated.

3. Burnett (1991) found that writing groups that engaged in constructive conflict were more productive than those that didn't. However, in verbal-visual collaboration I found that the less conflictive group was more successful. We need more research to determine productive levels of conflict in verbal-visual collaboration.

4. What is the effect of verbally-visually collaboratively composed messages upon their ostensible audience? An ethnography that traces in-agency conception through client adaptation through intended market reception is the next needed step in the study of verbal-visual collaborative composing of advertising.

5. What role does the oral presentation play in the presentation of verbal-visual documents to a client? How does it supplement and complement the proposed verbal-visual message?

6. We need to investigate further whether the verbal-visual topoi of similarity/contrast, contrast, and similarity are common in *effective* verbal-visual generation of ads and other documents. Does the use of visuals make much difference—change the incidence of these principles used? Speech, particularly in the classical rhetorical sense, has always made use of the visual, for example, in props. One thinks of the visual context of Marc Anthony's speech in *Julius Caesar,* a speech made over Caesar's dead body.

7. What are effective methods of teaching verbal-visual design to English majors? To art and photography majors? What are effective modes of training for workplace verbal-visual collaboration?

8. Finally, regarding the tip-ball's function in the system of creativity, do we need many ideas to come up with a good idea? Do bad ideas serve as a background against which a good idea stands out sufficiently to be chosen? Do we in addition need the salvageable elements that some junked concepts provide—do we need a junkyard of discarded concepts? Craig took "chore-reward" from a discarded concept. Jason appropriated a

tractor/dragster idea from a split painted tractor concept. Or do groups know enough about the standards of the domain and field that they can quit while they are ahead with a superior concept?

RECOMMENDATIONS FOR THE PRACTICE, TRAINING, AND TEACHING OF VERBAL-VISUAL COLLABORATION

The verbal-visual Internet is increasingly driving the economy and public life (Heath, 2000). The success of Barack Obama's online fund raising and the position of five Internet service and retailing companies in the Fortune 500 certainly attest to this fact. Training in verbal-visual composing is called for so that students are prepared to communicate ethically and effectively in such arenas, and such training is implied in the Conference on College Composition and Communication Position Statement on Teaching, Learning, and Assessing Writing in Digital Environments (Yancey et al., 2004). Moreover, collaborative verbal-visual composing is called for because of the need of writers and visual communication specialists to collaborate. Collaborative decision making involves skills such as "how to interrupt, latch onto the sentence of another speaker, illustrate with non-verbal means, and disengage from talk," skills themselves dependent on subskills such as presentation and identifying convincing evidence to persuade. Unless such skills are present, the group collaborative work cannot progress (Heath, 2000, p. 127). It is not enough to have knowledge of such skills as offering prompts, directing, challenging, and contributing information; one needs be able to apply them, both intra- and interorganizationally. As Des, Creative Director of Design and co-author of the campaign ultimately used by Agavez, told me, "I encourage my guys to . . . give me an argument. Because if they can argue . . .[for] their work, it means they understand it. That means they can sell it to the client. [If you] put something in front of me and say 'Well, I like it, . . .' that's not going to cut it with the customer" (TR 309). Even for the artists, the appropriate words, collaborative talk, was necessary to realize their designs. Artists at Heric also frequently had to summarize their arguments in writing in "cheat sheets" to help the account managers present their designs to clients in the artists' absence.

The preceding consideration of verbal-visual group composing leads to several specific suggestions for teaching and conducting verbal-visual collaboration. One can learn from the mistakes as well as strengths of professionals;[12] Neil and Jesse were professionals at a very high level of creativity, 20-year survivors in an extremely competitive business with little job security. Each took jobs at different agencies for a few years, where each continued to win many regional

---

[12] For more on how qualitative research can contribute to our understanding of composing, see Cross (1994b).

awards for advertising excellence, then rejoined, and in 2008 won numerous gold and silver awards. Craig took a job in a larger market and continues to succeed there. Jason became a Creative Director at Heric, adding a supervisory role. In short, all creatives continued to excel as verbal-visual collaborators.

Advice for Practitioners of Workplace Verbal-Visual Collaboration

Both large groups and dyads must focus on remaining mindful throughout the process. From the current study, we see that this focus can involve cognition in executing tasks and cognition coordinating the different tasks.

The brief and oral presentations of it should include all of the excellent elements of the Agavez brief, including communications objective, psychographic and demographic profile of audience, brand promise that relates product and benefit in interdependent relationship, reasons to believe, brand personality, and communication channels chosen (e.g., print, radio, online). In addition, reporting all consumer attitudes would help creatives hit the entire target.

Regarding dyadic verbal-visual creativity, Jason and Craig spent a lot of time staring off into space or at the floor to generate ideas. One certainly doesn't want to "fix" what isn't broken, but on the other hand, it might be worth experimenting to see if, after a thorough analysis of the campaign's rhetorical situation, that process can be sped up by using heuristics—systematic questions that help one investigate the subject and take action. Commercial invention devices could also be helpful. *IdeaFisher*, for example, although dated, is an immense set of heuristics, and it has a subset for advertising/promotion. *ThoughtOffice* is a spinoff that appears to also be useful. Moreover, the process could be shortened by systematically using the topoi, especially similarity/contrast, contrast, similarity, causation, obversion, facetious obversion, and the visual split image.

For those creating the ads, finding a coherent strategy appealing to the commonalities of conflicting constituencies is crucial. It may be a shortcut to focus upon a well-constructed brand promise, as Craig and Jason did, instead of reread and try to apply disparate parts of the brief. In terms of layout, positioning all elements in the right relationship communicating the strategy is crucial as is, even in a rough presentation, including all elements of the planned argument (instead of greeking). Creatives should record all concepts and concept elements generated in verbal-visual sketches with exact wording so that nothing is lost. In dry spells, these should be reviewed, as Neil did, to spark additional or modified ideas. Print ideas developed to the stage of onscreen layout should be printed out to be reviewed. Neil vetoed a pie chart concept that looked better when I printed it afterwards than it looked onscreen; ideas can look worse also in print because the colors are more vibrant onscreen because of the light projected through them (Locker, 2006).

Intermittent retraining is important to keep artists and writers operating optimally. Beyond technology upgrades, training should address also the fundamentals of the craft, such as visual design or written concision. Such training would have reminded Jesse that reverse type and all caps have low legibility.

In addition, if called for by integrated marketing campaigns, concepts should be able to be transposed into multiple media, including POS. Which parts of the message are communicated in which media should be determined at least preliminarily in the concepting stage and then finalized and delegated immediately after their acceptance as a campaign to show the client. Providing sufficient time for creatives to do mindful work is critical. Writing and visual design are time-consuming jobs, and work hours may extend significantly beyond a 40-hour week, whether in ad agencies, academia, or other work sites. But time is necessary to live as well. The all-nighters pulled by two artists during the Agavez campaign create bad health, low morale, and burnout and are not in anyone's long-term best interest. Three-dimensional artifacts and renderings appear to be particularly big time vampires. Time must be appropriately allotted for creating or rendering such works. Extended hours spent on numerous projects in a rushed, interrupted environment are not conducive to mindfulness, as Weick and Sutcliffe note:

> Accidents are not sudden, they are incubated and give off daily warning signals. This is why attention needs to be made more stable (i.e., norms and routines must specify and reward attention to intended objects) and more vivid (i.e., distractions need to be removed). (p. 517)

At Heric, the cognition of creating interrelating with the cognition of coordinating creatives (people popping into each other's offices and talking) was the standard approach. A major cause of this situation was the Heric culture's attitude toward speech and writing if not sensorium. Managers wrote a substantial amount and said that writing was crucial. Yet with e-mail, no creatives were unduly (or even duly) concerned. So managers typically did a lot of reporting on paper but communicating in person.

This orality-based approach to coordinating had been advocated by some researchers in the frenzied development era before the dot-com crash as an advisable paradigm for companies to deal with rapidly changing environment (e.g., Brown & Eisenhardt, 1998). However, the approach could be more of an obstacle than a catalyst. As one creative said, it may take three hours of thinking to get to a certain place. If he then had to stop to deal with interruption, he couldn't immediately get back to the place it took three hours to get to. He said closing the door didn't help—people interrupted anyhow. Also, I found that at Heric, it could get stifling hot quickly in some offices with the door closed.

Although solitude is needed at times, communication with other creatives also greases the collaborative wheels, and other coordination must go on. The answer in such situations is to not totally change the communication process, but rather to modify it. Organizations could have "quiet rooms" like graduate student library carrels where people can go and be undisturbed. That might be easier for copywriters than artists who need a lot of equipment. But one could put Apple G4s in the quiet rooms, or perhaps put people needing solitude in spare cubicles or offices. Or instead, it might be better to enforce a closed-door or cubicle policy—when the doors are closed or a sign is posted, interruptions aren't permitted. There would probably need to be a limit on how long interruptions could be stopped during one day. Still, freewheeling creative exchange should continue to be nurtured as well. The point is not for everyone to be silent but to access solitude when needed to generate or develop thought.

Another problem of coordination of the system of creativity was that managers had meetings brainstorming and choosing public relations and direct mail activities that creatives were not informed about until much later. By that point, some creatives had generated material that was no longer needed because the promotion was, for example, for fishing rather than golf. A solution is for the minutes of the account management strategy meetings to be written and e-mailed to creatives and to have that information included in a project status reports (see below). At Heric, oral announcement of the minutes would be needed also.

In addition to minutes of meetings, project status reports could help coordinate the collective creativity in a large, multimodal communication project. At Heric, after it was decided not to blow out all three campaigns in 3-D, one creative was preparing unnecessary POS materials for H-racks because he hadn't been informed. A brief project status report published every 3–5 business days, generated with project management software, would help curtail such dysfunction. Since in a status report all facets of the project would be listed and all accomplishments noted, everyone would know about any new directions the project was taking as well as have a sense of where they fit in the grand scheme. The logical person writing the status reports would be the coordinator of the project. Obviously, he or she would have to have more time than managers did then to do this report.

Implementing many of these suggestions could make an agency or other organization more of a print-based than oral-based culture. A danger is that some of the above suggestions collectively add a layer of bureaucracy, and reducing interaction may reduce collaboration. To hold and reward creatives' attention, minutes and reports would have to be short and substantive. Workplace writing skills stressing clarity, concision, and substance are called for. But the advantage is that collaboration could become even more focused—more consistently comprehensive yet within the problem space. A balance needs to be struck between being able to meet quickly and to share creative ideas without bureaucracy interfering, while creating sufficiently reviewable guidelines and information to keep groups and individuals thinking collectively across media within the scope of the project.

For all, addressing ethical issues as they arise is a part of successfully resolving the rhetorical problem because mindfulness is not just coordinated thought but coordinated, *ethical* thought, which effectively responds to all relevant dimensions of its context.

Advice for Instructors and Trainers

The following recommendations can be applied in teaching and can be adapted for on-site training:

An essential element we could teach to help students to situate writing in an increasingly visual communication is layout. Learning this technique requires a significant amount of time for independent work as well as group work to develop the visual thinking needed to contribute to a team. This approach can be applied in workplace training or in a business or technical writing class when teaching the sales brochure or letter unit by having students develop a central selling point (Locker, 2006, p. 135), not only in copy and tag line but also in visuals and layout. It could be applied in a first-year or advanced composition class in any verbal-visual group assignment (e.g., group research paper, group Web page for interest group or exploring theme, etc.). However, the chief criterion for including visuals must be that we illustrate to communicate, not communicate to illustrate.

As I noted previously (Cross, 2004 March), thumbnail sketches of layouts are where writer and artist can, if sufficiently versed in the technique, easily and effectively brainstorm possibilities, because thumbnails can be done relatively quickly, capturing and developing the rapid but in short-term memory evanescent thoughts, both fleeting and semiperceptible otherwise. They can also be done without the investment of time or the constraints of "the box"—the templates that can substitute for effective design. I learned this lesson in a newspaper-editing course as an MA student in journalism in 1978. One assignment was to create an original design for our daily newspaper. I created 13 different page designs, each on a six-column grid (see Figure 44). Doing so allowed me to create layouts that stressed the horizontal, the vertical, symmetry, or asymmetry. It allowed me to emphasize different news stories, sections (e.g., news digest), or other design elements such as the flag (the name of the paper). It allowed me to try different verbal-visual ratios (e.g., size of headline or picture, column inches of text to include). If one has calligraphic ability, one can represent many of the intra- as well as inter-, extra-, and supradesign elements classified by Kostelnick (1988) as time and purpose permit. Doing 13 versions gave me not only a range of solutions for the problem addressed, but also an awareness of the great flexibility and heuristic potential of the grid.

On the other hand, for a "tighter" version, which can help teams visualize color, form, and font combinations more accurately and alert designers to the technical problems entailed in a design concept, an artist and writer can use screen shots of essential design elements and cut and paste and move things around in a DTP program. I recently worked on redesign of the University of Louisville English

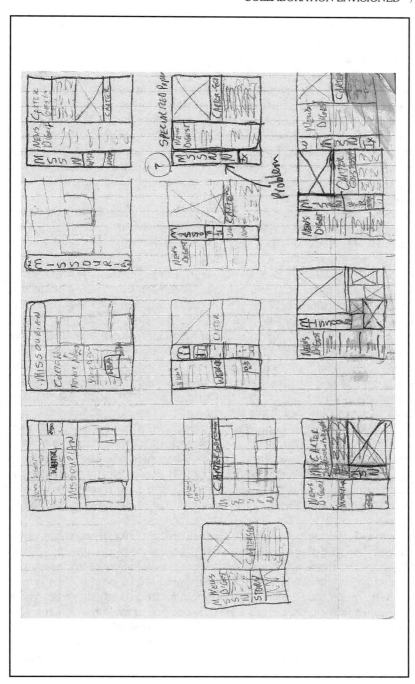

Figure 44. Thumbnail sketches of different configurations of design elements.

Department web page concept by taking a screen shot of the extant page, cutting out all to-be-revised parts, then redoing the field by using text and picture boxes to illustrate the revised design elements. Another advantage of this approach over thumbnail sketches is that one can work to scale. However, the approaches should not be mutually exclusive. I benefitted from reviewing the 13 page designs from Missouri first because they showed me numerous ways to arrange transposable design elements such as the flag. Before doing the tighter composition, I also benefitted from doing pencil thumbnail sketches on a 12-column grid field created by lined notebook paper turned sideways with the field reduced to scale. Doing so kept me conscious of all design elements and produced design problems that encouraged me to opt for a simpler but still effective gestalt in the tight version.

One caveat when presenting both penciled thumbnails and desktop published tighter renditions is that the DTP versions will win with an audience untrained in graphic design unless one is a very good freehand artist. Tight versions of weaker concepts trump penciled abstractions.

To be sure, templates can also be efficient solutions, particularly when teams lack graphic skills, tools, and time; but the development of desktop publishing has lowered the learning curve and increased the efficiency of such software. And even within templates, there are design decisions needed for various elements of the document. Thumbnails of templates could still allow more creativity and verbal-visual effectiveness than simply plugging the first-surfacing solution into a predesigned form. At the design stage, in most cases, it is better for verbal-visual collaborators to think first with a pencil and then with other tools (Brumberger, 2007; Cross, 2004). To begin, participants would do a number of thumbnail sketches to start working toward concepts and their layouts. However, as time permits, one should avoid premature selection: as Neil said, "you don't want to spend . . . time doing something that you don't think is . . . worth it. . . . But sometimes when you do them up on the computer they can come to life" (TR 68). Regardless of the form, the odds are that in the future, information workers will need to evaluate layouts if not produce them, and the earlier they can do that in the process effectively, the better.

Drawing and desktop publishing, of course, are not enough communication for collaboration. The physical setup needs to facilitate viewing drawings—with good lighting and tables or at least desks that can be adjoined are needed. If composing in a computer lab, wheeled chairs would help dyads or larger groups invent, draft, revise, and proofread together. Precise talk about verbal-visual elements is also needed, requiring a significant degree of multimodal literacy, or "metacognitive strategies that can be carried across multiple sites/texts/media" (Adler-Kassner, 2007). Students and professionals should know how the cognate elements of arrangement, emphasis, clarity, conciseness, tone, and ethos apply in verbal, visual, and verbal-visual realms. In group composing, they should also be able to articulate their strategies with these elements.

In industry, gatekeepers such as clients can become the primary audience and drive the text production at the expense of the ostensible audience and authors (Cross, 1994a). When pitching campaigns to gatekeepers then, it may be wise to go over a well-written creative brief first so the client and distributor temper their expectations to allow for the greatest appeal to customers. We have to be careful to avoid not only gatekeeper-based prose, but also gatekeeper-based visuals, because visuals are typically more influential. On the other hand, there must be an identifiable product, in our case not just any lawn mower, that the consumer takes away from the message, or the consumer will go out and buy just any lawn mower. So it's a balancing act between showing the benefit and showing the product. Also, because Neil and Jesse never got out of the greeking stage, it is recommended that although greeking may be helpful in an early design stage, the team needs to get out of it before the review if the complete idea is not communicated by the extant words and images and the audiences aren't properly accommodated in the partially developed ad.

We need to assign problems with complex audiences that encourage prioritizing audience appeals and then meeting needs in nonantagonistic and verbally-visually unified ways. Such assignments in workplace writing classes should not be infrequent. Because of the wide access to desktop and Web publishing technology and because of the multimedia technological lenses of a large and increasing share of the audience of American communication, we teachers of writing need to attend to visual communication more. We need to increase visual literacy of writers so that the lack of a visual language does not stifle their ability to come up with a successful concept in collaboration with graphic artists. A part of that visual literacy is, because we do not live in a value-free world, an ethic applied to the visual realm. Before any unit on verbal-visual composition is presented, students should do an ethical evaluation of a verbal-visual text assignment, in which ethical approaches including deontology and teleology are introduced, and students would (Hillocks, 1995) evaluate a verbal-visual text by an ethical approach in a series of activities initiated by a gateway activity. This procedure is an excellent introduction to visual design as well as formal ethics.

Within an ethical framework such as this one, the following example is one method of incorporating such an approach in a business or technical writing class. It assumes students would have had earlier instruction in persuasion, clarity, concision, communicating technical information, audience analysis, "you attitude," positive emphasis, and Toulmin logic (2004) along with ethics. Instruction in poetry composition and analysis is recommended, particularly for prospective copywriters. The following research-based unit includes the use of generative "topics" of verbal-visual composing, heuristics of verbal-visual invention called for by Lauer (2004, p. 161).

Brochure Assignment: Create a brochure promoting an event, organization, or product for a for-profit, government, or nonprofit organization. Use verbal and visual communication to produce this document.

Objectives:
- Students will become familiar with available desktop publishing program.
- Students will learn verbal-visual techniques of invention (concepting), design, evaluation, and elaboration.
- Students will learn techniques of collaboration and conflict management modes.

Day 1: Students are introduced to techniques of collaboration and constructive conflict. First, they learn productive conflict modes (compromise, smoothing, power, withdrawal, win-win) (Blake & Mouton, 1964) and practice them in cases. Students next role-play, reading quotes of writer and artist teams using collaborative moves described in this chapter and the rest of this book (e.g., offering prompts, challenging, contributing information, directing [Burnett, 1994]; see Figure 45 for an example).

Discuss afterwards how the concept of the "Another Satisfied Agavez Owner" emerges from the challenging and contributing of both members of the dyad: Jesse helps Neil explain and elaborate Neil's idea, then edits it so that it doesn't gag the gag; Neil helps Jesse explain the edit and revise the concept.

Next give pairs of students a sales-letter case problem of creating a document for the approval of two sometimes conflicting audiences—clients (manufacturers) and customers. Have one of each pair represent the interests of one of the two audiences, and have them employ all of the collaborative moves identified above. The instructor should videotape one of the most skillful pairs. Instructor analyzes the tape after class.

Day 2: The instructor brings the taped collaboration and conducts class analysis, pointing out strengths and weaknesses. Students learn rudiments of document design, including font choice (proportional spacing, large x height, variable line thicknesses, etc.), alignment and good continuation, figure-ground contrast, grid layouts, justification and rivers and lakes of white, visual center of page, quadrants of emphasis, symmetrical and asymmetrical design. Using thumbnail layouts, student groups then redesign a poorly designed flier.

Day 3: Students work separately today. First, they are introduced to generative topics of verbal-visual composing. They next identify examples of each provided by the instructor. Then, using a sketchpad, they do a close imitation of each of the kinds of verbal-visual relationships found in this study, changing only the words or the picture in each instance. Then they do loose imitations of each.

Day 4: Each student in each group brings in information about a product, event, service, or organization he or she wishes to promote. Groups convene and select a single topic for the brochure. Students then examine product, situation,

Have two students read the lines below

Neil: It's kind of like "another satisfied Agavez owner" on there. . . . You just show a shot of somebody . . . (**Directing**)

Jesse: Playing softball or something. (**Contributing Information**)

Neil: Yeah, it's just "another satisfied Agavez" shot.

Jesse: Okay.

Neil: But it's just a little—just like, you know. If there's any way we can get a trigger with it. I mean it kind of works. You might say there's a grilling scene going on. You can barely see [the mower] in the garage. And it would be great if the line . . . is like a real working line: Like "He's working hard" kind of thing." (**Directing**)

Jesse: I think it works like that. (**Challenging**)

Neil: Like what? (**Offering Prompts**)

Jesse: "Another satisfied Agavez owner." (**Challenging**)

Neil: "Yeah" (**Offering Prompts**)

Jesse: "not so much about working—it just ends in the shot. . . ." (**Challenging**)

Neil: Yeah, so you've just got the shot. (**Offering Prompts**)

Jesse: Uh—teeing off for . . . golf. (**Directing**)

Neil: Yeah, or just some beautiful fishing stock shots or something and down . . . it's the line. . . . (**Contributing Information**)

Jesse: Then you've got—

Neil: Yeah and then you have the tractor down at the bottom, and then you say, uh,—really drive it home with the strategic thing, that "you've got more important things to worry about" (**Challenging/Directing**)

Jesse: Right (**Offering Prompts**)

Neil: . . . And you have the opportunity to do the more important things. (**Challenging/Directing**)

Jesse: Right (**Offering Prompts**)

Figure 45. Practice verbal-visual collaboration exercise.

purpose, and audience and write a creative brief including the following headings: Communication Objective, Audience Profile, Brand Promise (central appeal of product, event, service, or organization), Reasons to Believe (evidence to support claims), and Brand Personality (e.g., smart, yet simple and no-nonsense).

To help students determine convincing relationships of the product and benefits, they should do node-and-link cognitive maps such as Figure 43 and be sure to identify the function of the links, the relationship between product and benefit.

Alternatively, before class, the teacher chooses the brochure topic and materials and writes the creative brief.

Day 5: Students meet and brainstorm brochure concepts in pairs. During brainstorming, using sketchbooks, groups practice various brainstorming techniques used by Craig, Jason, Neil, and Jesse—contrast, similarity, obversion, facetious inversion, different members of the same class, and such. Other visual approaches related to the classical topoi may also be used. Instructor circulates, coaching collaborations where indicated. Students should generate 3–4 strong verbal-visual concepts (sketches) based on the creative brief. Students should capture all concepts and concept elements generated, in verbal-visual sketches with exact wording so that nothing is lost.

Day 6: Each group reviews its brief, then selects the best concept using criteria based on the brief (they use weighted matrix to decide). Then instructor introduces thumbnail sketches. Each individual creates six different thumbnail sketches in class and for homework.

Day 7: Groups consider individual thumbnail sketches and if necessary create up to six different thumbnail sketch layouts for the chosen concept, experimenting with best placement of elements given document design principles. The group then chooses the best design.

Day 8: Students learn to create a business card with relatively simple and nearly ubiquitous Word-based desktop publishing program (*Microsoft Publisher* in *MS Office*) or the more effective and sophisticated *InDesign* or *QuarkXPress* if available. Key topics taught include grouping and layering. Students then learn how to create 6–8 panel brochures.

Day 9: Groups produce finished rough draft of brochure.

Day 10: Lecture on questionnaire design. Groups design document-testing questionnaire for brochure, incorporating questions focusing on verbal-visual elements of the cognate areas. Groups reproduce 17 copies of brief, brochure, and questionnaire for Day 11.

Day 11: Everyone individually reads and evaluates all other groups' brochures.

Day 12: Groups tally questionnaire responses (including writing summary of qualitative responses from open-ended questions), then write memo of revision directions based upon feedback. All audience objections must be addressed in the memo, along with action steps to improve brochure.

Day 13: Groups finish final copy of brochure and "roll out": displaying drafts and questionnaires, each group presents oral report with each person explaining one or more phases of the brochure-creation process. Final versions are then submitted to the instructor.

Skills subsequently could be reinforced in a service learning internship where students used verbal-visual composing to solve organizational problems.

The resources and knowledge needed to teach verbal-visual composing effectively in such a way span several disciplines in most if not all schools. Largely because of its need to develop specialized knowledge, academia has subdivided itself into formidable disciplines with long-standing traditions. Looking at the essentials of verbal-visual collaboration, however, we see at least four disciplines involved (see Figure 46).

Verbal-visual composing could be improved by integrating the expertise in several disciplines. With its stress both upon the written word and layout, journalism, along with its subdiscipline of photojournalism, occupies two points of the triangle. While graphic arts and writing are obvious components of verbal-visual collaboration, it may be surprising that communication is included. But as we've seen, dyadic collaboration not only relies largely upon talk to bring word and image together, but also in organizations, collaborators typically have to justify their verbal-visual creations orally. As an advertising manager told me at a tip-ball meeting, copywriters have to defend their words [and, we can infer, images] to everyone in the room. So a curriculum teaching this skill should span all mentioned disciplines. As total quality management has taught us, it is a mistake to make the boundaries of vertical chimneys of expertise impermeable. But there must be an infrastructure, reward system, collaborative training, and collegiality that support interdisciplinarity.

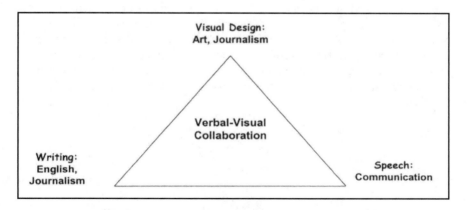

Figure 46. Medium-based disciplines involved in effective
verbal-visual collaboration instruction.

Another value of verbal-visual collaboration is that like writing across the curriculum, it can be used as a mode of learning in content courses. As noted above, what we know about imagery suggests that verbal-visual representations engage memory better than just words. The incorporation of visual and verbal processes and products in group projects could boost the learning gains associated not only with individuals in writing across the curriculum but also, as Heath has noted, with collaborative learning involving writing (2000, p. 124).

To what degree should instructors of rhetoric and composition, business, and technical communication teach verbal-visual collaboration? Rarely, of course, if the goal is simply ornamentation—one should use visual design to communicate, not communicate to get to use visual design. And because of writing's tremendous power to express, document, narrate, analyze, theorize, and synthesize, composition studies, with its extensive, interdisciplinary understanding of writing, needs to keep writing its "main event." But a statistic from the news business is germane: "Readership of cutlines (captions) is 10–15 per cent higher than that of stories" (Moen, 2000, p. 61). Given the increasingly Internet-driven nature of the economy and public discourse, and the paradigm shift for print documents brought in by relatively simple and inexpensive desktop publishing, the writer in search of images will no longer predominantly be the modernist poet in search of additional words, but instead the composer of persuasive, aesthetic, informative, or expressive discourse in search of visual images that help the writer discover and convey the subject. The writer thus must be able to create not only self-referential texts solely of words but also writing that serves a specialized rhetorical function while the visuals of a collaborator serve another function, both contributing to a larger message.

For most, acquiring this skill will require effective instruction in writing functioning as a complementary medium. Even if McLuhan's adage "the medium is the message" is wrong, the medium shapes the message, as Lowenstein points out (Merrill & Lowenstein, 1971, p. 18), the medium interacts and is interdependent with the message (Ong, 1971, p. 290), and the medium shapes the process of message production. Because of widespread media integration, access, and the resultant changing expectations of the reader, more often than not, even more than before in the history of print, verbal-visual genres will be the shape of words to come.

Methods

Ethnographic and qualitative methods were used to provide the best under-standing of verbal-visual collaboration within one of its (mostly) natural habitats, the system of creativity or the domain of practice and economic/organizational field (Csikszentmihalyi, 1996) within which the collaborating copywriters and artists based their decisions. This Appendix describes my methods of gathering and analyzing data, discusses my influence on the processes observed, and pro-vides a rationale for my mode of presentation and school of qualitative research.

No researcher enters the field *tabula rasa*—with a clean slate. It is the best we can do before accessing the site or soon afterward to make our preconceptions explicit so that our investigation is not conducted to reinforce tacit prejudices. When I went to Heric to study verbal-visual composing, I initially made my understandings of the subject as explicit as I could in a conceptual framework and then successively revised this framework to account for what I found in the field. To help create the conceptual framework, I conducted a review of research on collaborative verbal-visual composing in professional settings that confirmed the finding of Mirel and colleagues (1995) that "little research exists on collabor-ations between writers and graphic designers in industry."

DATA GATHERING

From mid-February through mid-May 2002, I collected data for 8 hours per working day in Heric Advertising Corporation—more than 460 hours. During fieldwork, I observed several artist-writer teams, audiotaping collaboration, back-ground, and retrospective interviews of any interactions I did not observe. Some 75 tapings were made. The audiotapes produced 1,000 pages of transcriptions. I also wrote 270 pages of observational, analytic, and reflexive field notes and collected 300 pages of visual documents and draft materials. I also collected related personal, agency, and client documents and e-mails. Discourse-based interviews were used to reveal tacit values determining composing decisions.

Besides observing creatives and their director in small- and large-group inter-actions, I also attended managerial strategy meetings and interviewed the campaign's three account managers, media buyer, traffic coordinator, production manager, research director, and agency president so that the community of practice could be rendered. Outside documents and agency interviews allowed me to trace the systemic context of the collaboration—the interrelation of agency, client, retailer, and consumers interviewed in market research.

From the extensive taping, notes, and document collection, I included the collaborators voices significantly in the study (Kirsch, 1997).

Five techniques during the study were used to authenticate my findings:

1. Spending a prolonged period at the site gathering data—more than 460 hours.
2. Attaining multiple time perspectives (Doheny-Farina & Odell, 1985).
3. Comparing several types of data (Yin, 1994).
4. Comparing the perspectives of numerous participants, including cross-case analysis of dyads.
5. Receiving feedback on my conclusions by presenting various findings at 11 national or international professional conferences.

DATA ANALYSIS

The 1,000 pages of audiotape transcriptions and 270 pages of field notes were coded. Copies were made of pages, and coded sections were cut and filed in paper files. In addition, each dyad's invention session was entered verbatim into Excel (see Figure 47) and each comment made in the session was coded in 24 different descriptive or analytic ways (see Table 7). Some 14,000 bits of qualitative data from these databases along with visual documents were involved in writing the manuscript.

Counts were done to compare incidences of various categories between dyads and between writers and artists. From these counts, percentages were calculated to be able to compare the different dyads' sessions: each session had a different length and number of comments. Looking at the numbers was typically not enough, however; that was normally followed by a review of the comments so coded and frequently surrounding comments to both cull telling examples and contextualize percentages in the evolving concepts and situations. I also used Excel's various graphs and charts to compare both veteran and "up and coming" dyads on pertinent analytic categories (Geisler, 2004).

Mode of Representation

Why choose the mode of representation used in Envisioning Collaboration? As a field that is responsible for postsecondary instruction in writing, we need to know much more about verbal-visual composing. To produce high-quality verbal-visual documents, the writers we train will often need to collaborate with artists. Thus both the need to learn how to compose verbal-visually at an expert level collaboratively and individually makes it necessary to document expert verbal-visual collaboration meticulously. To study these processes in their social context, the mode of representation of En*vision*ing Collaboration is case studies of dyadic composing nested within an ethnographic chronology. Case studies allow a fine-grained description and comparison that has allowed composition to formulate theories of composing (e.g., Emig, 1971). However, early case studies were criticized because they did not address real composing situations. To describe the social context within which participants made composing decisions, ethnographic chronology was used. Ethnographic findings are characterized by their circumstantiality (Geertz, 1983, p. 23), and chronology is typically used in ethnographies because it helps convey how circumstances influence behavior (Cross, 1994b, p. 163). The chronology is also used in discussing "institutions that are themselves organized on the basis of some seasonal cycle or rhythm" (Hammersley & Atkinson, 1983, p. 218). The "pitch" was not seasonal but was a recurrent cycle in the culture as central to advertising as the cycle of planting, growing, harvesting, and selling crops is to farming. From a stylistic standpoint, in places, I italicized visual words—words such as *overview* and *frame*work— to draw attention to the frequently tacit role of perception in our understanding of our world.

Locating the Ethnographer

The researcher is the critical instrument of the qualitative study, as Miles and Huberman note: "issues of instrument validity and reliability ride largely on the skills of the researcher. Essentially a **person** . . . is observing, interviewing, and recording, while modifying the observation, interviewing, and recording devices from one field trip to the next" [authors' emphasis]. The person needs to have familiarity with the object of study and its context (Miles & Huberman, 1994, p. 38). It thus is important to explain my development. I was introduced to extended narrative through my BA in English, with creative writing emphasis, from Miami of Ohio. My initial knowledge of graphic design and verbal-visual collaboration came while pursuing a master's in journalism at the University of Missouri, where I also studied communication theory and worked on the school's city daily, the *Columbia Missourian*, as a reporter, editor, and also published several photos there. Art Terry, former photo editor at *National Geographic* for 9 years, taught me photography and the photo essay that involved captions. Instruction in layout and design was attained in two courses: one in graphics, and another in newspaper editing and design, taught by Darrel Moen, whose textbook on newspaper layouts is a classic. I spent some late nights working on "thinking outside the box" but within the grid. I also had a course in advertising, and one in business journalism taught by Bill McPhatter, a reporter on sabbatical from

	A	B	C	D	E	F	G	H	I	J	K	L	M	N	O	P	Q	R	S	T	U	V	W	X
1	ot #	spkr	ver, vis cmt	aud attr	sub expl	insod said	subject's comment	prolif vv org princ. / rhet gram cogna te		Mov e	wells CZ	confl mod e	Clab style/ cons t	Rck ver vis init	Rck Vl rejla cc	actre i Agav	client oust	my expl	l agr disgr sub	sug used in ad	ad medk e	ad nam e	ad num ber	app aus e:
2	1	c	w	30-yr	doing something as honst a	s	smthg I cam up w right in a mtg: smt tht hit me: we kno mowng sux but at least yr lwnmr shoudn't	con	tone	incub 4	idea		dir	w			cust		a	d		sux	1	
3		c	o	wkhrd	[c puts chor rew on tabs below but this is about maze now]	s	chore u hav t go thru befor u can gt t reward	caus	clar	4.5	idea		dir	w	ac		cust	rhet-mea ns; rhet-br-	u	d	pti	maze	2	
4	2	c	o			s	chore u hav t go thru befor u can gt t reward	caus	clar	4.5	idea		dir	w	ac		cust	prom	u	d	pti	maze	2	
5	3	c	i	done	chore-reward(see cmt.2)	id	like rat in maze;start here and end up at fishg rod	caus	emph	4.5	idea		dir	w			cust			d	pti	maze	2	
6	202	o	i	done		sd	rat in maze w/cheese, or something laying over it	sm/cr	arr	4.5	idea		dir	i		ac	cust Agav ez	pro-w -con	d	d	pripos	maze	2	
7	203	i	i	done		s	the overlay thing?	sm/cr	arr	4.5	idea		op	i			cust Agav ez			d	pripos	maze	2	
8	204	c	i	done	like kids drawing	s	ur here and ur supposed t go all th way thru it	sim	arr	4.5	idea		ci	i			cust Agav ez -con	pro-w	d	d	pripos	maze	2	
9	205	i	i	done	Craig: do you see what Im sa	s	not exactly, I'm trying	sim	arr	4.5	idea		op	i			cust Agav ez			d	pripos	maze	2	
10	206	c	i	done		s	tak a reg lawn & do kid's thing tht has all the block	sim	arr	4.5	idea		dir	i			cust Agav ez -con	pro-w	d	d	pripos	maze	2	
11	207	i	i	done		s	but is this drawn on top of the lawn?	sim	arr	4.5	idea		op	i			cust Agav ez			d	pripos	maze	2	
12	208	c	i	done	done on a cmptr	sd	a whit line ov the lawn,tak u round, end isfishing hc	sim	arr	4.5	idea		dir	i			cust Agav ez -con	pro-w	d	d	pripos	maze	2	

							sim	aff	4,5	idea	op	i	cust Agavez	d	pripoč	maze	2
12	208	i	done		s	your start is the mower?	sim	aff	4,5	idea	op	i	cust Agavez	d	pripoč	maze	2
13	210	o	i	done	s	your start is wherever he is	sim	arr	4,5	idea	dr	i	cust Agavez	d	pripoč	maze	2
14	211	i	done		s	that could be all right. I dunno. [pause]	sim	arr	4,5	idea	op	i	cust Agavez	d	pripoč	maze	2
15	212	i	w	done	s	What does it say? What's the line?	sim	clar	4	idea	op	i	cust Agavez	d	pripoč	maze	2
16	213	o	w	done	I se cmogn ik Nike ligets m s	untelig. I dunno.	sim	clar	4,5	idea	oi	i	cust Agavez	d	pripoč	maze	2

Figure 47. Matrix used in data analysis.

Table 7. Names of Fields in Matrixes

Field A, 1: Number of Comment in Sequence

Field B, 2: Name of Speaker

Field C, 3: Whether Topic is Image, Word, or Concept

Field D, 4: Attribute from Brief Addressed

Field E, 5: Subject's Explanation of the Comment

Field F, 6: Whether Comment Inscribed or Said

Field G, 7: Subject's Comment

Field H, 8: Prolific Verbal or Visual Organizing Principle

Field I, 9: Rhetorical/Grammatical Description, Cognate Strategy

Field J, 10: Composing Move (e.g., 6--writing tag line)

Field K, 11: Creativity Phase (e.g., preparation, incubation)

Field L, 12: Conflict Management Mode

Field M, 13: Collaborative Moves (e.g., op=offering prompts)

Field N, 14: Comment Verbally or Visually Initiated

Field O, 15: Accepted/rejected by Chief Creative Officer a=accept, r=reject

Field P, 16: Accepted/rejected by Agavez after winning a, r

Field Q, 17: Primary Audience (if mentioned) is Customer, Client, MegaWorld

Field R, 18: My Analytic Code Explanation of Comment

Field S, 19: Based on the Evidence, My Agreement or Disagreement with
         Subjects' Reason[a]

Field T, 20: Suggestion Used in Final Ad or Discarded u=used, d=discarded

Field U, 21: Medium: pos, pri(nt),

Field V, 22: Ad's Eventual Name if it Survived

Field W, 23: Ad Number

Field X, 24: Pause Before (b) or After (a) Comment

---

[a]Used only in crucial situations.

Business Week. This course and the Missouri London Reporting Program, where
I reported on economics and NATO, were a foundation for my later organizational ethnographies. My foreign correspondence was published in newspapers
including the *Milwaukee Journal, San Francisco Chronicle*, and *Palo Alto Times*,
where I published a photograph along with a story.

While completing my second master's, in English at Ohio State University,
I conducted my first field research study (lasting 10 weeks), under the direction

of linguist Sara Garnes. This 1984 study was later published in *Computers and Composition* (Cross, 1990b). Five months were spent in the field during my second qualitative study, completed for a doctorate in English at Ohio State, directed by the committee of Edward Corbett, Kitty Locker, and anthropologist John Stewart. This study was later published in *Research in the Teaching of English* (Cross, 1990a). The study of small-group collaboration was then reconsidered through the additional lenses of gender and conflict theory and expanded to become *Collaboration and Conflict* (Cross, 1994b). My second full-length ethnography, *Forming the Collective Mind*, focused on large-group collaboration (2001).

I could describe my race, class, and gender, but to do so risks essentializing me and stereotyping my perspective (Charney, 2004, p. 587), not a goal of ethnography. Answering the question, "Who is the implied author of this text and why?" will reveal more about me than that. As Charney (2004) showed, it is not the case that only certain kinds of postmodern research, including critical ethnography (Blyler, 1996), have social and ethical value. We need many lenses, for we see darkly through the glass of our logics. I remain a reporter-theorist, employing techniques of participant-observation (Cross, 1994b).[1] My methods draw on the NCTE award-winning research of Broadhead and Freed (1986) and Doheny-Farina and Odell (1985), as well as Geisler (2004), Miles and Huberman (1994), Yin (1994), and other proven techniques of participant observation and data analysis cited in this study and employed in my earlier research.

Participation and observation balance each other and were employed in this study in the following ways. Participation (the observer's influencing that which was observed) took place through interpretation, reactivity, and empathy. Interpretation occurred in my selecting and interpreting facts. For example, I chose to describe the dyadic collaborations of 20-year veteran dyad and the young-Turk dyad because logistically I could only cover two as this event unfolded, and these were the most expert from the standpoint of tenure, awards, and site-assessed quality and were suggested to me. As it took 240 hours of 8-hour-a-day networking and knocking on doors to find a site and the dyads that were considered outstanding by the culture, I went with what was given to me. I also observed a male-female team later, but the data weren't as comparable because it was later in the process. Some data were also collected from the team whose ads Agavez ultimately used, but I could not study that process in detail because the artist had a motorcycle wreck and needed time to recover; also, details about their product would identify the companies. I also participated by choosing which data collected seemed most indicative of the object of study. The theories that best accounted for the data were also chosen for reasons explained in previous chapters.

---

[1] For a full rationale for this approach, please see Cross (1994b).

I also participated through a degree of reactivity—simply being there influences the processes at hand in some way. I lessened participants' career concerns about my being there by getting an agreement from management that my findings would not interfere with anyone's career. Management asked participants to sign human subjects releases, but they did not have to—I did not mention to management any person who did not sign one or participate, and all participants were informed in writing that they could drop out at any time. Motivation not to interfere with the creatives' work processes came from both wanting to capture these processes accurately and from knowing that if I got in the way sufficiently, I could be asked to leave at any point, something also stated on the human subjects releases. Although I had management backing, from what it took to get in the door, I knew that it wouldn't take much in the difficult environment everyone faced to be shown the door if creatives complained I was obstructing work.

I had to keep observing those work processes, however, and thus I persuaded management to quarter me on the creative floor rather than as they had planned on the executive floor next to the VP-Research and Planning. Stationed in a well-equipped office off a dark corridor of the cave, a nook potentially suitable nonetheless for Poe's cask of Amontillado, I asked creatives to call me when they were collaborating. As they were not always diligent in this calling (as Fortunato said, *"In pace requiescat"*), I also circulated sometimes during the day to be sure I wasn't missing anything. At one point near the end, Neil and Jesse were concerned that calling me in would interfere with the spontaneity of their reviewing Jesse's mock-ups. So I left my tape recorder with them, and they recorded such instances. Also, to avoid reactivity, I did not tape record the first words of Jesse and Neil's initial meeting, taking notes instead, but after a few minutes began taping while note taking. At times, after obviously taking out the tape recorder, I also put it on the floor to avoid its being conspicuous throughout the interaction.

My presence still was more than a (Linda) "Flower on the wall," an inevitable aspect of observational research. Jason said that at times "I've sat with Craig for half an hour and not said anything, just thinking," but he didn't want to create that "dead space" when he was taped; he said Craig felt more pressure also. However, when I asked if the outcome would have been different if I hadn't been there, he said, "You weren't in my car," referring to coming up with his split image idea away from Heric. "Our minds kept coming back to [the split image ad]," and they couldn't top it, he said. Jason was unsure if they could have come up with another idea had he been quieter. As to whether I had affected his process, Jason concluded, "I have no idea" (FN 225).

I remained quiet during meetings except when spoken to, with the exception noted in Chapter 3. Dazzled, as was Craig, with Jason's surreal yet strategic split image, I did concur in Craig's assessment that it was "cool." However, everyone that said anything about the concept in the large-group meetings—and many did—said the same thing, so I don't believe I influenced the process. I did not participate more (although I wanted to) because, as I told Neil and Jesse (see Chapter 2) when they asked me to "drop [a graph or chart idea] on the floor" to help them invent, I did not want to influence the processes. When asked this kind of question, as I was when managers under pressure prepared the night before Heric pitched to Agavez, I had to clarify my role as an unpaid researcher/ consultant. Had I charged for my observations and report, I could have been ordered to contribute to the ongoing process, losing my detachment, which was vital in documenting the processes accurately. It could have also greatly changed the process, which moved so quickly as it was, that I do not think my presence influenced it much. Both of these potential outcomes would have been detrimental to both Heric and me, especially as Heric won the pitch regardless.

Besides being asked a few times to collaborate actively, I was also asked for an audiotape of a past meeting to prove someone's point (that was later substantiated by others who had been there). However, because the audiotape would not have existed if I had not attended, and I didn't want to set a precedent, I did not give them the tape. I was also asked for some copies of some drawings that had been lost in the mailing to the Chief Creative Officer in Chicago. I did give these copies to the authors (who were not Jessie and Neil or Craig and Jason) because, for one thing, it seemed at very least fair to return to them the work they had created; as chance would have it, these authors were not later chosen to have their work presented to clients.

Participant-observers also participate through empathy. In striving to grasp the other participants' points of view, we become to varying degrees part of the site community. I felt this identification especially in the days immediately before the Agavez pitch—particularly at a weekend dry run of the pitch. I empathized with participants because I have spent many hours of overtime—if such a thing exists in academia—on my research projects. I also liked all participants—in part because of the amount of hard, intelligent work they put into the Agavez campaign, in part because they were, like people in English departments, interesting and fun to be around. The pressure and deadlines of high-stakes pitches, as noted above, could make creatives at times off-putting. However, Neil, who seemed particularly off-putting when I arrived, though never after that, gave me encouragement at a low point one day that had much to do with my finishing the fieldwork.

Participation is counterbalanced by observation, which manifests itself in objectivity, unobtrusiveness, aloofness. Observers strive to meticulously observe and depict actions (McCutcheon, 1981, p. 9) because, although pure objectivity is an unattainable ideal, as Geertz (1988) noted, "ethnography . . . is above all a rendering of the actual" (p. 143). My summary of methods above describes my observational approach. Roughly 7,500 hours were spent on observations, depictions, and analysis. Audiotapes, except for tangentially related background interviews, were transcribed at least twice because the initial transcriber's rendition of audiotapes that were at times hard to understand because of background noise, proved sketchy and in places inaccurate. I am indebted to a second transcriber, Nancy Henry, of the University of Louisville IESL Program, whose largely voluntary and painstaking retranscriptions saved the transcriptions and this study that depended upon them. In many key places, especially for the dyadic invention sessions, I went over the tapes again, sometimes several times to check and occasionally revise phrasings.

To corroborate inferences, more than one analytical method was used, as well as different kinds of data from several sources. The computer matrix brought together several kinds of data, including audiotape transcriptions, field notes, and documents. Several theoretical lenses were also employed to analyze findings. I relied upon materials coded by myself because the 7 hours of training I was able to provide a rater I tried employing 3 years into the study was in no way equal to my 4,000 hours of observation and analysis at that point. Insisting upon interrater reliability in such a situation would interfere with the validity of the study (Krippendorff, 2004, p. 213). As Geisler notes, "you may realize that your judgments are relying on knowledge so contextualized that you could not expect a coder to duplicate your judgments" (2004, p. 90). I found this to be the case when I tried to get interrater reliability on verbal, visual, and conceptual comments.

For example, a creative said the dyad needed to show the campaign "has legs." The rater rated this comment visual because of the literal interpretation of an addition or inclusion of legs in the campaign. However, I knew that "has legs" is advertising jargon for "able to be translated into messages in several media." As two of those media would be print and radio, I did not code the comment as "visual." Another disagreement occurred in coding a passage when an artist asked if a campaign needed to be "tight." I knew that "tight" is advertising jargon for "having a finished layout" and so ascribed the comment as visual; the rater did not understand the comment and did not code it either way. In other instances the rater coded a passage recounting the Creative Director's recommendations from another meeting as generative verbal or visual comments; however, I knew this was old information not generated by them and did not code it. For these and other reasons, our interrater reliability was somewhat below the suggested 0.7: .51.

Other works on methodology have also noted this problem (e.g., Cross, 1994b; Davies, 1999; McNealy, 1999). The rater did not understand the context well enough—the previous conversations, the subsequent products—to understand what the creatives were referring to. As Guba and Lincoln state, "The more time spent on site, the more unlikely it is that one will perceive selectively, will be guilty of misinterpretation or oversimplification" (1981, p. 148). Although I did not expect seemingly simple judgments regarding verbal or visual comments to be troublesome, they proved to be, and so I corrected any errors I identified in my coding and their kind (mostly ascribing whether a concept was chiefly verbal or visual) and thereafter relied upon my own iterative coding based upon my extensive and increasing knowledge of the context to provide the "reasonable consistency and stability" Miles and Huberman say is the main issue of reliability (1994, p. 278).

The study provided several other opportunities to review the coding. I initially coded transcriptions and computed percentages of incidence of certain coded behaviors in order to make a series of conference presentations. I then reviewed codes in writing a research report on case studies of two individual processes for Heric. Next, I reviewed and added codes to the collaborative transcriptions in putting them in an Excel database. Finally I reviewed the codes once again as I wrote a narrative of each verbal-visual collaboration, bringing together field notes, ads, sketches, policy documents, transcriptions, e-mails, and the like; finding some faulty transcriptions after listening to the sessions; finding something different than the initial reading of the transcripts indicated. I then recomputed percentages of the incidence of certain coded behaviors. As Geisler notes, coding is an iterative process, making it "priceless" to set up one's database so that automatic recomputations of percentages will occur when one changes one's codes on some of the data (2004, p. 101); because I chose to be more fine-grained than this approach and split certain codes, I had to do hand counts as well to add and subtract fractions of a code. These were checked. The information presented in this study is the result of many reviews of my own coding, which did change my coding and resultant portrayal of the composing processes as knowledge and reflexivity grew, something that one may expect, as Davies noted (1999, p. 93).

Davies also points out that "no ethnographic study is repeatable, either by another ethnographer or by the same ethnographer at another time" (p. 87). Indeed, only two of the primary participants in this study are still with Heric Advertising. However, I made my account as representative as possible of my nearly 7 years' study of these processes. Although participant-observation of one site such as Heric cannot claim the generalizabilty and replicability of experimental research, it can disprove categorical applicability of theories (e.g., Morgan, 1991) and provide grounded questions, hypotheses, and models such as those posed in Chapter 4 that may be further investigated by other kinds of studies at other sites.

To additionally offset participation, I strove to be unobtrusive in ways described above. Aloofness is a third way to counterbalance participation. I worked at being a detached reporter, for example, not trying to socialize with participants after hours even though it would have been enriching. Because participants and Heric had given me an office, computer, and time by keeping me in the loop and granting interviews, I strove to produce the most balanced account I could. Hence, I positioned my account between extremes caused by the overemphasis of one of four components of ethnography (Cross, 1994b).

One extreme is the researcher-centered view—ethnography using brief excursions as an excuse for ungrounded theory or tall tales. I spent more than 3 months in the field, covered the processes, analyzed the data, and presented much of it in this account to support descriptions and conclusions. To avoid overreliance on key informants, taped interviews were conducted with 21 individuals, in addition to numerous taped meetings involving participants.

Another extreme is the data-centered approach, which presents much insignificant data with insufficient analysis. In the field, I worked very hard to stay within the boundaries of the study and its focus upon dyadic composing for the Agavez pitch, turning down, for example, an offer from Craig to study the dyad composing for another account subsequently. Envisioning Collaboration integrates theory from business and technical writing, composition, psychology, graphic design, philosophy (Langer, 1957), advertising, management, and media theory to explicate collaborative verbal-visual composing processes and products. Beyond that, it employs techniques of data analysis from linguistics and qualitative research.

A third extreme is basing the account solely on the point of view of the participants. One danger of uncritically embracing the rationales of participants is to not provide that which is typically requested of the researcher—a relatively independent account that can give participants another informed perspective on their actions. While always considering the perspective of participants, I strove to avoid any chance of writing a "puff piece" by using a preponderance of data to support conclusions wherever possible. To avoid vested interests, as noted, I did not request or receive payment for this research, and I have not worked with the company in any other capacity.

The last extreme is to create an account that agrees with the current theory of the discipline and members of its community even though data and the researcher's experience do not support this view. Although informed by what I knew from past experience and the few preliminary studies on verbal-visual collaboration, I took an inductive approach, selecting Piaget, Csikszentmihalyi, and several rhetoricians and philosophers of the visual as the best way to explain processes and products, only well over 2 years after leaving the field. I thus positioned my account between four methodological extremes that can invalidate studies.

Coda

One feels at this point having reached the pinnacle of a fairly tall mountain. Although it is tempting to think one has climbed it alone,[2] it is only through the teamwork and support of those mentioned in the acknowledgments section of this book that such a vista could be seen and, one hopes, communicated.

**"Another few weary steps and there was nothing above us
but the sky."
—Sir Edmund Hillary**

---

[2] For more on the relation of the support team to the ethnographer in my approach to ethnography, see Cross, 2001, p. 252.

Works Cited

Adler-Kassner, L. (2007). (cited with no further information in NCTE (2008) Multimodal literacy key terms.) Retrieved September 8, 2008, from http://www.ncte.org/edpolicy/multimodal/about/122819.htm

Aldag, R. J., & Fuller, S. R. (1993). Beyond fiasco: A reappraisal of the groupthink phenomenon and a new model of group decisions processes. *Psychological Bulletin, 113,* 533–552.

Allen, N. (2002). Telling our stories in pictures. In N. Allen (Ed.), *Working with words and images.* Westport, CT: Ablex Publishing.

American Heritage Dictionary of the English Language (4th ed.). (2000). *Obvert.* Retrieved December 9, 2008, from http://www.bartleby.com/61/77/O0017700.html

Anderson, P. V. (2007). *Technical communication: A reader-centered approach.* Boston, MA: Thomson-Wadsworth.

Arnheim, R. (2004). *Art and visual perception: A psychology of the creative eye* (Rev. ed.). Berkeley, CA: University of California Press.

Asch, S. (1952). *Social psychology.* Englewood Cliffs, NJ: Prentice-Hall.

Baird, R. N., Turnbull, A. T., & McDonald, D. (1987). *The graphics of communication: Typograpy, layout, design, production* (5th ed.). New York: Holt, Rinehart, and Winston.

Bakhtin, M. M. (1981). Discourse in the novel. In M. Holquist (Ed.), *The dialogic imagination* (C. Emerson & M. Holquist, Trans.; pp. 259–422). Austin, TX: University of Texas Press.

Barabas, C. (1990). *Technical writing in a corporate culture: A study of the nature of information.* Norwood, NJ: Ablex.

Barker, R. T., & Stutts, N. B. (1999). The use of narrative paradigm theory in assessing audience value conflict in image advertising. *Management Communication Quarterly, 13*(2), 206–244.

Baron, R. (2005). So right it's wrong: Groupthink and the ubiquitous nature of polarized group decision making. *Advances in Social Psychology, 37,* 219–253.

Baron, R. M., & Misovich, S. J. (1999). On the relationship between social and cognitive modes of organization. In S. Chaiken & Y. Trope (Eds.), *Dual-process theories in social psychology.* New York: The Guilford Press.

Baumgarten, N. (2005) *The secret agent: Film dubbing and the influence of the English language on German communicative preferences. Towards a model for the analysis of language use in visual media.* Dissertation zur Erlangung des Grades der Doktorin der Philosophie beim Fachbereich Sprach,- Literatur- und Medienwissenschaft der Universität Hamburg vorgelegt von by Nicole Baumgarten aus Elmshorn Hamburg [Retrieved from Bibliothek Hamburg. http://www.sub.uni-hamburg.delopus/volltexte/2005/2527/pdf/Dissertation_Baumgarten.pdf].

Bernhardt, S. (1986). Seeing the text. *College Composition and Communication, 37*(1), 66–68.

Bernhardt, S. (1996). Visual rhetoric. In T. Enos (Ed.), *Encyclopedia of rhetoric and composition* (pp. 747–749). New York: Garland.

Blake, R., & Mouton, J. (1964). *The managerial grid: Key orientations for achieving production through people.* Houston, TX: Gulf.

Blyler, N. R. (1996). Narrative and research in professional communication. *Journal of Business and Technical Communication, 10*(3), 330–351.

Bohn, W. (2002). *The rise of surrealism.* Albany, NY: SUNY Press.

Bolls, P. (2008, September 11). *This is your brain on media: Producing media for the mind in a digital age.* Paper presented at the Missouri School of Journalism Centennial, Columbia, MO.

Bourdieu, P. (1984). *Distinction.* Cambridge, MA: Harvard University Press.

Broadhead, G. J., & Freed, R. C. (1986). *The variables of composition.* Urbana, IL: NCTE.

Broadkey, L. (1987). Modernism and the scene of writing. *College English, 49,* 396–418.

Brown, J. S., & Gray, E. S. (1995, November). The people are the company. *Fast Company.* Retrieved 5/13/10 from http://www.fastcompany.com

Brown, S. L., & Eisenhardt, K. M. (1997). The art of continuous change. *Administrative Science Quarterly, 42*(1), 1–34.

Brown, S. L., & Eisenhardt, K. M. (1998). *Competing on the edge: Strategy as structured chaos.* Boston, MA: Harvard Business School Press.

Brumberger, E. R. (2005). Visual rhetoric in the curriculum. *Business Communication Quarterly, 42*(4), 328-333.

Brumberger, E. R. (2007). Making the strange familiar: A pedagogical exploration of visual thinking. *Journal of Business and Technical Communication, 21*(4), 376–401.

Burke, K. (1950). *A rhetoric of motives.* Berkeley, CA: University of California Press.

Burke, K. (1962). *A grammar of motives, and a rhetoric of motives.* New York: World.

Burnett, R. (1994). Interactions of engaged supporters. In L. Flower, D. L. Wallace, L. Norris, & R. Burnett (Eds.), *Making thinking visible: Writing, collaborative planning, and classroom inquiry* (pp. 73–81). Urbana, IL: National Council of Teachers of English.

Burnett, R. E. (1991). Conflict in the collaborative planning of coauthors: How substantive conflict, representation of task, and dominance relate to high-quality documents. *Dissertation Abstracts International* 52/04, 1236. (UMI No. 9126935).

Cameron, D. (2008, September 1). Value of direct-to-consumer drug advertising oversold, study finds. (Press Release). Cambridge, MA: Harvard Medical School Office of Public Affairs. Retrieved March 18, 2009, from http://hms.harvard.edu/public/news/ss0808/090108_soumerai.html

Cardona, M., & Dipasquale, C. (2002, March 18). Economy gets shot in arm as positive signs emerge. *Advertising Age, 73*(11), 8.

Carliner, S. (2001). Emerging skills in technical communication: The information designer's place in a new career path for technical communicators. *Technical Communication, 48*(3), 156–177.

Carlson, L., Grove, S. J., & Doerch, M. J. (2003). Services advertising and integrated marketing communications: An empirical examination. *Journal of Current Issues and Research in Advertising, 25*(2), 69–82.

Carpenter, E. (1966). The new languages. In E. Carpenter & M. McLuhan (Eds.), *Explorations in communication* (pp. 162–179). Boston, MA: Beacon Press.

Chao, L. L., & Martin, A. (1999). Cortical regions associated with perceiving, naming, and knowing about colors. *Journal of Cognitive Neuroscience, 11*(1), 25–35.

Charney, D. (2004). Empiricism is not a four-letter word. In J. Johnson-Eilola & S. Selber (Eds.), *Central works in technical communication* (pp. 567–593). New York: Oxford University Press. Reprinted from *College Composition and Communication, 47*(4), 567–593.

Chase, W. G., & Simon, H. A. (1973). Perception in chess. *Cognitive Psychology, 4,* 55–81.

Connors, R. J. (1993). Actio: A rhetoric of written delivery (Iteration two). In J. F. Reynolds (Ed.), *Rhetorical memory and delivery* (pp. 65–77). Hillsdale, NJ: Lawrence Erlbaum Associates.

Corbett, E. P. J. (1990). *Classical rhetoric for the modern student.* New York: Oxford University Press.

Costanzo, W. (1986). Film as composition. *College Composition and Communication, 37,* 79–86.

Cross, G. A. (1988). Editing in context: An ethnographic exploration of editor-writer revision at a midwestern insurance company. *Dissertation Abstracts International,* 49/08, 2195. AAT 8820277. ProQuest Document Number 744249231.

Cross, G. A. (1990a). A Bakhtinian exploration of factors affecting the collaborative writing of an executive letter of an annual report. *Research in the Teaching of English, 24*(2), 173–203.

Cross, G. A. (1990b). Left to their own devices: Three basic writers using word processors. *Computers and Composition, 7*(2), 47–58.

Cross, G. A. (1994a). *Collaboration and conflict.* Cresskill, NJ: Hampton Press.

Cross, G. A. (1994b). Ethnographic research in business and technical writing: Between extremes and margins. *Journal of Business and Technical Communication, 8*(1), 118–134.

Cross, G. A. (1994c). Recontextualizing writing: Roles of written texts in multiple media communications. *Journal of Business and Technical Communication, 8*(2), 212–230.

Cross, G. A. (2001). *Forming the collective mind.* Cresskill, NJ: Hampton Press.

Cross, G. A. (2004, February). *Sharpening individual creativity: An analysis of the individual composing processes of a copywriter and a graphic artist at Heric Advertising, Inc.* (pseudonym). Report submitted to Heric Advertising, Inc. Louisville, KY: Author.

Cross, G. A. (2004, March). *Preparing students for shared territory: Composition in the visual age.* Paper presented at the plenary session, Research Network. Conference on College Composition and Communication, San Antonio, TX.

Cross, G. A. (2008). Individual verbal-visual composing processes of artist and copywriter in advertising. Manuscript in preparation, University of Louisville.

Csikszentmihalyi, M. (1996). *Creativity: Flow and the psychology of discovery and invention.* New York: HarperCollins.

Davies, C. A. (1999). *Reflexive ethnography.* London: Routledge.

Davis, Scott. (2005). Marketers challenged to respond to changing nature of brand building [Electronic version]. *Journal of Advertising Research, 45,* 198–200, Cambridge University Press. Retrieved on February 5, 2007, from http://journals.cambridge.org/action/displayIssue?jid=JAR&volumeId=45&issueId=02#

DELINEATE. (2007a). *Brand equity.* Retrieved March 24, 2008, from http://delineate.co.nz/the-branding-dictionary/

DELINEATE. (2007b). *Visual identity.* Retrieved March 24, 2008, from http://delineate.co.nz/the-branding-dictionary/

De Pelsmaker, P., Guens, M., & Vanden Bergh, J. (2001). *Marketing communications.* Harlow, UK: Financial Times/Prentice Hall.

Dick, R. (2006). Does interface matter? A study of Web authoring and editing by experienced Web writers. *Business Communication Quarterly, 69*(2), 203–215.

Doheny-Farina, S., & Odell, L. (1985). Ethnographic research on writing: Assumptions and methodology. In L. Odell & D. Goswami (Eds.), *Writing in nonacademic settings* (pp. 503–525). New York: Guilford.

Donnell, J. (2005). Illustration and language in technical communication. *Journal of Technical Writing and Communication, 35*(3), 239–271.

Dragga, S., & Gong, G. (1989). *Editing: The design of rhetoric.* Amityville, NY: Baywood.

Ede, L., & Lunsford, A. (1984). Audience addressed/audience invoked: The role of audience in composition theory and pedagogy. *College Composition and Communication, 35,* 155–171.

Ellul, J. (1965). *Propaganda: The formation of men's attitudes.* New York: Vintage.

Emig, J. (1971). *The composing processes of twelfth-graders.* Urbana, IL: National Council of Teachers of English.

Engardio, P., Roberts, D., & Bremmer, B. (2004, December 6). The China price: Special report. *BusinessWeek,* 3911, 102-112.

Fahnestalk, J. (2001). Arrangement. *Encyclopedia of rhetoric* (pp. 40–52). Oxford, UK: Oxford University Press.

Faigley, L. (1985). Nonacademic writing: The social perspective. In L. Odell & D. Goswami (Eds.), *Writing in nonacademic settings* (pp. 503–535). New York: Guilford.

Faigley, L., George, D., Palchik, A., & Selfe, C. (2004). *Picturing texts.* New York: W. W. Norton & Co.

Flower, L. (1994). *The construction of negotiated meaning.* Carbondale, IL: Southern Illinois University Press.

Flower, L., & Hayes, J. R. (1981). A cognitive process theory of writing. *College Composition and Communication, 32*(4), 365–387.

Flower, L., & Hayes, J. R. (1984). Images, plans, and prose: The representation of meaning in writing. *Written Communication, 1*(1), 120–160.

Flower, L., & Hayes, J. R. (1994). The cognition of discovery: Defining a rhetorical problem. In S. Perl (Ed.), *Landmark essays on writing process* (pp. 63–97).

Hermagoras Press. Mahwah, NJ: Lawrence Erlbaum Associates. Reprinted from *College Composition and Communication, 31*(1), 21–32.

Foss, S. K. (1993). The construction of appeal in visual images: A hypothesis. In D. Zarefsky (Ed.), *Rhetorical movement: Essays in honor of Leland M. Griffin* (pp. 210–224). Evanston, IL: Northwestern University Press.

Foss, S. K. (2004). Framing the study of visual rhetoric: Toward a transformation of rhetorical theory. In C. A. Hill & M. Helmers (Eds.), *Defining visual rhetorics* (pp. 303–313). Mahwah, NJ: Lawrence Erlbaum Associates.

Fuller, S. R., & Aldag, R. J. (1998). Organizational Tonypandy: Lessons from a quarter century of the groupthink phenomenon. *Organizational Behavior and Human Decision Processes, 73,* 163–184.

Gage, J. (1980, February). Philosophies of style and their implications for composition. *College English, 41,* 615–622.

Geertz, C. (1983). *Local knowledge: Further essays in interpretive anthropology.* New York: Basic Books.

Geertz, C. (1988). *Works and lives.* Stanford, CA: Stanford University Press.

Geisler, C. (2004). *Analyzing streams of language.* New York: Pearson/Longman.

George, D. (2002). From analysis to design: Visual communication in the teaching of writing. *College Composition and Communication, 54*(1), 11–39.

Grice, R., & Krull, R. (2001). 2001: A professional odyssey. *Technical Communication, 48*(2), 135–144.

Guba, E. G., & Lincoln, Y. S. (1981). *Effective evaluation.* San Francisco, CA: Jossey-Bass.

Haas, C., & Witte, S. P. (2001). Writing as embodied practice. *Journal of Business and Technical Communication, 15*(4), 413–457.

Hagan, S. M. (2007). Visual/verbal collaboration in print. *Written Communication, 24*(1), 49–83.

Hammersley, M., & Atkinson, P. (1983). *Ethnography: Principles in practice.* London: Tavistock.

Handa, C. (2004). *Visual rhetoric in a digital world.* Boston, MA: Bedford/St. Martin's.

Havilland, W. A. (1980). *Cultural anthropology* (3rd ed.). New York: Holt.

Hayakawa, S. I. (1978). *Language in thought and action* (4th ed.). New York: Harcourt Brace & Company.

Hayes, J. R. (1989). *The complete problem solver.* Hillsdale, NJ: Erlbaum.

Heath, S. B. (2000). Seeing our way into learning. *Cambridge Journal of Education, 30*(1), 121–132.

Hillocks, G. (1995). *Teaching writing as reflective practice.* New York: Teacher's College Press.

Himley, M. (1991). *Shared territory: Understanding children's writing as works.* New York: Oxford University Press.

Hope, D. S. (2004). Gendered environments: Gender and the natural world in the rhetoric of advertising. In C. A. Hill & M. Helmers (Eds.), *Defining visual rhetorics* (pp. 155–177). Mahwah, NJ: Erlbaum.

Howes, D. (1991). *The varieties of sensory experience: A sourcebook in the anthropology of the senses.* Toronto: University of Toronto Press. Retrieved 6/24/08 from http://www-personal.umich.edu/~jaylemke/new.htm

Hutchins, E. (1995). *Cognition in the wild.* Cambridge, MA: MIT Press.

Innis, R. E. (2007). Placing Langer's philosophical project. *The Journal of Speculative Philosophy, 21*(1). Retrieved June 15, 2008, from http://muse.jhu.edu/journals/journal_of_speculatie_philosophy/v021/21.1innis02.html

Janis, I. (1982). *Victims of groupthink* (2nd ed.). Boston, MA: Houghton Mifflin.

Jarvis, C. (2005). *Strategy making and adhocracy.* Business Open Learning Archive. Retrieved November 6, 2008, from http://www.bola.biz/mintzberg/adhocracy.html

Johar, G. V., Holbrook, M. B., & Stern, B. B. (2001). The role of myth in creative advertising design: Theory, process, outcome. *Journal of Advertising, III*(2), 1–25.

Jones, J. P. (2004). *Fables, fashions, and facts about advertising: A study of 28 enduring myths.* Thousand Oaks, CA: Sage.

Karis, B. (1989). Conflict in collaboration: A Burkean perspective. *Rhetoric Review, 8*(1), 113–126.

Keep, C., McLaughlin, T., & Paramar, R. (2008). Closure. *The Electronic Labyrinth.* Retrieved June 13, 2008, from http://elab.eserver.org/hf10286.html

Kellogg, R. T., Olive, T., & Piolat, A. (2007). Verbal and visual working memory in written sentence production. In M. Torrance, L. Van Waes, & D. Galbraith (Eds.), *Writing and cognition: Research and applications* (pp. 97–108). Amsterdam: Elsevier.

Kenney, K. (2004). Building visual communication theory by borrowing from rhetoric. In C. Handa (Ed.), *Visual rhetoric in a digital world* (pp. 321–343). Bedford/St. Martin's. Reprinted from *Journal of Visual Literacy, 22*(1), 53–80.

Kimura, D. (1999). *Sex and cognition.* Cambridge, MA: MIT Press.

Kinneavy, J. (1971). *A theory of discourse.* New York: Oxford.

Kirsch, G. (1997). Multi-vocal texts and interpretive responsibility. *College English, 59*(7), 191–202.

Knobloch, L., & Brannon, C. H. (1984). *Rhetorical traditions and the teaching of writing.* Upper Montclair, NJ: Boynton/Cook Publishers.

Koffka, K. (1935). *Principles of gestalt psychology.* New York: Harcourt.

Koslow, S., Sasser, S. L., & Riordan, E. A. (2003). What is creative to whom and why? Perceptions in advertising agencies. *Journal of Advertising Research, 43*(1), 96–110.

Kostelnick, C. (1988). A systematic approach to visual language in business communication. *Journal of Business Communication, 25*(3), 29–49.

Kostelnick, C. (1989). Process paradigms in design and composition: Affinities and directions. *College Composition and Communication, 40*(3), 267–281.

Kostelnick, C., & Roberts, D. D. (1998). *Designing visual language.* Boston, MA: Allyn & Bacon.

Kress, G. (2006, October). *"Re-arranging" narrative: A timeless form in an era of instability.* Paper presented at the Thomas R. Watson Conference in Rhetoric and Composition, Louisville, KY.

Kress, G., & van Leeuwen, T. (1996). *Reading images: The grammar of visual design.* London: Routledge.

Krippendorff, K. (2004). *Content analysis.* Thousand Oaks, CA: Sage.

Kroeber, A. L., & Kluckhohn, C. (1963). *Culture: A critical review of concepts and definitions.* New York: Vintage Books.

Langer, S. (1957). *Problems of art.* New York: Charles Scribner's Sons.

Lauer, J. (2004). *Invention in rhetoric and composition.* West Lafayette, IN: Parlor Press & The WAC Clearinghouse.

LeFevre, K. B. (1987). *Invention as social act.* Carbondale, IL: Southern Illinois University Press.

Lester, P. M. (1995). *Visual communication: Images with messages.* Belmont, CA: Wadsworth.

Lindemann, E. (2001). *A rhetoric for writing teachers* (4th ed.). New York: Oxford University Press.

Locker, K. O. (2006). *Business and administrative communication* (7th ed.). Boston, MA: McGraw-Hill Irwin.

Markham, R., & Hynes, L. (1993). The effect of vividness imagery on reality monitoring. *Journal of Mental Imagery, 17,* 159–170.

Marsh, C. (2007) Aristotelian causal analysis and creativity in copywriting. *Written Communication, 24*(2), 168–197.

Mazzocco, P., & Brock, T. C. (2006). Understanding the role of mental imagery in persuasion. In L. R., Kahle & K. Chung-Hyun (Eds.), *Creating images and the psychology of marketing* (pp. 65–78). Mahwah, NJ: Lawrence Erlbaum Associates.

McCutcheon, G. (1981). On the interpretation of classroom observations. *Educational Researcher, 10*(5), 5–10.

McLuhan, M. (1964). *Understanding media* (2nd ed.). New York: Signet.

McNealy, M. S. (1999). *Strategies for empirical research in writing.* Boston, MA: Allyn & Bacon.

McQuarrie, E. F., & Mick, D. G. (2003). The contribution of semiotic and rhetorical perspectives to the explanation of visual persuasion in advertising. In L. M. Scott & R. Batra (Eds.), *Persuasive imagery: A consumer response perspective* (pp. 191–219). Mahwah, NJ: Erlbaum.

Merrill, J. C., & Lowenstein, R. L. (1971). *Media, messages, and men.* New York: David McKay Co.

Miles, M., & Huberman, A. M. (1994). *Qualitative data analysis* (2nd ed.). Beverly Hills, CA: Sage.

Miller, C., & Selzer, J. (1985). Special topics of argument in engineering reports. In L. Odell & D. Goswami (Eds.), *Writing in nonacademic settings* (pp. 231–249). New York: Guilford.

Mintzberg, H., & Quinn J. (1988). *The strategy process: Concepts, contexts and cases* (3rd ed.). New York: Prentice Hall.

Mirel, B., Allmendinger, L., & Feinberg, S. (1995). Collaboration between writers and graphic designers in documentation projects. *Journal of Business and Technical Communication, 9*(3), 259–288.

Moen, D. (2000). *Newspaper layout and design: A team approach.* Ames, IA: Iowa State University Press.

Morgan, G. (1986). *Images of organization.* Beverly Hills, CA: Sage.

Morgan, M. (1991). The group writing task: A schema for collaborative assignment making. In N. R. Blyler & C. Thralls (Eds.), *Professional communication: The social perspective.* Newbury Park, CA: Sage.

MSN Encarta. (2006). *Gnarly.* Retrieved May 18, 2006, from http://encarta.msn.com/dictionary_/gnarly.html

Myers, I. B., & McCaulley, M. H. (1985). *Manual: A guide to the development and use of the Myers-Briggs type indicator.* Palo Alto, CA: Consulting Psychologists Press.

National Council of Teachers of English. (2005). *Multimodal literacies: NCTE Guideline.* Retrieved August 4, 2008, from http://www.ncte.org/about/over/positions/category/media/123213.htm

Odell, L., & Katz, S. (2005). *Writing in the visual age.* Boston, MA: Bedford/St. Martin's.

Oldham, G. R., & Cummings, A. (1996). Employee creativity: Personal and contextual factors at work. *Academy of Management Journal, 39*(3), 607–634.

Ong, W. (1971). *Rhetoric, romance, and technology.* Ithaca, NY: Cornell University Press.

Ong, W. (1979). *Interfaces of the word.* Ithaca, NY: Cornell University Press.

Ong, W. (2002). *Orality and literacy: The technologizing of the word.* London: Routledge.

Orlando, S. (2007). Women are right: Men are clueless holiday shoppers, says retail expert. *University of Florida News.* Retrieved January 5, 2006, from http://news.ufl.edu/2000/12/10/clueless/

Owsley, W. G. (1972). *Class notes. Art appreciation.* Oxford, OH: Miami University.

Paivio, A. (1986). *Mental representations: A dual coding approach.* New York: Oxford University Press.

Perelman, C., & Olbrechts-Tyteca, L. (1971). *The new rhetoric.* Notre Dame, IN: University of Notre Dame Press.

Peter, L. (1993). *Peter's quotations: Ideas for our time.* New York: Collins.

Phillips, B. J. (2003). Understanding visual metaphor in advertising. In L. M. Scott & R. Batra (Eds.), *Persuasive imagery: A consumer response perspective* (pp. 297–310). Mahwah, NJ: Erlbaum.

Phillips, B. J. (2000). The impact of verbal anchoring on consumer response to image ads. *Journal of Advertising, 29*(1), 15–24.

Piaget, J. (1971). *Biology and knowledge* (B. Walsh, Trans.). Chicago, IL: University of Chicago Press.

Pope-Ruark, R. (2008). Challenging the necessity of organizational community for rhetorical genre use: Community and genre in the work of integrated marketing communication agency writers. *Business Communication Quarterly, 71*(2), 185–194.

Porter, J. E. (1986). Intertextuality and the discourse community. *Rhetoric Review, 5*(1), 34–47.

Portewig, T. C. (2004). Making sense of the visual in technical communication: A visual literacy approach to pedagogy. *Journal of Technical Writing and Communication, 34*(1&2), 31–42.

Publisher's Information Bureau. (2009, January 13). 2008 magazine advertising shows effects of soft economy. *Magazine Publishers of America.* Retrieved March 19, 2009, from http://www.magazine.org/advertising/revenue/by_ad_category/pib-4q-2008.aspx

Pupipat, A. (1998). Scientific writing and publishing in English in Thailand: The perception of Thai scientists and editors. *Dissertation Abstracts International, 59*(7A), 2476.

Ramey, J. W. (2000). The confluence of visual and verbal rhetoric: Toward a pedagogical theory of the imagetext. (Doctoral dissertation, University of Louisville, 2000). *Dissertation Abstracts International, 61*, 3981.

Reuter, W. (2007, May 14). German parliament condemns China's "Laogai" camps. Berlin: *Der Spiegel.* Retrieved August 14, 2008, from http://www.spiegel.de/ international/germany/0,1518,483308,00.html

Rosner, M. (2001). Theories of visual rhetoric: Looking at the human genome. *Journal of Technical Writing and Communication, 31*(4), 391–413.

Rothenberg, R. (1995). *Where the suckers moon: The life and death of an advertising campaign.* New York: Vintage Books.

Russell, J. T., & Lane, W. R., (2002). *Otto Kleppner's advertising procedure* (15th ed.). Upper Saddle River, NJ: Prentice-Hall.

Russell, J. T., & Verrill, G. (1986). *Otto Kleppner's advertising procedure* (9th ed.). Englewood Cliffs, NJ: Prentice Hall.

Sadoski, M., Kealy, W. A., Goetz, E. T., & Paivio, A. (1997). Concreteness and imagery effects in the written composition of definitions. *Journal of Educational Psychology, 89,* 518–526.

Schober, W. (1998, December). P-O-P Times/POP design trends survey 1999. *P-O-P Times: The news publication of point-of-purchase advertising, display, and packaging,* pp. 36–52.

Schriver, K. (1997). *Dynamics of document design.* New York: John Wiley & Sons.

Selzer, J. (2004). The composing processes of an engineer. In J. Johnson-Eilola & S. A. Selber (Eds.), *Central works in technical communication* (pp. 317–324). New York: Oxford University Press. (Reprinted from *College Composition and Communication, 34*(2), 178–187).

Smith, H. (Writer) & Young, R. (Writer & Director). (2004). Is Wal-Mart good for America? In T. Mangini (Production Manager), *Frontline.* Boston, MA: WGBH.

Smock, F. (2005, August 21). Original, engaging: Skinner's *Salt Water Amnesia* is a worthy collection of poetry. *The Courier Journal.* Book Section.

Soto, P. (2006). *Introduction.* In M. Serrats (Ed.), *Point of purchase.* New York: Collins/ Design HarperCollins Publishers.

Stewart, D. C. (1988). Collaborative learning and composition: Boom or bane? *Rhetoric Review, 7*(1), 58-83.

Encyclopedia Britannica Micropaedia IX. (1974). *Surrealism.* 692/2. Chicago: Encyclopedia Britannica, Inc.

Tiano, A., & Keep, L. (Producers). (2008).*The Brain Fitness Program.* Arlington, VA: PBS.

Thera, N. (1996). *The heart of Buddhist meditation.* York Beach, MN: Samuel Weisner.

Thera, N. (1997). *The power of mindfulness.* Buddha Dharma Education Association, Inc. Retrieved December 10, 2008, from http://www.buddhanet.net/pdf_file/ powermindfulness.pdf

Toulmin, S. (2004). *The uses of argument.* Cambridge, UK: Cambridge University Press.

Vanden Bergh, B., & Stuhlfaut, M. (2006). Is advertising creativity primarily an individual or social process? *Mass Communication & Society, 9*(4), 373–397.

Vygotsky, L. (1978). *Mind in society: The development of higher psychological processes.* M. Cole et al., Eds.). Cambridge, MA: Harvard University Press.

Wallis, C., & Steptoe, S. (2006, December 18). How to bring our schools out of the 20th century. *Time, 168*(25), 50–56.

Webb, J., & Keene, M. (1999). The impact of discourse communities on international professional communication. In C. R. Lovitt & D. Goswami (Eds.), *Exploring the rhetoric of international professional communication: An agenda for teachers and researchers* (pp. 81-109). Amityville, NY: Baywood.

Weick, K. E., & Roberts, K. (1993). Collective mind in organizations: Heedful inter-relating on flight decks. *Administrative Science Quarterly, 38,* 357–381.

Weick, K. E., & Sutcliffe, K. M. (2001). *Managing the unexpected.* San Francisco, CA: Jossey-Bass.

Weick, K. E., & Sutcliffe, K. M. (2006). Mindfulness and the quality of organizational attention. *Organization Science, 17*(4), 514–524.

Wells, W., Burnett, J., & Moriarty, S. (1995). *Advertising principles and practice.* Englewood Cliffs, NJ: Prentice Hall.

White, S. D. (2005, March 16). *Brand equity.* Retrieved August 15, 2008, from http://ezinearticles.com/?Brand-Equity&id=20703

Willerton, R. (2005). Visual metonymy and synecdoche. *Journal of Technical Writing and Communication, 35*(1), 239–271.

Williams, J. (2007). *Style: Lessons in clarity and grace* (9th ed.). New York: Pearson/Longman.

Wysocki, A. F., & Lynch, D. A. (2007). *Compose, design, advocate.* New York: Pearson/Longman.

Yancey, K. (2004, March 25). *Chair's address.* Paper presented at the 2004 conference on College Composition and Communication, San Antonio, TX.

Yancey, K., Lunsford, A., McDonald, J., Moran, C., Neal, M., Pryor, C., et al. (2004). CCCC Position Statement on Teaching, Learning, and Assessing Writing in Digital Environments. Retrieved July 3, 2008, from http://www.ncte.org/cccc/resources/positions/123773.htm

Yin, R. (1994). *Case study research: Design and methods* (2nd ed.). Thousand Oaks, CA: Sage.

Young, J. W. (1944). *Technique for producing ideas.* Chicago, IL: Advertising Publications, Inc.

Author-Subject Index